Quantitative Methods in the Humanities and Social Sciences

Quantitative Methods in the Humanities and Social Sciences is a book series designed to foster research-based conversation with all parts of the university campus – from buildings of ivy-covered stone to technologically savvy walls of glass. Scholarship from international researchers and the esteemed editorial board represents the far-reaching applications of computational analysis, statistical models, computer-based programs, and other quantitative methods. Methods are integrated in a dialogue that is sensitive to the broader context of humanistic study and social science research. Scholars, including among others historians, archaeologists, new media specialists, classicists and linguists, promote this interdisciplinary approach. These texts teach new methodological approaches for contemporary research. Each volume exposes readers to a particular research method. Researchers and students then benefit from exposure to subtleties of the larger project or corpus of work in which the quantitative methods come to fruition.

More information about this series at http://www.springer.com/series/11748

Masako Fidler • Václav Cvrček
Editors

Taming the Corpus

From Inflection and Lexis to Interpretation

Springer

Editors
Masako Fidler
Department of Slavic Studies
Brown University
Providence, RI, USA

Václav Cvrček
Institute of the Czech National Corpus
Charles University
Prague 1, Czech Republic

ISSN 2199-0956 ISSN 2199-0964 (electronic)
Quantitative Methods in the Humanities and Social Sciences
ISBN 978-3-319-98016-4 ISBN 978-3-319-98017-1 (eBook)
https://doi.org/10.1007/978-3-319-98017-1

Library of Congress Control Number: 2018957139

This Springer imprint is published by the registered company Springer Nature Switzerland AG
The registered company address is: Gewerbestrasse 11, 6330 Cham, Switzerland

Contents

Chapter 1
Introduction

Václav Cvrček and Masako Fidler

Empirical linguistics has always gravitated towards quantification. With the advent of electronic corpora—large, searchable sets of natural language data, quantification has become part and parcel of linguistic studies. In the past few decades in particular, we have witnessed a "quantitative turn" in various schools of linguistics (cf. Janda, 2013 for cognitive linguistics) and in the digital humanities which was further accelerated by the advent of text corpora. This volume aims to showcase a variety of recent quantitative approaches that "tame the corpus"; it shows how language corpora can be used for research questions of interest to students and scholars in the humanities and social scientists.[1] It simultaneously fills a lacuna in mainstream English-based quantitative linguistic studies by demonstrating that quantitative methods applied on inflectional language may reveal novel phenomena.

This introduction presents our position with respect to quantitative language data analysis. We first revisit the apparent "quantitative–qualitative dichotomy" to show that there are features shared by quantitative and qualitative analyses. We then discuss the advantages of quantitative data and statistical evaluation. The chapter closes with an overview of the studies in this volume.

[1] The volume was inspired by the Workshop on Quantitative Text Analysis for the Humanities and Social Sciences, which the editors organized at Brown University on April 8 and 9, 2016.

V. Cvrček (✉)
Institute of the Czech National Corpus, Charles University, Prague 1, Czech Republic
e-mail: vaclav.cvrcek@ff.cuni.cz

M. Fidler
Department of Slavic Studies, Brown University, Providence, RI, USA
e-mail: masako_fidler@brown.edu

M. Fidler, V. Cvrček (eds.), *Taming the Corpus*, Quantitative Methods in the Humanities and Social Sciences, https://doi.org/10.1007/978-3-319-98017-1_1

A Quantitative–Qualitative Dichotomy

Quantitative and qualitative approaches are commonly viewed in opposition to each other. The comparison between the two approaches potentially leads to oversimplification[2]: quantitative approaches are often considered more reliable, more precise, more inductive, and allow more convincing generalizations and hypothesis testing than qualitative approaches; qualitative approaches are viewed as subjective, focused on a specific instance, exploratory (allowing for defining the problem or establishing a hypothesis), and deductive. Contrary to such a popular impression, however, each approach has its strengths and weaknesses. Qualitative research may obtain in-depth knowledge of a particular sample (e.g., through the close reading of a single literary text), revealing a wide range of questions/hypotheses about the text (e.g., metaphors used, prominent motifs, intertextual links, and allusions). The trade-off is that the researcher's claim is based on a small sample. Quantitative research usually starts with a narrowly focused observation (e.g., the relative prominence of individual words) from a larger population (e.g., the entire corpus of texts written by one author or texts of one epoch). This type of research may lead to overarching conclusions. Its trade-off is that many details may be omitted as unimportant or irrelevant to the research question. In other words, we may either examine a small number of instances of the phenomenon under scrutiny very carefully, or a large number of instances superficially. Regardless of efforts and funds, each type of research has its own omnipresent trade-off.

Quantitative and qualitative approaches moreover share certain properties. Qualitative research may involve some minimum "quantification" when some recurrent patterns are noted.[3] Quantitative research presupposes a "qualitative delimitation" of categories: for example, types of nouns or parts of speech must be qualitatively defined before their frequencies can be calculated. To cite Herdan, "[t] here is no sharp dividing line between qualitative and quantitative methods, but only transition comparable to that from large scale to small sca[l]e maps" (1966, p. 2). If neither approach can exist in isolation, then we can expect that both approaches would also *share* some advantages as well as disadvantages.

One crucial concept to capture such advantages and disadvantages of both approaches is *reductionism*. In any research—qualitative and quantitative alike, we have to make a decision on what to include in our investigation. Researchers usually pick only those available (or noticeable) features that appear relevant to the research question and ignore the rest. Consequently, each description is shaped by a

[2] Superficial Internet search often leads one to have such an impression, cf. https://www.orau.gov/cdcynergy/soc2web/content/phase05/phase05_step03_deeper_qualitative_and_quantitative.htm and https://keydifferences.com/difference-between-qualitative-and-quantitative-research.html#ComparisonChart. Accessed 25 May 2018.

[3] Even a singular appearance represents quantity (=1) and the difference between a single or no occurrence may result in ascribing an important property to the phenomenon under examination or not. But usually, even in qualitative studies, multiple examples demonstrating a hypothesis are better than one.

combination of what has been found and what has been left aside (either knowingly or unknowingly): we select specific categories, terms, a point of view, and/or a methodology. This problem of reducing the research input is usually mentioned in relation to quantitative studies; in order to examine some phenomenon quantitatively, we have to zoom in on a limited and manageable amount of features. But the same problem can be found in qualitative research as well; the researcher may consider a broader context of relations interacting with the target phenomenon, but it is impossible to include all the potential influences (e.g., all intertextual links). What usually happens in qualitative analysis is that the researcher discusses only those aspects of his/her choice, to the exclusion of other aspects.[4] Both quantitative and qualitative approaches thus may suffer from reductionism to varying degrees.

Likewise, a degree of *reliability* is of concern to both quantitative and qualitative studies. It is likely that examination of a large sample (at the corpus level) leads to substantive conclusions about the target language phenomenon. The reliability of the researcher's findings, however, will depend on the level of reductionism: reducing a complex system to a few easy-to-quantify variables may point to interesting results, but this inevitably leads to a schematic description with some important parts missing. On the other hand, if one examines the same research question qualitatively in a single text with an eye to a wide range of interacting factors, the study may yield valid results so long as its findings can be applied to other texts. In order to achieve reliable results, then, we need both methods.

Degrees of reductionism can also affect degrees of *objectivity* and *subjectivity*—properties that are often attributed to quantitative and qualitative research, respectively. Quantitative methods can be qualified as objective, *provided* that the categories they use (e.g., parts of speech, as mentioned above) are validated by convincing qualitative research.

There is yet another property that supposedly divides qualitative and quantitative methods: *inductive* vs. *deductive reasoning*. Qualitative methods are often associated with the former and quantitative methods with the latter (Rasinger, 2008, p. 11). In quantitative studies, it is common practice to impose a statistical model on the data (especially in situations where many models are available) based on our general assumptions about the gathered evidence; this approach clearly involves deductive reasoning. However, we may find also counterexamples. Corpus-driven (Tognini-Bonelli, 2001) or data-driven quantitative studies are built on inductive reasoning; they assume that the theory has to be optimized for large amounts of data (and not the other way around). As for qualitative studies, often described as inductive, they can be deductive by approaching the target subject with pre-formulated theory or by describing the subject within an established concept or point of view (as in critical discourse analysis). Clearly, the boundaries between quantitative and qualitative studies are not as discrete as they appear.

[4] Unlike many quantitative studies, where the amount of reduction is sometimes explicitly acknowledged. Johnson states that in fact any (statistical) inference about the data is guessing; what quantitative methods can help us with is to quantify how reliable our guesses are (2008, p. 3).

Furthermore, there is also a perception that qualitative study yields a *hypothesis*, which should consequently be *tested* quantitatively. This is not always the case. Both qualitative and quantitative approaches share an exploratory potential. Sometimes, the underlying phenomena are visible only from the perspective of larger data (collocations in corpus linguistics being an obvious example). Sometimes, important aspects can be spotted only through detailed qualitative study. New hypotheses may arise from both directions.

Why the Use of Corpus and Quantitative Methods?

In spite of the shared features between qualitative and quantitative methods, the latter nonetheless has significant additional and possibly more important advantages, given the increasing need for empirical evidence in linguistics. One of them—as we as editors see it—is that quantitative methods are likely to produce testable (or falsifiable, cf. Popper, 1959 [2005]) outcomes. There are two important aspects of quantitative methods: each result can be replicated on the original data (everyone is allowed to rerun the experiment and verify if the reported results are based on solid analysis); and each method can be normally applied to different data (which allows for testing the limits of generalization). In contrast, qualitative analysts lacking large data sets and statistics would have to make extraneous efforts to do the same.

The second advantage of a quantitative approach is that it is supported by existing mathematical and statistical methods. An elaborated system of dealing with quantifiable variables already exists ready to use, with well-described (although sometimes complex and hard to understand) limitations and pitfalls. In addition, mathematics is an artificial system that does not bear any false connotations. In order to understand why this is an advantage, we must recognize that there is a metaphor at the core of any scientific description (e.g., the development of languages as a tree spreading out branches). By translating language features into counts and frequencies, we use a mathematical "metaphor," which has the advantage of being a universally comprehensible but simultaneously artificial system unburdened by connotations. This property is hard to find outside of mathematics.

The third advantage of quantitative approaches is that they allow "*interobjectivity*"—the possibility of seeing similar patterns in different fields of study. By this principle, we may compare such things as the similarity of word frequency distribution (known as Zipfian distribution) to the distribution of population within the cities of a country. By recognizing similar patterns across different disciplines and objects of study, we can enhance our own understanding of language and bring new inspiring ideas into its description.

Finally, there is a practical motivation to use quantitative methods. Although both quantitative and qualitative studies may be empirical, only the former assumes that generalization is possible only after the examination of representative data samples. This was not an issue in the past, but with the advent of large electronic corpora, one now has to search for a method capable of *taming the once unthinkable amount of data*.

Taming the Corpus

Quantification, with all its shortcomings and deficiencies, is still the only way to deal with the large corpora, which are increasingly used to produce findings about language, literature, and society. Besides describing linguistic phenomena, such as collocability of words (e.g., Gries, 2013) or language variability (e.g., Biber and Conrad, 2009) to name at least a few, quantitative methods applied to large language data empower scholars to explore social issues, e.g., media portrayal of refugees and asylum seekers (Baker and McEnery, 2005). Quantitative methods also help capture global themes predominant in the national literatures and historical documents (Jockers, 2013).

Such studies largely focus on the lexicon, which plays several important roles in the production of text and our perception of the world. Words occurring at unexpectedly high frequencies, for example, point to prominent topics—word frequencies can reveal what readers find striking in a text, especially when contrasted against a background of other corpora. Word clusters can help identify phrases or formulaic expressions in large collections of discourse samples. The use of such lexicon-centered methods understandably originated from the study of texts in English, a language with little explicit grammatical marking.

This book examines lexis as well as smaller grammatical units that can be objectively identified—detailed components in phonology and morphosyntax (syllable structure, modifier-modified agreement, and grammatical case). This line of research is made possible by the explicit grammatical marking of Czech and the large and well-documented language data available through the Czech National Corpus (henceforth CNC). CNC (see https://www.korpus.cz) is one of the most robust and well-balanced language corpora in the world and the most developed corpus of any Slavic language. Since its establishment in 1994, the CNC project has been continuously mapping Czech in different domains; several series of corpora have been developed and maintained, namely a synchronic written corpus (currently with four billion words), a spoken corpus (focusing on unprepared informal dialogues with 6.4 million words), and a diachronic corpus (covering the period from the fourteenth century to 1945). CNC also contains parallel-language corpora (InterCorp) that facilitate contrastive research in more than thirty languages (245 million words in Czech, 1.87 billion in aligned texts of other languages); InterCorp is valuable not only for its size (it is one of the largest and the most diverse among the Slavic parallel corpora available) but also for its careful design and manually checked core section in fiction. Moreover, CNC is equipped with web-based software tools with continually updated functions. These tools ensure a large number of possibilities to probe language on multiple levels: translation between languages, collective perceptions of language, and analysis of literary and political texts.

The aim of this book is to showcase multiple approaches to language, literature, and society. The volume demonstrates diverse methods, which range from "simple" quantification as a means of description to sophisticated statistical methods employed for the purpose of revealing new phenomena.

Section 1 (*Words, rhymes, and grammatical forms*) deals with phonotactics, poetic structure, morphological complexity used to differentiate literary style, and native speakers' sense of grammaticality—issues pertinent to linguistic typology, cognition and language, and literary studies. The article by Neil Bermel, Luděk Knittl, and Jean Russel probes the relationship between language exposure and speakers' performance on production and ratings tasks. Frequency data from CNC is used as a proxy for language exposure. Jiří Milička and Hana Kalábová explore vowel phonotactics in Czech words and word stems. The authors identify s vowel length and vowel front-/backness. Radek Čech and Miroslav Kubát propose a computational method to measure the morphological richness of texts (an index of utmost importance in inflected languages), thereby finding a way to quantitatively characterize author styles. Petr Plecháč applies a quantitative method to poetry. The author develops a method to identify frequent rhyme pairs in poetry corpus by collocation extraction technique and uses the output as a training set for machine learning. The method is tested on poetry corpora in three different languages (Czech, English, and French) with high accuracy.

Section 2 (*Not only "lost" in translation*) takes us to interlanguage relations. Lucie Chlumská takes the "top-down view." She compares the prominent n-grams and POS-grams (n-grams consisting of part-of-speech tags) in translated Czech and in the English source texts. She examines the viability of "translation universals" that are independent of linguistic similarities or differences between the original and the translated texts. While confirming such universal tendencies in Czech–English translations, the author argues that no component claimed to belong to the category of a translation universal can be distinctly isolated; translated texts manifest a combination of properties. Moreover, the author discusses the specificities of cross-linguistic comparison based on POS-grams and n-grams in the two typologically different languages. David Danaher takes the bottom-up view, looking at the specific sociocultural contexts in which lexis is embedded. He analyzes collocations to study the semantics of *lidskost* (often translated as "humanity," "humanness," or "humaneness") and related words as used in Václav Havel's writings. Combining quantitative and qualitative methods, the author traces the contexts that molded the semantics of these words. Danaher's collocation analysis illustrates how words come to defy translation because of their usage in socioculturally specific contexts that have evolved over the past centuries. The issues in this section are important regardless of the size of the target language (the language into which a text is translated). Admittedly, complexity in translation is an issue for midsized and smaller languages as target languages since translated texts constitute a large part of literary production. However, it is also an important issue in larger target languages spoken by a large monolingual population that has little access to the original texts.

Section 3 (*Understanding discourse*) demonstrates how quantitative analysis of texts can contribute to our understanding of society and connects the volume to legal language (Kieran Williams), construction of gender (Adrian Zasina), and discourse position and implicit ideology (Masako Fidler and Václav Cvrček). Williams' study demonstrates how collocations can identify potential costs of the general public's misunderstanding legal language. As an illustration, the author uses words from the 2017 Czech gun bill, written with the intention of creating a constitutional right to keep and bear arms, to assist the state in protecting national security. By comparing the usage of crucial terms used both in the gun law and in non-legal texts, Williams suggests a "marked misalignment" between the two usages that could gravely affect compliance with and enforcement of the gun law. Zasina uses corpus data to investigate gender representation of politicians in Czech daily newspapers. His study serves as a springboard to consider a need to go beyond identifying explicit gender stereotypes, and to construct a more complex conceptual model to interpret subtle attributes used on male and (especially) female politicians. Fidler and Cvrček take the basic concept of keyword analysis, a corpus linguistic method used to identify prominent words in text ("aboutness"), as a starting point, but both extend and add to its functionality. The "Multi-level Discourse Prominence Analysis" provides information about a text's overarching rhetoric and helps to objectivize the ideological content of news. It takes advantage of the inflectional morphology of Czech (via analysis of prominent morphs) to unpack implicit and recurrent messages in texts, and more importantly has the potential to reveal implicit ideology at a deeper (perhaps subconscious) level.

Taming the Corpus presents a variety of quantitative approaches to language, literature, and society. The volume attempts to show how quantitative methods can be further empowered by utilizing features that are characteristic of an inflectional language. The editors hope that the book will spark interest in thus-far underutilized grammatical markings in many other languages that could potentially enhance objectivity and precision in quantitative methods.

Acknowledgments The publication of this volume was made possible by support from grant *Progres* Q08 *Czech National Corpus* implemented at the Faculty of Arts, Charles University and the Humanities Research Grant from Brown University. Special thanks goes to Mathew Amboy and Faith Su from Springer who saw through the entire publication process and Marek Nekula for thoughtful and helpful comments on the manuscripts. The editors would also like to thank Andrew Malcovsky for copyediting work. Last but not least, many thanks to Lída Cvrčková Porkertová and Vlastimil Fidler for their support and patience.

References

Baker, P., & McEnery, T. (2005). A corpus-based approach to discourses of refugees and asylum seekers in UN and newspaper texts. *Journal of Language and Politics, 4*(2), 197–226.

Biber, D., & Conrad, S. (2009). *Register, genre, and style*. Cambridge, UK: Cambridge University Press.

Gries, S. T. (2013). 50-something years of work on collocations. *International Journal of Corpus Linguistics, 18*(1), 137–165.

Herdan, G. (1966). *The advanced theory of language as choice and chance*. Berlin, Germany: Springer.

Janda, L. A. (Ed.). (2013). *Cognitive linguistics: The quantitative turn*. Berlin, Germany: De Gruyter Mouton.

Jockers, M. L. (2013). *Macroanalysis. Digital methods and literary history*. Urbana, IL: University of Illinois Press.

Johnson, K. (2008). *Quantitative methods in linguistics*. Malden, MA: Blackwell publishing.
Popper, K. (1959) [2005]. *The logic of scientific discovery*. London, UK: Routledge.
Rasinger, S. M. (2008). *Quantitative research in linguistics. An introduction*. London, England: Continuum.
Tognini-Bonelli, E. (2001). *Corpus linguistics at work*. Amsterdam: John Benjamins.

Part I
Words, Rhymes, and Grammatical Forms

Chapter 2
Do Users' Reading Skills and Difficulty Ratings for Texts Affect Choices and Evaluations?

Neil Bermel, Luděk Knittl, and Jean Russell

Abstract In our contribution, we consider how corpus data can be used as a proxy for the written language environment around us in constructing offline studies of native-speaker intuition and usage. We assume a broadly emergent perspective on language: in other words, the linguistic competence of individuals is not identical or hardwired but forms gradually through exposure and coalescence of patterns of production and reaction. We hypothesize that while users presumably all in theory have access to the same linguistic material, their actual exposure to it and their ability to interpret it may differ, which will result in differing judgments and choices. Our study looks at the interaction between corpus frequency and two possible indicators of individual difference: attitude towards reading tasks and performance on reading tasks. We find a small but consistent effect of task performance on respondents' judgments but do not confirm any effects on respondents' production tasks.

Keywords Czech morphology · Variation · Overabundance · Acceptability judgments · Experimental linguistics · Usage-based approach

Introduction[1]

Considerable attention has been devoted to whether all native speakers of a language access the same linguistic structures and material in similar ways, and whether, having accessed it, their use of and reaction to language (what we will call *linguistic behavior*) differ as well in predictable ways. There is accumulating

[1] This research was carried out as part of the project "Acceptability and forced-choice judgements in the study of linguistic variation," funded by the Leverhulme Trust (RPG-407). The support of the Trust is gratefully acknowledged.

N. Bermel (✉) · L. Knittl · J. Russell
University of Sheffield, Sheffield, UK
e-mail: n.bermel@sheffield.ac.uk; l.knittl@sheffield.ac.uk; j.russell@sheffield.ac.uk

M. Fidler, V. Cvrček (eds.), *Taming the Corpus*, Quantitative Methods in the Humanities and Social Sciences, https://doi.org/10.1007/978-3-319-98017-1_2

evidence that intra-speaker variation can point to differences in linguistic behavior that are not random or insignificant.

We can propose that speakers' varying backgrounds (i.e, their *exposure* to language) affect language in use (i.e, their *output* or their *evaluation of input*). In other words, if we call what underlies this linguistic behavior a "grammar," each speaker's is subtly different. Corpus data can, if carefully used, be hypothesized to represent this "exposure" to at least the written form of the language, which is the tack we will take in this study.[2] In doing so, we aim to add to the evidence showing how corpus frequency can be useful in detecting and predicting our use of language.

Background

Evidence has, at times, pointed to vocabulary size, education, profession, and reading recall abilities as factors differing from subject to subject that affect one's "personal" linguistic behavior, and these differences have been found in syntax, word-formation, and inflectional morphology. While we might try to explain away differences resulting from regional or age variation as the product of language shift and change, it is harder to do so with e.g. educational or professional differences.

In a series of articles, Dąbrowska has tracked some of these differences in speaker backgrounds, which, she shows, lead to differences in both linguistic performance and linguistic judgments. Dąbrowska (2008) looked at a sample of users stratified by educational background and assessed their performance on a production task. She concluded that "the results… revealed large individual differences in speakers' ability to inflect unfamiliar nouns which were strongly correlated with education" (2008, p. 941). Having attempted to eliminate some possible confounding factors, she concluded, "We can be reasonably confident… that the observed differences in scores in the other conditions reflect genuine differences in linguistic proficiency" (2008, p. 945). A logical deduction from that might have been that more educated speakers had larger vocabularies; however, Dąbrowska did not find enough evidence for this, saying, "…the results do not support the hypothesis that the critical variable is vocabulary size, although they do not unequivocally rule it out" (2008, p. 949). In a later study, she examined judgments of sentence well-formedness given by linguists and nonlinguists, and found that:

> Linguists' judgments are shown to diverge from those of nonlinguists. These differences could be due to theoretical commitments (the conviction that linguistic processes apply 'across the board,' and hence all sentences with the same syntactic structure should be equally grammatical) or to differences in exposure (the constructed examples of this structure found in the syntactic literature are very unrepresentative of ordinary usage) (2010, p. 1).

[2] Fidler and Cvrček's (2015) study of keyword analysis in Czech presidential New Year speeches uses this approach to good effect to demonstrate how different types of exposure, in the guise of reference corpora, can be used to model differing potential receptions of a text.

While Dąbrowska was cautious in her conclusions about whether educational differences and vocabulary size can be so closely linked, other researchers have made the connection between linguistic behavior and vocabulary size more directly. For example, Frisch & Brea-Spahn (2010) found that vocabulary size, as measured by the results of a word familiarity rating task, correlates with acceptability scores on a word-formation task. They noted:

> Participants with a larger vocabulary in English were more accepting of low probability nonwords in English. It appears that those with greater vocabulary knowledge are more likely to have experienced improbable phonological constituents, and may also have a lower threshold for "unacceptable" nonwords, if their threshold is based on a likelihood estimate from their individual lexicon (2010, p. 345).

Reading abilities also affect judgments: Staum Casasanto, Hofmeister, & Sag (2010) investigated how differences in reading span interact with judgements.[3] Reading span task scores were highly significant predictors of acceptability scores on a task involving the syntax of embedded clauses, e.g, *The nurse from the clinic supervised the administrator who scolded the medic while a patient was brought into the emergency room* (Staum Casasanto et al. 2010, p. 224). They concluded that

> [P]articipants' reading span scores predict sentence judgments differently for different types of manipulations. Participants with higher reading spans tend to judge ungrammatical sentences as being worse than their low-span counterparts do, yet they tend to judge difficult sentences as being better than participants with lower reading spans (2010, p. 228).

A further set of factors that have been shown to contribute to analyses of linguistic behavior are those that derive from analyses of the task performance itself. For example, Divjak demonstrates that ratings given on "filler" items—in other words, items designed to distract the respondent, rather than the test items themselves—are in fact the best predictor of how a respondent rates the test items (in this instance manipulating the complement of certain verbs). This suggests that an overall *individual* variation in how people use rating scales can account for some of the differences we see; Divjak terms this "non-linguistic variability" (2016 [2017], p. 14). Bermel, Knittl, & Russell show that respondents' ratings of the *less* common of two variants are the best predictor of how they answer on a production task. In other words, looking at the ratings for the lesser-used ending {a} in the genitive singular rather than the more-common {u} gives us the best chance of predicting which ending native speakers will insert in a gap-filling task (2015a, pp. 304–306).

In summary, then, it seems that a variety of speaker-specific factors can influence linguistic behavior. Some of these, such as educational attainment and profession,

[3] Reading span tasks ask participants to read unconnected sentences, memorizing the final word of each sentence, which they then must recall later. There is some dispute about what exactly they are measuring (Hupet, Desmette, & Schelstraete, 1997), but as Conway et al. point out, they have been widely used nonetheless to assess how we tap into our working memory's storage and processing functions: "The task is essentially a simple word span task, with the added component of the comprehending of sentences. Subjects read sentences and, in some cases, verify the logical accuracy of the sentences, while trying to remember words, one for each sentence presented" (Conway et al., 2005, p. 771).

appear to be nonlinguistic factors but may in fact be linked to an individual's linguistic abilities. Others, including vocabulary size (either measured via the self-reported familiarity of words or accuracy on a semantics test) and reading span test scores, are more overt measures of reading proficiency. A third group effectively measures the respondent's attitude towards the given features or towards survey data in general.

If many of these factors impinge on our ability to read and interpret, it stands to reason that there will be a link between a proxy for the external "textual world," such as a corpus, and the sorts of answers respondents give on surveys. In the next section, we will consider how this relates to our own research data.

Corpus Data

For a number of years now, we have been looking at places in the Czech conjugational and declensional systems where a syntactic "slot" has multiple exponents whose usage is not clearly differentiated, a situation described variously as *competition* (Lečić, 2015), *variation* (Bermel & Knittl, 2012a, 2012b; Bermel et al., 2015a, 2017) or *overabundance* (Thornton, 2012).[4]

In common with other Slavic languages, Czech is highly inflected, and thanks to a series of far-reaching phonological changes over the last millennium, the conditions for deploying its broad assortment of inflectional material are not always clear (see Bermel & Knittl, 2012b, pp. 93–95 for a fuller discussion).[5] Consequently, while we are able to describe clearly for some syntactic slots what exponent is used there, for others there is considerable variation. Exponents may be described using a list-type approach ("the following lexemes use exponent A; others use exponent B") or using a collection of rules of thumb ("borrowings, multisyllabic stems, and labial consonant stems prefer exponent C; others prefer exponent D").[6] In addition to places where choice is clear-cut, there exists a transitional band of items where both exponents are used in some measure.

[4]An example of clearly differentiated usage is, e.g, between the exponents {em} and {ou} in the instr. sg.: the former is used with masc. and neut. nouns, while the latter appears with fem. nouns. The only place we get overlap—e.g, *s (v)okurkem* ~ *s (v)okurkou* 'with cucumber'—is where the gender of the noun is unstable across dialects. When usage is not clearly differentiated, often some factors or tendencies can be identified that contribute to choice, but none that clearly demarcate it.

[5]A further contributory factor to the persistence of variation in Czech may be the relatively weak position of the standard, which does not function as a common speech variety across the vast majority of the country (see, e.g, Sgall, 2011, p. 183, one among many texts that could be cited in this regard). Attempts at standardizing one or another variant tend to be perceived as applying only to formal written texts.

[6]Compare, for example, the appearance of fleeting [e] in the fem. and neut. gen. pl. and the description of the masc. animate nom. pl. exponents {i}~{ové}~{é} in Grepl et al. (1995), pp. 248–249, 256–257. The first is described in terms of a default form and the conditions under which insertion takes place, while the latter variation is described using overlapping semantic, phonological, and suprasegmental criteria that may apply. The same approach is used in the normative Internet Language Manual (Ústav pro jazyk český 2004).

In English, with its relatively impoverished inflectional morphology, the best higher-frequency environment in which to study this is the overlap between the so-called strong and weak verb classes in the past tense and the perfect, and it has been studied from various angles over the past several decades (Albright & Hayes, 2003; Bybee & Slobin, 1982; Chandler, 2010; Eddington, 2000; Haber, 1976; Prasada & Pinker, 1993, etc.).[7] In Czech, this overabundance is widespread across both verbal and nominal morphology (e.g, Bermel 2004a, 2004b, 2010; Bermel, Knittl, & Russell, 2015b); in particular, nominal morphology, with seven cases, two numbers, and between 10 and 15 major declension patterns for nouns, is a fertile area for the study of competition between variant forms.

Our research involved testing three such slots in Czech where this phenomenon occurs. Two of these are from the so-called hard masculine inanimate declension pattern (exemplar word *hrad* 'castle'). As a result of the merger and reorganization of the dominant o-stem class and the smaller u-stem class that had evidently already begun in proto-Slavic, in Czech the u-stem endings have spread widely across the old o-stem lexical stock in the genitive singular (gen. sg.) and the locative singular (loc. sg.), while the old o-stem endings have also penetrated the much smaller group of nouns that previously formed the u-stem class. The third is the result of a younger innovation in which feminine nouns inherited from the Proto-Slavic i-stem pattern (exemplar word *kost* 'bone') have acquired to a greater or lesser degree the exponents of the old Proto-Slavic ja-stem pattern (exemplar word *růže* 'rose') in the gen. sg. and most plural cases, forming a new pattern (exemplar word *píseň* 'song') whose membership is not all that clearly defined.

The Czech National Corpus

Our main interest was to see whether exposure had an impact on the way Czechs perceived these variant forms as well as how they used them. Our proxy for *exposure* was the Czech National Corpus (CNC), specifically the frequency with which forms occur in it.

By CNC, we mean specifically its layer of synchronic representative corpora of written language (SYN2000, SYN2005, SYN2010, and SYN2015).[8] Each of these corpora contain roughly 100 million tokens (excluding punctuation) and are *representative* in that they contain a mixture of text types, broken down at top level into *publicistika* 'journalistic texts,' *odborná* or *oborová literatura* 'specialist or non-fiction texts,' and *beletrie* 'imaginative texts.'[9] Attempts at producing *balanced* cor-

[7] Latinate nouns (*octopi~octopuses*, etc.) are another area where variation can be looked at in English, but it has been an area of more research in derivational morphology, where variation is more widespread (*normality~normalcy*, etc.). However, derivational morphology is not seen as having the same impact on our understanding of utterance structure and the creation of "grammatical" meaning as does inflectional morphology.

[8] On our proxies for *perception* and *use,* see the "Methodology" section below.

[9] This term is more often translated as "fiction," but in the CNC corpora prior to SYN2015, it

Table 2.1 Text-type breakdown (top level) in the SYN corpora

	SYN2000 (%)	SYN2005 (%)	SYN2010 (%)	SYN2015 (%)
Journalistic texts	60	33	33	33.33
Specialist texts	25	27	27	33.33
Imaginative texts	15	40	40	33.33

pora based on research into reading habits gave a variety of results, summarized in Table 2.1.[10]

It is hard to tell without access to the comparative research underlying these changes, but there is a clear shift in favor of a more equal balance of text types, simplifying the task of comparing results from various text types within the corpus.[11]

Our results drew on both the SYN2010 and SYN2005 corpora (Čermák et al. 2005; Křen et al. 2010). Our goal was to identify nouns that exhibit variation in usage in the cases targeted. We conducted targeted searches in SYN2005 using the corpus search engine to retrieve all word forms with a particular shape and grammatical tag, e.g, ending in <u> and tagged as a masc. inanimate gen. sg. noun, or ending in <a> with the same tag.[12] We then compared the resulting lists to find variant forms of a word, e.g, *jazyku/jazyka*, which represented the variation sought.

For each case, the lists of lemmas (with each ending and with both endings) ran to many thousands of items, so a manageable process was needed for verifying the data and catching potential errors. Our method is described in detail in Bermel and Knittl (2012b, pp. 97–98), but in brief: all concordances with the less frequent ending were verified manually, token by token, as were examples of the more frequent ending when it appeared in variation. We also removed all "nonwords" from the lists and looked at any errors in the lemmas, which are often a sign that mistagging may have occurred.

These measures did not remove all erroneous forms retrieved, which would have been a much larger job, but they eliminated a large number of them. Even so, the effect on our overall statistics was not all that evident: for most lexemes, the proportions remained roughly constant. We thus arrived at three lists of lexemes where there was variation between two forms in the cases in question.

includes examples of the genre *literatura faktu:* creative nonfiction such as memoirs, travelogues, etc.

[10] The latest corpus in the series, SYN2015, is not balanced in this fashion; see *inter alia* Čermák, Králík, and Kučera (1997) on the research underlying the original corpora and Cvrček, Čermáková, and Křen (2016) on the composition of SYN2015.

[11] A programmatic explanation for this shift away from "real-world balance" towards "text-type balance" is given in Cvrček et al. (2016).

[12] When lemmatization succeeds, the CNC always disambiguates and resolves in favor of one assignment for each place in the tag (unlike, for example, the Russian National Corpus, where ambiguities are never resolved and all possible tags are associated with a token). This disambiguation is partially rule-based and partially the result of a heuristic correction based on manual tagging of a portion of the corpus. When lemmatization fails, typically due to a very rare or poorly formed (misspelled) word form, no morphological analysis can take place and the form is tagged as *nerozpoznaný* 'unrecognized'; our searches will not have picked up such forms.

One early outcome of this work is that *variation* is a gradient feature. Looked at in absolute terms, we find variation with very high-frequency lexemes as well as very low-frequency lexemes. The proportion of case exponents in one vs. another form is also distributed along a scale: for one word, ending {1} may predominate, whereas for another word it might be ending {2}, and that dominance might be overwhelming or less strong. The only consistent observation is that few lexemes, other than those of low frequency or those where there is some sort of semantic motivation, exhibit equipollent distribution, e.g, both endings {1} and {2} occur in roughly even proportions. Where the variation is unmotivated or only partly motivated, there is almost always some sort of skew to the dominance of one exponent.

Over the past few years, we have used these lists, and a few others compiled in the meantime, to test various hypotheses about frequency. In particular, Bermel et al. (2017) demonstrated that proportional frequency of forms had a consistent effect, at least on the sort of tasks we were asking respondents to perform.

Using Corpus Data in Surveys

The nature of a survey using native-speaker respondents imposes limits on the amount of corpus data that we can test. Respondents fatigue easily; with a high number of short, repetitive tasks, we decided that we could not ask them to spend more than 15–20 min on the survey without risking their attention flagging. We had the advantage of being able to pay respondents, which proved a useful motivational tool, but even so, the number of factors we could include was constrained. In this round, then, we looked at proportional frequency only. It was operationalized by choosing lexemes that fell into one of six proportional bands. The first questions to address are: why use bands at all; why, if so, do we use six bands; and why were those particular boundaries selected for them?

What we are calling *bands* are often termed *bins*: all data found in a particular range is treated as having the same value. We might assume that the best option would always be to retain all precise values and thus not use any bands or bins: surely, it must be more precise to retain the information that lexeme C has exponent {1} 13.7% of the time, while lexeme D has exponent {1} only 12.5% of the time. However, retaining this level of precision has an impact on the way we test our data. It implies a level of precision that in the real world may not exist, i.e, that because a 100-million-word corpus has those particular values, a native speaker will be more likely to favor exponent {1} in lexeme C than exponent {1} in lexeme D, and will be correspondingly more likely to use it in the first scenario than the second. For this reason, tests using bins may prove to be more realistic if we believe that corpora are best interpreted as a rough guide to the linguistic environment rather than an exact one; and that our abilities to track this linguistic environment may be approximate rather than precise.

To reduce at least one aspect of uncertainty, we limited our choice of nouns to those where at least 100 tokens in the case in question were found in a 100-million-token corpus (1 ipm). While this is admittedly an arbitrary level, we felt that it was necessary to ensure the validity of results. A set with four tokens of exponent {1} and two tokens of exponent {2} gives a proportional frequency of 67%:33%, but if only two tokens had been different, the proportions would have been reversed. With a sample of $N \geq 100$, the chance of this happening is correspondingly reduced.

We set the number of bands and the particular boundaries between them opportunistically. For us, the most important criteria were that we get enough granularity in the results to be able to draw clear conclusions, and that we draw the boundaries around our bins in such a way that each of them represents a meaningful number of items. If we create a bin with few or no items in it, the information it yields will be limited and we will have a severely constrained choice of lexemes to use in our survey. In other words, we are not proposing that these specific bands have any inherent meaning themselves, i.e, that using six bands instead of seven indicates a rougher granularity of response overall, or because a word falls into the fifth instead of the sixth band that its behavior is qualitatively different. Instead, we are testing the usefulness of a scale itself: whether the proportional frequency of items in the linguistic environment makes a difference to people's judgments and choices.

For our purposes, then, the most important feature of a scale is that the bands each contain adequate numbers of lexemes for us to construct a survey, and that the survey contain enough levels to assess the variation properly. How we assess the variation has an effect on (and is affected by) the statistical measures chosen.

Previously, for example, we had experimented with seven bands and four bands. The latter had little granularity and thus results were not as clear as we had hoped, while the former presupposed a "central" band with roughly equal proportions of each exponent—which, as it turned out, were very difficult to find. This is because, as mentioned in the section "The Czech National Corpus," unmotivated and partially motivated variation tends to result in a skew dominance, where one exponent predominates in the vast majority of circumstances. In other words, where a firm criterion for choosing one form over another is lacking, frequency itself becomes a criterion, with users perceiving one form as "default" or "normal" and the other as "rare" or "unusual" to varying degrees. In the end, we went with a division into six unequally sized bands that allowed us a reasonable choice of lexical items for each band. The middle two bands were much broader (35% each), while the outside bands were very narrow (1% each), as this is where we find the greatest number of lexemes with variant forms.

We further restricted our choice of lexemes by checking our findings in both SYN2005 and SYN2010, two corpora with identical high-level structures (see Table 2.1 above). To warrant inclusion in our survey, a lexeme had to fall into the same proportional frequency band in both corpora. The resulting set of nouns can be seen in Table 2.2.

Table 2.2 Proportional bands used in this survey

Feature	{a} vs. {u}	{e/ě} vs. {u}	{i} vs. {e/ě}
0–1%	*podzim* 'autumn'	*zákaz* 'prohibition'	*tvrz* 'fortress'
	chodník 'sidewalk'	*úvod* 'introduction'	*poušť* 'desert'
1–15%	*záchod* 'toilet'	*parlament* 'parliament'	*příď* 'bow'
	kožich 'fur'	*soud* 'court, case'	*spoušť* 'havoc, trigger'
15–50%	*dvorek* 'courtyard'	*kanál* 'sewer, channel'	*nit/niť* 'thread'
	velín 'control room'	*sklad* 'storeroom'	*nať* 'greens, stem'
50–85%	*lesík* 'little wood'	*tenis* 'tennis'	*loď* 'ship'
	komín 'chimney'	*spis* 'file, record'	*trať* 'track'
85–99%	*čtvrtek* 'Thursday'	*balkon* 'balcony'	*ocel* 'steel'
	národ 'nation'	*zápas* 'contest, match'	*moč* 'urine'
99–100%	*oběd* 'dinner'	*stůl* 'table'	*bezmoc* 'powerlessness'
	sklep 'cellar'	*byt* 'apartment'	*čelist* 'jaw'

Methodology

Our main hypothesis was that respondents' performance on production and evaluation tasks would vary depending on speakers' reactions to reading tasks. However, we know from the previous research that other factors have repeatedly been shown to be a dominant influence on these sorts of tasks; therefore, we also hypothesize that the effect of reading-task factors will be *smaller* than those of other known contributing factors, such as the proportional frequency of these forms as observed in, e.g, corpora.

Our survey was constructed by drawing sentence-long contexts from the Czech National Corpus wherever possible.[13] Two basic versions of the questionnaire were created: a production variant, where respondents were to input the missing endings of words, and an evaluation variant, where respondents were to rate each ending's acceptability on a scale from 1 (completely normal) to 7 (unacceptable). The same sentences were used as triggers in both basic versions.

Gap-filling sentences were presented in the following format:

6. Z poušt__ vál horký vítr.

'A hot wind blew from the *desert*_____'

Ratings tasks were presented in the following format, with both possible forms displayed in context:

[13] Sometimes these sentences needed to be modified—typically shortened to remove extraneous material, but also sometimes substituting lexical items to achieve a more "neutral" effect for the trigger. This was to avoid respondent reactions directed not at the target feature but at some other aspect of the text that was irrelevant, which could confound the results. In some instances (esp. with rarer lexemes), no suitable sentence could be found, and so we looked for sentences with synonyms or other lexemes close in meaning and substituted the target word in order to create the trigger.

32.

	1(+)	2	3	4	5	6	7(-)
Pracovali jsme od časného rána do **obědu**.	○	○	○	○	○	○	○
Pracovali jsme od časného rána do **oběda**.	○	○	○	○	○	○	○

'We worked from early morning through to *lunch (obědu/oběda)*.'

As can be seen, there was no particular attempt to hide what was being tested. This derived partly from experience and partly from the structure of the survey. In a gap-filling survey, it is clear what is being tested, and so to hold conditions constant with the evaluation task, we needed to highlight the word concerned in the same way. On the matter of the naturalness of this sort of task, see, e.g, Bermel and Knittl (2012b, pp. 243–245).

Each target word appears in the survey twice, in two different syntactic contexts. One context is that most favored for the given case, i.e, for the genitive an adnominal construction (indicating possession or characteristic) and for the locative a location with the preposition *v* 'in' or *na* 'on.' The other context was a less common one, i.e, genitive after a non-motion preposition such as *vedle* 'next to' and *během* 'during' or for the locative a non-locational preposition or meaning. We had previously found that ratings were sensitive to context (Bermel & Knittl, 2012a, 2012b), hence its inclusion here.

The survey was supplied to users recruited via colleagues, family, and friends on Surveymonkey. Each user read and responded to 36 triggers mixing a variety of features. A reading skills test followed, and then a further 36 triggers as at the beginning.

Within each basic version (gap-filling and ratings), the test questions were thus divided into two "blocks" (before/after reading skills test). Half the respondents took block A before block B; the other half took block B before block A. Within blocks, the order of questions was randomized.[14]

The reading skills test contained two specially written passages. These happen to contain the test words, but respondents were not asked to do anything with them in this part of the study—instead, we were interested in their reading abilities overall and how those might have affected their responses to the triggers (see the discussion in section "Background"). We aimed to create one passage that would be comprehensible to ordinary readers, so as not to intimidate respondents and induce them to abandon the task, but we needed at least one passage to be considerably more difficult to ensure that not all respondents were at ceiling on the reading task as a whole.[15]

[14] Surveymonkey did not support randomizing question order across two separate locations in a survey, so the constituent triggers of a block always had to remain in that block.

[15] If all respondents are at ceiling, the task will not serve to isolate relevant factors, as we cannot distinguish among the respondents based on performance.

We tested our passages for "readability" using online tools at readability-score.com and read-able.com. The tests used on these sites (Flesch Kincaid Reading Ease and Grade Score, Gunning Fog Score, SMOG index, Coleman Liau Index, and Automated Readability Index) consider factors such as sentence length, word length, and number of syllables per word. For a language like Czech with a relatively "shallow" orthography, they can be predicted to give reasonable results. Our first text was rated "easily understandable by 11–12 year olds," while the second was rated as having postgraduate-level complexity, which confirmed our intuitive evaluations of them.[16]

Following each passage, there were four questions. The first asked respondents to evaluate, subjectively, their experience of reading. *Jak pochopitelný je podle vás tento text?* 'How comprehensible did you find this text?' Possible answers ranged from *1—Velmi snadno* 'Very easy' to *7—Velmi špatně* 'Very poor.' The intermediate points 2–6 were numbered but not named. The remaining three questions were multiple-choice comprehension checks and were designed to test the precision or accuracy of the respondent's reading skills.

In one version of the passages, most test words appeared with the "expansive" exponents {u} (masc. gen.), {u} (masc. loc.), and {e/ě} (fem. gen.), which are the endings that appear most frequently in these slots and are historically on the rise. In the other version, most test words appeared with the "recessive" features {a} (masc. gen.), {ě/e} (masc. loc.), and {i} (fem. gen.), which appear less frequently overall in the slot and are historically on the wane.[17]

There were thus eight basic possible permutations (task type (2) × block order (2) and reading passages (2)). The assignment of respondents to these eight basic versions was done randomly by the survey software.

In summary, the features we considered as possible factors are listed in Table 2.3, along with the manipulations we undertook to make them usable for the type of statistical analysis.[18]

[16] Read-able.com warned us, "Ooh, that's probably a bit too complicated. Have you thought about using smaller words and shorter sentences?"

[17] Forms that were unrepresented in the corpus or represented only sporadically were not used, so as not to create the impression of an unnatural text. Instead, for those lexemes the common form was inserted.

[18] See further for information on ANOVAs. The assumptions of ANOVA include a dependent variable with interval values and a limited number of "levels" per factor. A seven-point scale such as the one we use for our ratings is considered to give *ordinal* values (showing order or priority but where there is no demonstrable mathematical relationship between the values) rather than *interval* values (showing points on a scale with a demonstrable mathematical relationship: equally spaced, each double/ten times the preceding, etc.). However, when the number of respondents exceeds 100, ordinal values such as our impressionistic seven-point scale give equally good results. We created levels for our factors by "binning" responses to get 4–6 groups for each factor. We practiced good data hygiene here by defining our bins prior to analysis rather than afterwards and by ensuring that bins with very small numbers of respondents were amalgamated with other bins.

Table 2.3 Factors in the analysis

Between-subjects factors (individual differences between respondents)			
Variable	*Data type*	*Manipulation*	*Resulting type*
Age	Interval	Binned: 18–25, 26–35, 36–45, 46+	Ordinal
Region	Nominal	Bohemia, Moravia	Nominal
Reading test accuracy ("Reading Accuracy")	Interval	Multiple-choice questions correct out of 6	Interval
Perceived difficulty of text ("Perceived Difficulty")	Ordinal	Sum of two ratings, one per text	Ordinal
Within-subjects factors (features of the data seen by all respondents)			
Variable	*Data type*	*Manipulation*	*Resulting type*
Proportional frequency of items in a corpus ("Proportional Frequency")	Interval	Binned as in Table 2.2 above	Ordinal
Syntactic context of item in the trigger ("Context")	Nominal	One highly typical context and one less typical context	Nominal
Ending rated (ratings task only) ("Ending")	Nominal	Exponent: {a}, {u}, {i}, {e/ě}	Nominal
Dependent variable			
Rating (ratings task only)	Ordinal	Value from 1 (best) to 7 (worst)	Ordinal
Ending Selected (gap-filling task only)	Nominal	Frequency with which expansive ending is chosen (value 0 > *n*)	Interval

Results

305 Czech native speakers completed our surveys. Of those, 151 completed the gap-filling task and 154 completed the ratings task. The assignment to one or another task was made randomly by the survey program.

Between-Subjects Variables

Our respondents are from a cross-section of Czech society, although they cannot be said to be a proportional representation of it. Younger, more educated, female respondents predominate compared to their numbers in society as a whole. The survey has this in common with others of its type (see Bermel et al., 2015a, pp. 291–292). Only the geographic distribution between two major speech regions (Bohemia vs. Moravia/Silesia) is proportional to the populations in those bins. The breakdown is given in Table 2.4.

As previously mentioned, the between-speakers variables that interested us most in this study were those that involved reading skills. The first, given in Fig. 2.1, concerns the accuracy of answers to the six multiple-choice reading comprehension

Table 2.4 Biographical details

Age and region			Education and gender		
	Group	*N*		Group	*N*
Age Group	18–25	122	Education	Primary school	41
	26–35	63		Technical school	7
	36–45	43		Secondary school	106
	46+	77		Tertiary education	151
Region	Bohemia	182	Gender	Male	101
	Moravia	123		Female	204

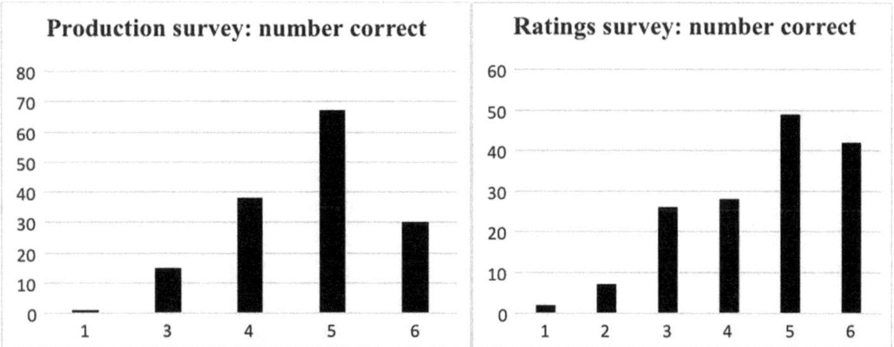

Fig. 2.1 Accuracy on the reading comprehension test: production vs. ratings

questions.[19] The second, given in Fig. 2.2, concerns respondents' perceptions of difficulty of the texts. In both instances, results are given separately for those completing the production version of the survey and those completing the ratings version of the survey.

In Fig. 2.1, the x-axis represents the number of correct answers per respondent, and the y-axis represents the number of respondents. We can see that the bell curve is skewed towards the right: on average, people answered more questions right than wrong, so the top of the curve is at 5/6 correct answers.

This compares with Fig. 2.2, where we have more centered bell curves. The scores in Fig. 2.2 represent the sum of ratings on two questions following the texts, both of which asked, 'how difficult did you find this text?.' Ratings were given on a scale from 1 (very easy) to 7 (very difficult): thus a summed score of 7 could represent a judgment that one text was very hard (6) while another was very easy (1), or alternatively that both texts were of moderate difficulty (3, 4). The mode (most common score) was 6 for those taking the production version of the survey and 7 for those taking the ratings version, suggesting that few people found both texts easy or both texts difficult.

[19] Reading comprehension texts and questions are available on request from the corresponding author (n.bermel@sheffield.ac.uk).

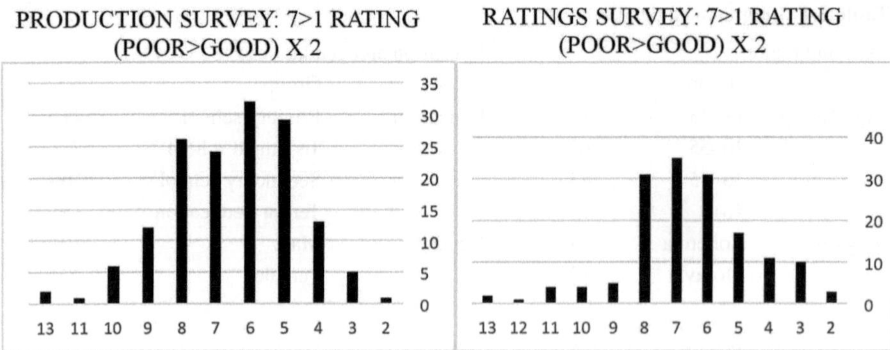

Fig. 2.2 Difficulty: production vs. ratings

One problem with bell curves like those in Figs. 2.1 and 2.2 is that some data are quite sparse. On the accuracy questions, no one got all questions wrong, and the number of respondents getting 1–2 questions right is also vanishingly low. This was particularly notable in the production survey, where only 1 respondent scored just 1 correct question and none scored only 2 correct questions.

On the difficulty rating, the scores could run from 14 (both texts maximally difficult) to 2 (both texts maximally easy). For the production cohort, only one respondent rated both texts as maximally easy and few people rated both texts as difficult (only three respondents between 11 and 14 points). For the evaluation cohort, three people rated both texts as maximally easy and a further three gave between 12 and 14 points.

Thus, although a bell curve appears in all four graphs, the sparseness of data at the ends of the bell curve (points on the scale with 0–2 answers) means that results may not appear significant.

Results of Production Task

Repeated measures ANOVAs were carried out to ascertain the influence of proportional frequency ("mixture" of forms) and sentential context (how the form is syntactically connected to the rest of the sentence) on the frequency of choice of the "expansive" (historically ascendant) endings. ANOVA is a statistical test that compares sets of data to show which of a series of entered factors had a statistically significant effect and how the overall effect is apportioned out among the factors.

Statistical significance is given by the p-value, which assesses the chance that the result is random (e.g, the result of "noise" or an unbalanced sample). We say we have a significant (noteworthy) result if $p < 0.05$ (a 5% or less chance that this result is non-replicable).

The partial eta-squared (η^2) value can be used to detect the size of the contribution of the given factor. The value is always between 0 and 1, with larger values (towards 1) representing a greater size of effect.[20]

Region of origin and age groups were entered as between-subjects ("biographical") factors, alongside the self-rated difficulty of the text and the number of correct comprehension-check answers (see Table 2.3).

In our results, there were occasional significant "biographical" factors, but they differed from feature to feature. For the masc. gen. sg., Region was the only significant feature: F (1, 132) = 9.85, $p < 0.003$, partial $\eta^2 = 0.07$. For the masc. loc. sg., there was a significant interaction between Region and Proportional Frequency: F (4.18, 551.26) = 2.65, $p < 0.04$, partial $\eta^2 = 0.02$. For the fem. gen. sg., we found a significant interaction between Perceived Difficulty and Proportional Frequency: F (41.61, 549.24) = 1.50, $p < 0.03$, partial $\eta^2 = 0.10$, and Reading Accuracy: F (4, 132) = 3.31, $p < 0.02$, partial $\eta^2 = 0.09$. All these significant results were sporadic and had small effect sizes.

In sum, we found no consistent evidence that reading scores or other biographical data (i.e., between-subjects variables) consistently influence the production task.

Results of Evaluation Task

Repeated measures ANOVAs were carried out to ascertain the influence of proportional frequency ("mixture" of forms as found in the corpus) and sentential context on the acceptability rating of forms. The particular exponent chosen also becomes an independent variable, because we have separate ratings for each exponent seen (see Table 2.3).

Region of origin and age group were entered as between-subjects ("biographical") factors, alongside the self-rated difficulty of the text and the number of correct comprehension-check answers.

In examining our analyses, we will be interested in: (1) which factors seem to have the largest effects and (2) which factors crop up most consistently across all three features examined, regardless of effect size.

Masculine Genitive Singular {a} vs. {u}

In the masc. gen. sg., we found two major effects (based on the F value and the partial η^2 value, which is derived in part from it). These were both connected with the proportional frequency in the corpus of the ending tested. The first in Table 2.5 suggests that the largest effect is due to the frequency of the ending tested in the corpus relative to the frequency of the untested ending. A second, medium-sized

[20] We also report, but do not discuss, the F value, which is the ratio of between-groups variances to within-groups variances. An F value of 1 tends to confirm the null hypothesis.

Table 2.5 Significant factors in the masc. gen. sg

Feature	*F* values	*p* value	Part. η^2	Effect size
Proportional Frequency * Ending	F (3.53, 468.95) = 538.45	$p < 0.001$	0.80	Large
Proportional Frequency	F (4.30, 571.74) = 63.66	$p < 0.001$	0.32	Medium
Context	F (1, 133) = 20.60	$p < 0.001$	0.13	Small
Prop. Frequency * Ending * Age Group	F (10.58, 468.95) = 6.38	$p < 0.001$	0.13	Small
Context * Proportional Frequency	F (4.78, 635.26) = 17.04	$p < 0.001$	0.11	Small
Age Group	F (3, 133) = 4.86	$p < 0.004$	0.10	Small
Prop. Frequency * Reading Accuracy	F (21.49, 571.74) = 1.70	$p < 0.03$	0.06	Small
Ending * Region	F (1, 133) = 5.95	$p < 0.02$	0.04	Small
Prop. Frequency * Age Group	F (12.90, 571.74) = 2.05	$p < 0.02$	0.04	Small
Prop. Frequency * Ending * Region	F (3.53, 468.95) = 2.61	$p < 0.05$	0.02	Small

Asterisks indicate an interaction between two or more features

effect is that of Proportional Frequency itself, which suggests that, e.g, when a lexeme has more skewed proportion of endings, these will be rated overall higher or lower than a lexeme whose endings are proportionally more equal in the corpus.

There were a number of minor effects, which are listed in order of decreasing effect size in Table 2.5. These minor effects (where the *F* value and the partial η^2 value are much smaller) frequently involve interactions with Proportional Frequency, suggesting that they are not equally distributed across all the lexemes studied. Instead, for example, Reading Accuracy scores play a role in people's ratings, but only for certain lexemes based on their placement on the proportional frequency scale (again, suggesting that respondents react differently to words whose alternate forms have a skewed representation vs. those whose forms have a more equal representation in the corpus).

In contrast to the production task, where age played no role, Age Group shows up three times in the results of the evaluation task, suggesting that there are more general differences in how people of different ages reacted, and Age Group has specific interactions with corpus frequency. However, the frequency with which one form was produced vis-à-vis the other seems not to have differed significantly across the age groups.

Masculine Locative Singular {ě/e} vs. {u}

The two major effects in the masc. loc. sg. were identical to those in the gen. sg. The minor effects are listed in Table 2.6. As with the gen. sg., many of the minor effects also include Proportional Frequency, indicating that they are not equally distributed across all words but take account of skewed vs. equal representation of variant forms in the corpus. Reading Accuracy showed up again, in interaction with Proportional Frequency. Age Group also showed up, by itself and in two

Table 2.6 Significant factors in the masc. loc. sg

Feature	*F* values	*p* value	Part. η^2	Effect size
Proportional Frequency * Ending	F (3.36, 447.13) = 465.63	$p < 0.001$	0.78	Large
Proportional Frequency	F (4.21, 560.21) = 79.90	$p < 0.001$	0.38	Medium
Context * Diff. Rating	F (11, 133) = 2.31	$p < 0.02$	0.16	Small
Prop. Frequency * Ending * Diff. Rating	F (36.98, 447.13) = 1.49	$p < 0.04$	0.11	Small
Prop. Frequency * Ending * Age Group	F (10.09, 447.13) = 5.07	$p < 0.001$	0.10	Small
Prop. Frequency * Age Group	F (12.64, 560.21) = 3.61	$p < 0.001$	0.08	Small
Context	F (1, 133) = 10.42	$p < 0.003$	0.07	Small
Age Group	F (3, 133) = 3.19	$p < 0.03$	0.07	Small
Prop. Frequency * Reading Accuracy	F (21.06, 560.21) = 1.75	$p < 0.03$	0.06	Small
Context * Proportional Frequency	F (4.87, 647.15) = 8.19	$p < 0.001$	0.06	Small

Table 2.7 Significant factors in the fem. gen. sg.

Feature	*F* values	*p* value	Part. η^2	Effect size
Proportional Frequency * Ending	F (3.63, 482.91) = 510.25	$p < 0.001$	0.79	Large
Proportional Frequency	F (4.18, 555.88) = 73.89	$p < 0.001$	0.36	Medium
Ending * Diff. Rating	F (11, 133) = 2.30	$p < 0.02$	0.16	Small
Prop. Frequency * Ending * Diff. Rating	F (39.94, 482.91) = 1.92	$p < 0.002$	0.14	Small
Prop. Frequency * Ending * Age Group	F (10.89, 482.91) = 4.10	$p < 0.001$	0.09	Small
Context	F (1, 133) = 11.04	$p < 0.002$	0.08	Small
Prop. Frequency * Reading Accuracy	F (20.90, 555.88) = 1.79	$p < 0.02$	0.06	Small
Context * Proportional Frequency	F (4.60, 612.30) = 3.62	$p < 0.005$	0.03	Small
Prop. Frequency * Region	F (4.18, 555.88) = 2.37	$p < 0.05$	0.02	Small
Prop. Frequency * Ending * Region	F (3.63, 482.91) = 2.59	$p < 0.01$	0.02	Small

interactions. Difficulty Rating showed up twice in the minor effects, both in interactions with features of the sentences presented (Context and Proportional Frequency by Ending).

Feminine Genitive Singular {i} vs. {ě/e}

The two major effects in the fem. gen. sg. were identical to those seen in both masc. sg. cases. The minor effects are listed in Table 2.7. The continuing significance of Proportional Frequency is shown here as well. Additional factors in this analysis include Reading Accuracy, Region, Context, and Difficulty Rating.

Significant Factors in Common

Certain factors showed up in two or three of our cases. In two cases, we found significant effects of the following factors or interactions of factors:

- Age Group
- Proportional Frequency * Ending * Region
- Proportional Frequency * Ending * Difficulty Rating
- Proportional Frequency * Age Group

In all three cases, we found significant effects of the following factors or interactions of factors:

- Proportional Frequency * Ending
- Proportional Frequency
- Proportional Frequency * Ending * Age group
- Context
- Context * Proportional Frequency
- Proportional Frequency * Reading Accuracy

Discussion

We noted above a difference between the two sorts of tasks completed by our respondents. The production task showed sporadic significant contributions by features or interactions of features but no sign of consistent, significant effects in any one area. The number of significant features was much greater with the ratings task, and the primary problem facing the researcher is to distinguish which of them to single out for further investigation.

Avoiding Type I Errors

A Type I error, or a "false positive" result, occurs when our statistical test reports that the connection noticed is not the result of chance, i.e, is a significant predictor of future behavior, when in fact it is probably not significant and nothing should be read into it. However, the number of apparently anomalous positive results here deserves comment. We can explain them in two ways. One possibility is that there really is an effect here, but it is not general to the category of "morphological overabundance" and we can thus draw no further conclusions from it. For example, there may be a feature of one or two of the words used that we did not account for, and what we are actually looking at is a feature limited to a particular lexeme or small set of lexemes. Another possibility is that the appearance of a significant result is a side effect of having a large number of variables and interactions. Significance is of course nothing more than an estimation of the probability that the results are down to chance, and hence if enough variables and interactions are included, the probability rises that at least one of them will register as significant. The probability of these occasional "false positives" is increased by the fact that our surveys were relatively large, with over 150 participants each; analyses of larger cohorts are more prone to return small effects as significant.

For this reason, we focused our attention on factors that held constant across all three of the features studied. Doing so reduced the chance that we would be committing a Type I error.

Explaining Variations in Ratings

Most of the variation in ratings is accounted for by the effects of the interaction between proportional frequency of forms in a corpus (Proportional Frequency) and the specific variant ending used (Ending). In other words, the relative frequency with which language users see one form vs. another in the "real world" around them (as represented by corpus data) constitutes the largest influence on their ratings of those forms.

A second, medium-sized effect is always Proportional Frequency by itself, which indicates that, regardless of which variant is involved, different ratios between variants affect our judgments. A skewed ratio of forms (say, 99:1) is treated differently than a more balanced ratio of forms (say, 5:1 or 3:1), and this operates regardless of which specific variant is in question.

These findings are entirely in line with our previous investigations (Bermel & Knittl, 2012a, 2012b; Bermel et al., 2015a, 2015b, 2017). These identified the proportional frequency of items in a corpus as the largest attributable factor in respondents' ratings of those items and a large factor in how respondents selected one or the other variant. We also proposed that the absolute frequency of forms was the largest attributable factor in respondents' selection of one of two available forms.

Some variation in our ratings is attributable to the syntactic context in which the lexeme is situated. This again is in line with the previous findings. Bermel and Knittl (2012b) had found a larger and more consistent effect of Context, but that difference is probably down to the different structure of the study. Our earlier study had focused on two variables only: Proportional Frequency and Context (4 levels), and so tested a wider variety of contexts, allowing for more detailed results. In the current study, the addition of other factors made it impractical to include more than two levels of Context without the survey becoming unwieldy for respondents. The current analysis is consequently less fine-grained, so the importance of this factor is suppressed.

Most interestingly for our current purposes, we identified a consistent small effect of the interaction between Proportional Frequency and Reading Accuracy: Better reading scores indicate more positive ratings, with the most positive ratings (i.e, closer to 1 than 7) coming from those who had moderate-to-high scores on the reading accuracy task.

As can be seen in Fig. 2.3, the effect was more noticeable for words where both endings are better attested (middle four bands), as opposed to those where one end-

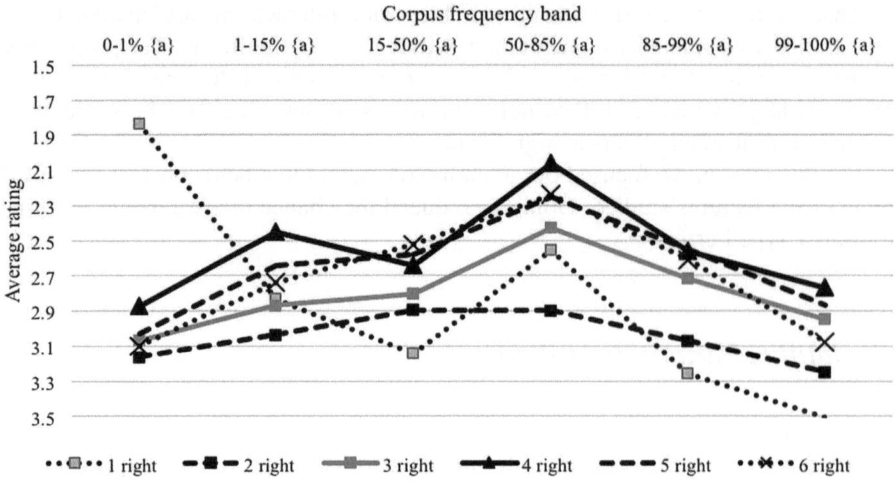

Fig. 2.3 Text comprehension accuracy vs. frequency of {a} ending for masc. gen. sg

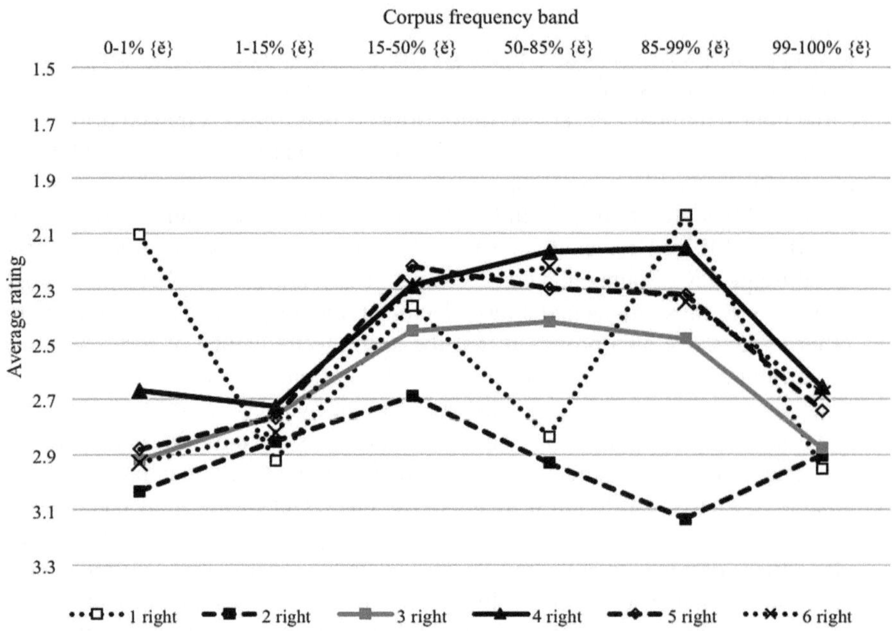

Fig. 2.4 Text comprehension accuracy vs. frequency of {ě/e} ending for masc. loc. sg

ing is completely predominant (outer two bands). Similar, but not identical, patterns can be observed in Figs. 2.4 and 2.5, for the masc. loc. sg. and the fem. gen. sg., respectively.[21]

[21] The anomalous shape of the "1 right" band has to do with the fact that only two respondents fell into this bracket, so the reactions are highly dependent on individual idiosyncrasies.

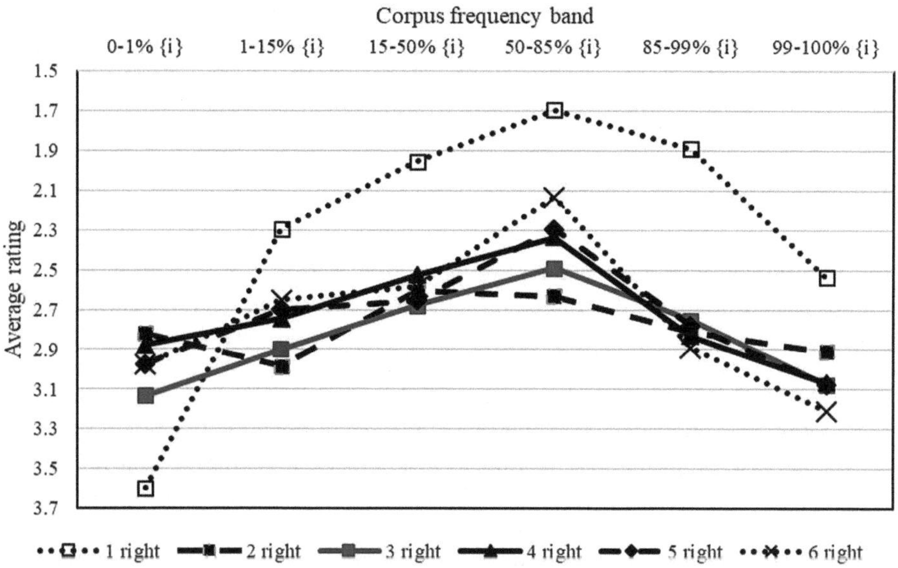

Fig. 2.5 Text comprehension accuracy vs. frequency of {i} ending for fem. gen. sg

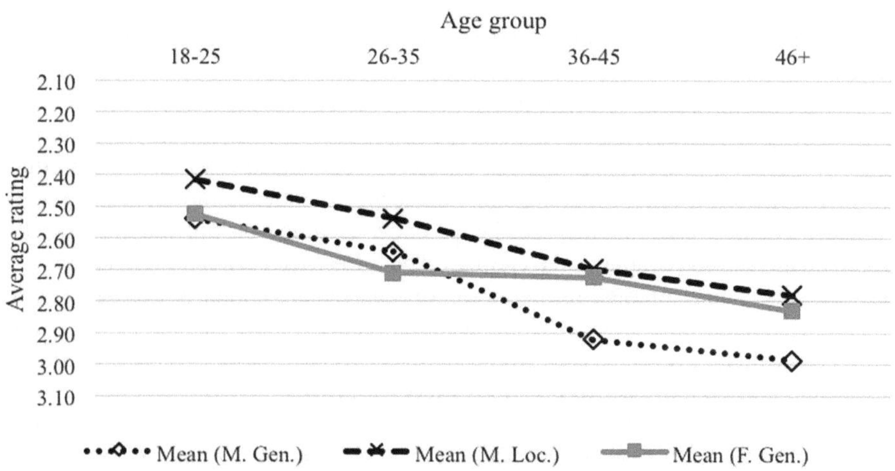

Fig. 2.6 Mean rating by age group

Age plays a surprisingly consistent role in choices, as can be seen in Fig. 2.6. Across all features studied, older people are less susceptible to rate items positively (the lower the number, the more positive the rating).

This result was surprising, as age had not emerged in our previous surveys as a consistent and significant factor.

Of our two reading tasks, difficulty ratings registered as influential for ratings on two out of our three features, but only accuracy on the comprehension checks registered as influential for all three features. We noted that this variation is strongest for slots where both forms are represented in the corpus in more than sporadic fashion (>1%).

Conclusions

In our original hypotheses, we had proposed that performance on production and ratings tasks would vary depending on speakers' reactions to reading tasks. The first part of this hypothesis—concerning the production task—was not confirmed. The second part—concerning the ratings task—was confirmed. We only felt confident proposing one of the two reading tasks—the accuracy test—as a reliable indicator, as the other task only registered significant for two of the three features studied.

We had also proposed that the effect of these between-subjects, user-dependent factors would be smaller than those of other known contributing factors based in the language, such as the proportional frequency of these forms as observed in, e.g, corpora. This part of the hypothesis was confirmed. In other words, the frequency with which we meet variant forms in written discourse is the prime determiner of how we select among those variant forms and how we evaluate them. Factors that differentiate between individuals based on their abilities or life histories (age, gender, region of origin, education, and reading ability) play a secondary role or no discernible role.

We noted that neither reading task seemed to influence production tasks in cells where there is overabundance. In retrospect, the ability to comprehend a text and answer questions correctly might not be closely connected with how we produce forms. However, levels of reading skills do seem to influence ratings tasks in cells where there is overabundance: the better one's accuracy on our reading test, the more positively one evaluates the endings. The difference between high-scorers and low-scorers is more marked for items where speakers are regularly exposed to both forms. This made us wonder whether accurate readers might turn out to be broader or more proficient readers, who would be likely to have more exposure to written texts, and thus be more accepting of a variety of forms.

Age showed up in these studies as a significant factor, whereas in our other studies of the same features its effect had not been significant. Users of different ages may not have significantly different mechanisms for judging and producing case endings, but nonetheless they appear to react differently to linguistic stimuli that attempt to influence their behavior, such as our reading passages and tests. It may be that the greater linguistic experience of older speakers results in a different pattern of response.

Our hypothesis regarding wider exposure and higher ratings would lead us to expect, therefore, that older respondents would have had more exposure to a larger number of forms and thus be more positive about a greater variety of them. However, the results were in fact the exact opposite: Age Group came out as a significant factor in the evaluation tasks, but the older the group, the less positive overall were the ratings. This means that the two variables in question here (reading accuracy and age) are not covariate, as they do not share in producing the same result. Greater exposure over time, as opposed to over quantity and variety of texts solely, seems to lead, paradoxically, to a hardening of opinion, giving indirect evidence for preemption ("how speakers learn what not to say" (Goldberg, 2011, p. 132)). It suggests that preemption, like other cognitive processes, does not finish at some "critical age" but continues to operate through adulthood.

Another way to look at this is to see age as a counterweight to growing vocabulary and increased exposure. Mulder and Hulstijn (2011) show that certain high-effort tasks present evidence of cognitive decline among speakers from age 18 to 75; however, more automatic production tasks are rated as showing little to no decline over time. We might expect that as our exposure to texts grows over time, our reaction times might slow as we have to process additional, internally conflicting data with our slowing reflexes, but yet this seems not to be the case for the vast bulk of routine work that we do as speakers. Our findings support the hypothesis that preemption can provide a partial explanation as to why our production time does not rise to that same extent.

Our study thus suggests that respondents access the linguistic knowledge represented in corpora in various ways: *lexically* (through a mental representation of lexical frequency), *contextually* (organizing language material by relations that can be perceived in corpus data), *experientially* via *skilled reading* (through the accuracy of one's grasp of texts, possibly indicative of the intensity of prior engagement in reading activities), and *experientially* via *length of exposure* (through a changing attitude to language over time as experience accretes and the mind compensates for the growing volume of resource at its disposal). The first two factors—which are largely shared by speakers—play a predominant role, but the last two—which show differences between speakers—play a small but significant role, showing how the type, quality, and length of exposure to language data changes our perception of it.

References

Albright, A., & Hayes, B. (2003). Rules vs. analogy in English past tenses: A computational/experimental study. *Cognition, 90*, 119–161.

Bermel, N. (2004a). V korpuse nebo v korpusu? Co nám řekne (a neřekne) ČNK o morfologické variaci v tvarech lokálu [*V korpuse* or *v korpusu*? What the Czech National Corpus will (and will not) tell us about morphological variation in locative case forms]. In Z. Hladková & P. Karlík (Eds.), *Čeština – univerzália a specifika 5* (pp. 163–171). Prague, Czech Republic: Nakladatelství Lidové Noviny.

Bermel, N. (2004b). Jak často se vyskytují (vyskytujou) tzv. hovorové tvary 1. os. j. č. a 3 os. mn. č. v Českém národním korpusu? [How often do the so-called colloquial forms of the 1 sg. and 3 pl. occur in the Czech National Corpus]? In P. Karlík (Ed.), *Korpus jako zdroj dat o češtině* (pp. 29–40). Brno, Czech Republic: Masarykova univerzita.

Bermel, N. (2010). Variace a frekvence variant na příkladu tvrdých neživotných maskulin [Variation and the frequency of variants in hard masculine inanimate nouns]. In S. Čmejrková,

J. Hoffmannová, & E. Havlová (Eds.), *Užívání a prožívání jazyka* (pp. 135–140). Prague, Czech Republic: Karolinum.

Bermel, N., & Knittl, L. (2012a). Corpus frequency and acceptability judgments: A study of morphosyntactic variants in Czech. *Corpus Linguistics and Linguistic Theory, 8*, 241–275.

Bermel, N., & Knittl, L. (2012b). Morphosyntactic variation and syntactic environments in Czech nominal declension: Corpus frequency and native-speaker judgments. *Russian Linguistics, 36*, 91–119.

Bermel, N., Knittl, L., & Russell, J. (2015a). Morphological variation and sensitivity to frequency of forms among native speakers of Czech. *Russian Linguistics, 39*, 283–308.

Bermel, N., Knittl, L., & Russell, J. (2015b). From standard to norm through the lens of corpora and native speakers. *Prace Filologiczne, 67*, 21–43.

Bermel, N., Knittl, L., & Russell, J. (2017). Frequency data from corpora partially explain native-speaker ratings and choices in overabundant paradigm cells. *Corpus Linguistics and Linguistic Theory*. https://doi.org/10.1515/cllt-2016-0032.

Bybee, J. L., & Slobin, D. I. (1982). Rules and schemas in the development and use of the English past tense. *Language, 58*, 265–289.

Čermák, F., Doležalová-Spoustová, D., Hlaváčová, J., Hnátková, M., Jelínek, T., Kocek, J. et al. (2005). *SYN2005: A genre-balanced corpus of written Czech.* Prague, Czech Republic: Ústav Českého národního korpusu FF UK, from www.korpus.cz

Čermák, F., Králík, J., & Kučera, K. (1997). Recepce současné češtiny a reprezentativnost korpusu (Výsledky a některé souvislosti jedné orientační sondy na pozadí budování Českého národního korpusu) [The reception of contemporary Czech and corpus representativity: Results and some relevant points of a preliminary sounding done during the building of the Czech National Corpus]. *Slovo a slovesnost, 58*, 117–123.

Chandler, S. (2010). The English past tense: Analogy redux. *Cognitive Linguistics, 21*, 371–417.

Conway, A. R., Kane, M. J., Buntin, M. F., Zach Hambrick, D., Wilhelm, O., & Engle, R. W. (2005). Working memory span tasks: A methodological review and user's guide. *Psychonomic Bulletin & Review, 12*, 769–786.

Cvrček, V., Čermáková, A., & Křen, M. (2016). Nová koncepce synchronních korpusů psané češtiny. *Slovo a slovesnost, 77*, 83–101.

Dąbrowska, E. (2008). The effects of frequency and neighbourhood density on adult speakers' productivity with Polish case inflections. *Journal of Memory and Language, 58*, 931–951.

Dąbrowska, E. (2010). Naive v. expert intuitions: An empirical study of acceptability judgments. *The Linguistic Review, 27*, 1–23.

Divjak, D. (2017). The role of lexical frequency in the acceptability of syntactic variants: Evidence from *that*-clauses in Polish. *Cognitive Science, 41*, 354–382. First published online 2016: 1–26.

Eddington, D. (2000). Analogy and the dual-route model of morphology. *Lingua, 110*, 281–298.

Fidler, M. U., & Cvrček, V. (2015). A data-driven analysis of reader viewpoints: Reconstructing the historical reader using keyword analysis. *Journal of Slavic Linguistics, 23*, 197–239.

Frisch, S., & Brea-Spahn, M. (2010). Metalinguistic judgments of phonotactics by monolinguals and bilinguals. *Laboratory Phonology, 1*, 345–360.

Goldberg, A. (2011). Corpus evidence of the viability of statistical preemption. *Cognitive Linguistics, 22*, 131–153. https://doi.org/10.1515/COGL.2011.006

Grepl, M., Hladká, Z., Jelínek, M., Karlík, P., Krčmová, M., Nekula, M., et al. (1995). *Příruční mluvnice češtiny [A grammar handbook of Czech]*. Prague, Czech Republic: Nakladatelství Lidové noviny.

Haber, L. R. (1976). Leaped and leapt: A theoretical account of linguistic variation. *Foundations of Language, 14*, 211–238.

Hupet, M., Desmette, D., & Schelstraete, M.-A. (1997). What does Daneman and Carpenter's reading span really measure? *Perceptual and Motor Skills, 84*(2), 603–608.

Křen, M., Bartoň, T., Cvrček, V., Hnátková, M., Jelínek, T., Kocek, J., et al. (2010). *SYN2010: A genre-balanced corpus of written Czech.* Prague, Czech Republic: Ústav Českého národního korpusu FF UK, from www.korpus.cz

Lečić, D. (2015). Morphological doublets in Croatian: The case of the instrumental singular. *Russian Linguistics, 39*, 375–393.

Mulder, K., & Hulstijn, J. H. (2011). Linguistic skills of adult native speakers as a function of age and level of education. *Applied Linguistics, 32*, 475–494.

Prasada, S., & Pinker, S. (1993). Generalization of regular and irregular morphological patterns. *Language and Cognitive Processes, 8*, 1–56.

Sgall, P. (2011). Perspektivy standardní češtiny [Perspectives on standard Czech]. In E. Hajíčová & J. Panevová (Eds.), *Jazyk, mluvení, psaní* (pp. 180–204). Prague, Czech Republic: Karolinum.

Staum Casasanto, L., Hofmeister, P., & Sag, I. (2010). Understanding acceptability judgments: Additivity and working memory effects. In *Proceedings of the 32nd annual conference of the Cognitive Science Society* (pp. 224–229). Austin, TX: Cognitive Science Society.

Thornton, A. (2012). Reduction and maintenance of overabundance: A case study on Italian verb paradigms. *Word Structure, 5*, 183–207.

Ústav pro jazyk český. (2004–2017). *Internetová jazyková příručka [The internet* language *manual]*. Jazyková poradna: Ústavu pro jazyk český, from http://prirucka.ujc.cas.cz/

Chapter 3
Vowel Disharmony in Czech Words and Stems

Jiří Milička and Hana Kalábová

Abstract This corpus study describes vowel phonotactics in Czech words. The results suggest that some probabilistic patterns are employed in Czech: some vowel combinations are overrepresented, while others are underrepresented. A syllable containing a short front vowel tends to be followed by a syllable with a long front vowel. A long front vowel is typically followed by a back vowel and a long back vowel tends to be followed by a short vowel; thus, an interesting circular dissimilative pattern can be observed. An explanation of the phenomena can be facilitated by the Shannonian theory of communication. The analysis was performed both on words and word stems (i.e, words without endings), obtaining different results.

Keywords Corpus linguistics · Quantitative linguistics · Czech · Hungarian · Phonotactic patterns · Vowel harmony

Introduction: Vowel Harmony and Disharmony

Vowel harmony is a long-distance assimilatory process found in many languages all over the world. It refers to important phonotactic patterns in these languages. These patterns originate from the process of vowel-to-vowel assimilation found in earlier stages in the history of some languages, which results in vowels that are similar to each other in some way (Ohala, 1994). The phenomenon is known from the Uralic and Turkic languages, but there are many other languages from different language families that show similar patterns of vowel harmony. For example, Finnish allows only front (/y/, /ö/, /ä/) or back vowels (/u/, /o/, /a/) in a single word; the co-occurrence of "harmonically neutral" vowels (/i/, /e/), however, is not constrained

---

J. Milička (✉) · H. Kalábová
Institute of Comparative Linguistics, Faculty of Arts, Charles University,
Nam. Jana Palacha 2, Praha 1, Czech Republic

M. Fidler, V. Cvrček (eds.), *Taming the Corpus*, Quantitative Methods in the Humanities and Social Sciences, https://doi.org/10.1007/978-3-319-98017-1_3

(Suomi, McQueen, & Cutler, 1997). Word endings have two possible forms, so that the vowel type of the root triggers the vowel harmony in the rest of the word: *talo* → *talossa* ('house' → 'in a house'), *sänky* → *sängyssä* ('bed' → 'in a bed').

The term *vowel disharmony* in the traditional sense of the word is used to refer to a *violation* of the vowel harmony patterns (for example, *olympialaiset* 'the Olympic games' in Finnish contains both front [/y/] and back vowels [/o/, /a/]) (Johnson, 1980). However, in this paper we do not use this term to refer to an aberration. Patterns of vowel disharmony in this study concern a *tendency* to accumulate dissimilar vowels in neighboring syllables in words. In contrast to languages in which vowel disharmony/harmony is documented as a consistent pattern, the target of this study focusing on Czech is most likely a tendency or a somewhat weaker pattern. We therefore use a methodology that is sufficiently robust to detect varying degrees of probabilistic tendencies.

This study will examine the tendencies of vowel combinations in Czech. Admittedly, this is not the first study on the possible existence of vowel harmony or disharmony patterns in a language that does not follow explicit rules of vowel harmony; a study on tendencies towards vowel harmony in French has already been conducted (Nguyen & Fagyal, 2008). Poldauf (1969) noticed that there is a tendency in Czech morphology towards vowel disharmony between the stems and their case endings, e.g, nouns that contain /a/ as the last vowel of the stem (as in *hrad* 'castle') tend to be assigned paradigms that do not contain /a/ in the ending (e.g, *hradu* 'castle, gen sg' instead of *hrada* 'castle, gen sg,' which is also theoretically possible). There is a recent attempt at a comprehensive description of Czech phonotactics (Bičan, 2011), but it is not based on a corpus linguistic paradigm.[1] Other studies by the same author (Bičan, 2015a, 2015b) test hypotheses regarding Czech vowel length, but these are based on a list of transcribed lexemes.[2]

Data

The data were extracted from the SYN2010 corpus (Křen et al., 2010)—a synchronic corpus of written Czech comprising 100 million tokens. The corpus contains fiction (40%), technical literature (27%), and journalistic texts (33%).

The SYN2005 corpus (Čermák et al., 2005) and SYN2015 corpus (Cvrček, Čermáková, & Křen, 2016; Křen et al. 2015, 2016) were also used to check the variability of the results across different datasets. The three corpora are comparable with each other, except that the text-type composition of SYN2015 differs slightly: fiction makes up 33.33%, nonfiction 33.33%, and journalistic texts 33.33%. In all cases, the least frequent words (frequency <10) were omitted.

[1] Paradigm in the Kuhnian sense (Kuhn, 1962).

[2] *Phonological Lexical Corpus*, which is not a corpus in the traditional sense; it is a list of lexemes (available at http://www.ujc.cas.cz/phword) (Bičan, 2015c).

Word stems were obtained by means of lemmatization of this corpus (Hnátková, Křen, Procházka, & Skoumalová, 2014; Petkevič, 2014). For example, the word form *vínovici* ('wine brandy, acc sg') is a compound of the stem *vínovic* and the ending *-i*. The stem extraction is carried out automatically by the following algorithm: (1) find all word forms of the given lemma; (2) find the longest string that is shared across all of the word forms of the given lemma: for example, the word form *vínovici* ('wine brandy, acc sg') belongs to the lemma *vínovice* ('wine brandy, nom sg'), but other inflected word forms are different—*vínovicích* ('wine brandy, loc pl'), *vínovicemi* ('wine brandy, instr pl'), *vínovic* ('wine brandy, gen pl'), etc.; therefore, the shortest shared stem is *vínovic*. In some paradigms, all endings share the same initial vowel (for example, the adjectival endings *-í*, *-ích*, *-ími*). Therefore, (3) if the last phoneme in the word is a vowel, truncate the last phoneme (only in inflected parts of speech).

The algorithm is far from being 100% reliable (in a random sample of 100 lemmata 93 were correct) as it fails to resolve forms with stem alternations such as *pes* ('dog, nom sg,' the stem is *pes-*)—*psa* ('dog, gen sg,' the stem is *ps-*), along with difficulties with the possessive ending *-ův,* which alternates with the form *-ov-*, e.g, *otcův* ('belonging to father nom sg')—*otcovi* ('belonging [nom pl] to the father'). It also fails to resolve suppletive forms such as *člověk* ('person')—*lidé* ('people'). The vast majority of word types are non-alternating and non-suppletive, but these alternating and suppletive word forms are the most frequent ones. The precision of the stemming algorithm is thus quite low. Therefore, we consider the results measured on this dataset to be only supplementary. Instead, we use results measured on the original word forms as our primary data.

As our work concerns Czech data, it is necessary to present a brief overview of the Czech vowel system. Czech has a five-vowel system wherein each vowel also has a long variant (as illustrated in Table 3.1). In this study, length (quantity) is marked by a short diagonal stroke above the letter (*acute accent*), as in Czech orthography. The vowels are presented in Table 3.1. Long /í/ is phonetically more raised than its short counterpart /i/ and short /a/ is phonetically more fronted than its long counterpart /á/. Long /ó/ is excluded from our analysis, as it occurs only in loanwords and interjections. The Czech vowel system also contains three diphthongs /au/, /eu/, and /ou/. The first two appear only in loanwords, so we also exclude them from analysis (for details, see Dankovičová, 1999, p. 72).

The Czech syllable nucleus can also be formed by a syllabic /r/, /l/, or /m/ in addition to the vowels (Palková, 1994, p. 367). In this study, we include these syllabic consonants in tables and figures, as their usage is quite common in Czech and they constitute an integral part of the phonological system, but we do not take them

Table 3.1 Czech vowel system (Dankovičová, 1999)

	Front	Central	Back
High	/i/ /í/		/ú/ /u/
Middle	/e/ /é/		/ó/ /o/
Low		/a/ /á/	

into account in the front–back vowel dichotomy analyses of vowel subset relations, since we cannot treat them as either front or back vowels.

Method

Description

The core of our method is straightforward: all pairs of neighboring vowels, diphthongs, and syllabic /r/ and /l/ in the corpus are recorded. Word boundaries are "not crossed"; in other words, only vowel pairs within individual words are taken into account. In addition to word types, word tokens were also taken into consideration; for example, the word *vínovici* ('wine brandy—singular dative') occurs three times in SYN2010, and thus the vowel pairs /í–o/, /o–i/ and /i–i/ were each counted three times in our statistics. By *word token*, we mean the form identified by the standard Czech National Corpus tokenization, i.e, the orthographical word rather than the *phonological word.*

The mere frequency of each vowel pair, however, is insufficient. We need to know whether the vowel pair is underrepresented or overrepresented, i.e, whether the vowel pair frequency is higher or lower than in a hypothetical situation in which the language system is completely neutral regarding any vocal harmony or disharmony. The most straightforward way to do that is to compare the measured values with the following random model:

> The relative frequency of the bigram $f(a; b)$ is equal to the absolute frequency of the bigram $(a; b)$ divided by the number of all bigram tokens. The theoretical relative frequency of the bigram $f'(a; b)$ is equal to the product of the relative frequency of the vowel $f_1(a)$ on the first position of all bigrams and the relative frequency of the vowel $f_2(b)$ on the second position. This simple idea yields the following formula of the metric $M(a; b)$, which is calculated as a ratio of the measured relative frequency of the bigram to the theoretical value:

$$M(a;b) = \frac{f(a;b)}{f'(a;b)} = \frac{f(a;b)}{f_1(a) f_2(b)} \tag{3.1}$$

The metric is easy to interpret:

$M(a; b) > 1$ indicates that the bigram is overrepresented
$M(a; b) < 1$ indicates that the bigram is underrepresented

Due to the corpus size, the absolute frequencies of the vowels and bigrams are overwhelming; therefore, the confidence intervals are small in all cases, and will not be shown in the analysis.

Example: Hungarian

The usage of the metric can first be exemplified by an analysis of the Hungarian National Corpus.[3] This section will show that the method results in reasonable outcomes that are consistent with this well-studied phonotactic system.

Hungarian has front, back, and "neutral" (or unrounded front) vowels (Vago, 1976). The list of the vowels is presented in Table 3.2. The neutral vowels are shown in boldface. Hungarian is a good example of a language with quite strict phonotactic patterns for vowels: one stem can contain only front or only back vowels. However, neutral vowels can co-occur with any vowel (Rounds, 2001, pp. 10–11).

Table 3.3 is comprised of the 10 most overrepresented vowel pairs in the Hungarian corpus. The example words are the first occurrences of the vowel pair in the alphabetically ordered list of words (the same principle is applied to all words in Table 3.4). Therefore, the examples are not frequent or even "prototypical" words; they are here just to instantiate the usage of the vowel pair in real language. Since the study does not concern the meaning of the examples but rather their form, they are not translated into English. This comment applies to the Czech tables (5, 6, 10, and 11) as well.

The strongest connections between vowels are represented in the weighted directed graph in Fig. 3.1. The vertices represent vowels and they are arranged to the shape of the vowel triangle diagram; the edges (the lines connecting the vowels) stand for the vowel pairs tend to be overrepresented: the higher the metric value, the thicker the lines. The arrows point from the first vowel of the pair to the second.

Table 3.4 contains the 10 most underrepresented vowel pairs in Hungarian. The most underrepresented vowel pairs are depicted in the directed graph (Fig. 3.2). The higher the inverse of the metric value, the thicker the lines. (That is, the thickness of a line is proportional to $\frac{1}{M(a;b)}$.)

Table 3.2 Hungarian vowel system (Vago, 1976)

	Front		Back	
	Short	Long	Short	Long
High	**/i/** /ü/	**/í/** /ű/	/u/	/ú/
Mid	/ö/	**/é/** /ő/	/o/	/ó/
Low	**/e/**		/a/	/á/

[3] Details on the Hungarian National Corpus and the data are available at http://corpus.nytud.hu/mnsz/index_eng.html (Oravecz, Váradi, & Sass, 2014).

Table 3.3 The 10 most overrepresented vowel pairs in the Hungarian corpus

Vowel a	Vowel b	Example	Abs. freq.	Rel. freq. *f*(*a*; *b*)	*M*(*a*; *b*)
ű	ö	acéltűkön	253,746	0.0011	10.425
ö	ö	ablakcsörömpölés	1,773,146	0.0077	9.676
ü	ö	ablakfüggönyeit	673,899	0.0029	9.069
í	ű	acélszínű	132,462	0.0006	5.259
ő	ö	abbafejeződött	308,998	0.0013	4.052
ű	ű	acélgyűrűket	21,651	0.0001	3.585
ű	é	ablakfűtést	357,960	0.0015	3.341
ö	ű	abortuszszörnyűség	138,216	0.0006	3.039
ú	ú	acélhúrú	23,555	0.0001	2.826
í	ó	ablakbenyílóban	405,127	0.0018	2.674
ő	é	ablakemelőjének	888,716	0.0038	2.648

Table 3.4 The 10 most underrepresented vowel pairs in Hungarian

Vowel a	Vowel b	Example	Abs. freq.	Rel. freq. *f*(*a*; *b*)	*M*(*a*; *b*)
a	ő	adatbőséggel	44,089	0.00019	0.036
o	ü	abroszcsücskökkel	14,730	0.00006	0.035
í	ú	alapdíjú	902	0	0.034
ű	ó	attitűdgyógyítás	975	0	0.027
ü	u	dühhullám	1651	0.00001	0.023
o	ő	acélexportőr	17,253	0.00007	0.022
ö	ó	állóeszközmódszer	5451	0.00002	0.02
ü	a	adásszünnap	7372	0.00003	0.011
u	ő	adjunktusnő	1836	0.00001	0.009
u	ü	abortuszüggyel	905	0	0.008
ü	ó	Büróba	586	0	0.005

As the diagrams in Figs. 3.1 and 3.2 demonstrate, the metric that we use fully exposes the Hungarian phonotactic patterns described above. It is worth mentioning that /e/ and /é/ seem to be positively connected to the front vowels and negatively connected to the back ones. This finding supports the idea that /e/ and /é/ should not be classified as "neutral" vowels, an approach that was discussed in Ringen and Kontra(1989).

Results

Words

The Hungarian phonotactic patterns for vowels in neighboring syllables have been described by linguists in a deterministic way. Thus, it should be easy to capture them by statistics. For Czech, however, we do not expect straightforward results.

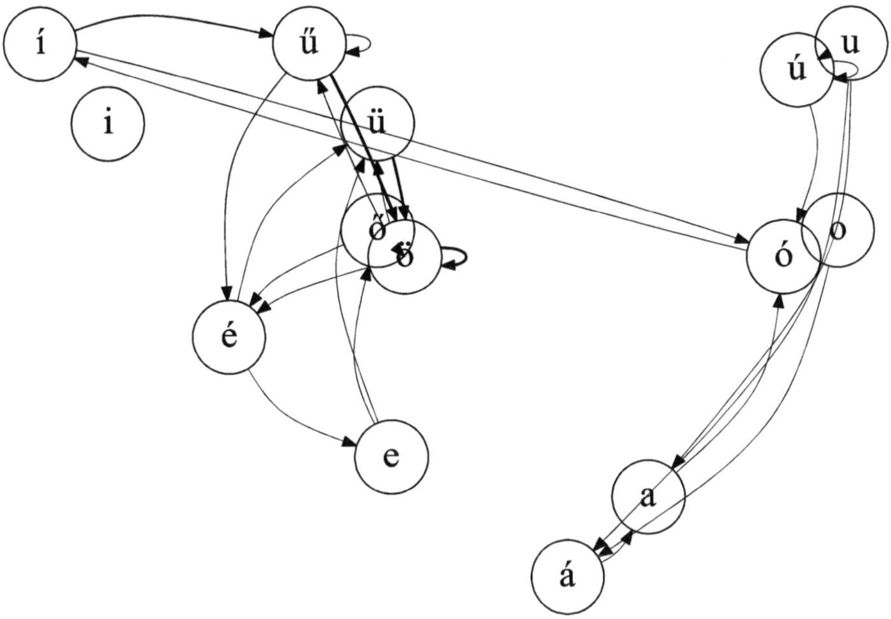

Fig. 3.1 Triangle diagram of Hungarian vowels—the most overrepresented vowel pairs

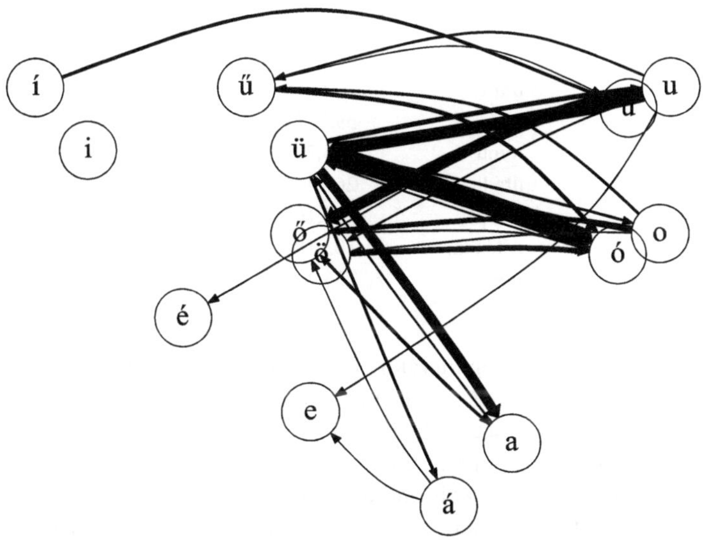

Fig. 3.2 The triangle diagram of the Hungarian vowels—the most underrepresented vowel pairs

Table 3.5 The 30 most overrepresented vowel (or diphthong or syllabic /r/ and /l/) pairs in the Czech corpus SYN2010

Vowel a	Vowel b	Example	Abs. Freq.	Rel. Freq. *f*(*a*; *b*)	*M*(*a*; *b*)
é	o	svého	883,014	0.008063	3.734
ú	l	úplně	35,565	0.000325	3.726
r	l	navrhl	13,735	0.000125	2.121
l	é	plné	23,626	0.000216	2.083
é	l	pohlédl	18,571	0.00017	1.891
ú	e	může	576,450	0.005264	1.707
l	e	úplně	96,931	0.000885	1.693
r	í	první	239,028	0.002183	1.662
e	l	řekl	245,332	0.00224	1.625
ú	o	způsobem	367,153	0.003353	1.597
í	ú	měsíců	118,587	0.001083	1.555
é	u	systému	156,540	0.001429	1.539
u	r	udržet	40,416	0.000369	1.536
í	a	například	1,240,022	0.011323	1.514
u	ou	budou	180,129	0.001645	1.510
l	ou	plnou	7599	6.94E−05	1.444
u	e	bude	1,855,063	0.01694	1.429
o	á	možná	1,775,271	0.016211	1.356
e	í	který	4,527,600	0.041344	1.350
á	ú	států	113,228	0.001034	1.326
e	é	které	1,396,715	0.012754	1.320
á	í	žádný	1,185,796	0.010828	1.315
r	u	trhu	85,264	0.000779	1.271
ú	r	úmrtí	8669	7.92E−05	1.267
í	á	říká	397,733	0.003632	1.253
o	u	tomu	1,906,292	0.017407	1.231
ú	a	úřadu	260,445	0.002378	1.208
a	r	patrně	93,101	0.00085	1.205
á	a	základní	1,103,188	0.010074	1.204
i	é	lidé	735,435	0.006716	1.203

The mere fact that the existing literature does not discuss strict phonotactic patterns for Czech vowel combinations signals that patterns, if any, might be nondeterministic and subtler than is the case with Hungarian.

Let us have a look at the list of the most overrepresented vowel pairs for Czech (Table 3.5). Only "native" vowels and diphthongs were taken into account: that is, /ó/, /au/, vowels with an umlaut and other relatively rare vowel combinations of foreign origin were excluded.[4]

The most overrepresented vowel pairs from Table 3.3 are depicted in Fig. 3.3; the thicker the line, the more overrepresented the vowel pair.

[4] The full dataset for this study can be found at http://www.milicka.cz/kestazeni/vowels.zip.

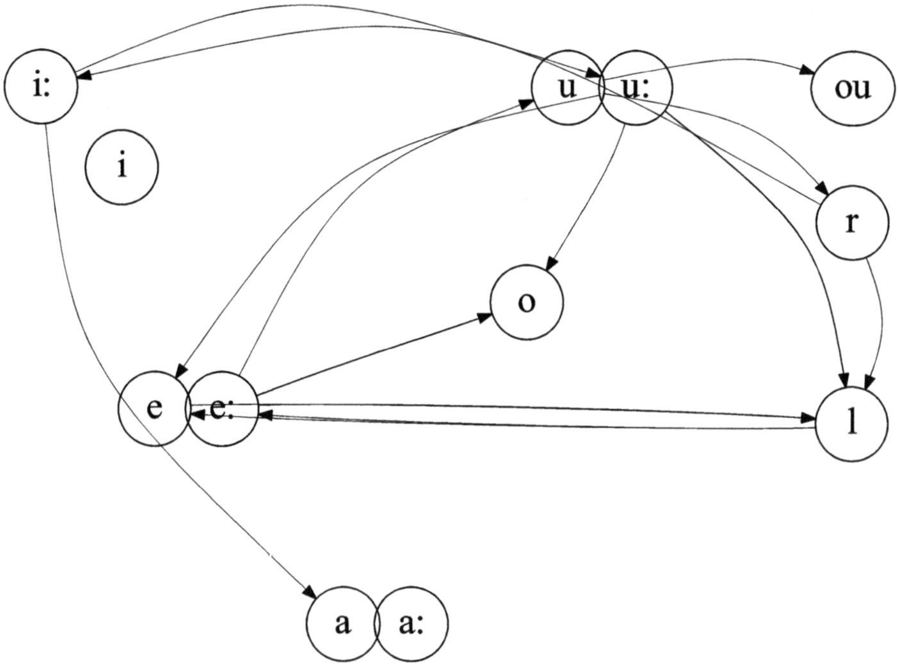

Fig. 3.3 Triangle diagram of Czech vowels—the most overrepresented vowel pairs

We note that the metric M for the most overrepresented pairs in Czech texts is much lower than the values for Hungarian. While the edges in Hungarian (Fig. 3.1) are more vertically oriented (i.e, from a front vowel to another front one, from a back vowel to another back one), those in the Czech graph are more horizontal. Moreover, there is no tendency to repeat the same vowel in two successive syllables.

The most underrepresented vowel pairs are listed in Table 3.6.[5] We can see that some vowel pairs are so rare that some of the example words are abbreviations. The schema of the most striking tendencies is depicted in Fig. 3.4.[6]

The overall picture of these overrepresented and underrepresented pairs suggests that there are some tendencies to restrict certain combinations in the vowel pairs. For further examination, we first define the following groups of vowels:

short front vowels: the set of [/i/, /e/];
long front vowels: the set of [/í/, /é/];
short back vowels: the set of [/u/, /o/];
long back vowel: the set of [/ú/].

[5] As you can see, abbreviations were not excluded from the corpus. This is why some of the rare and underrepresented vowel pairs are instantiated by abbreviations; otherwise, their frequency would be even lower.

[6] The black "smudge" near the /r/ vertex is a thick "loop edge." This means that the /r/–/r/ pairs are really rare.

Table 3.6 The 30 most underrepresented vowel (plus the diphthong /ou/ or syllabic /r/ and /l/) pairs in the Czech corpus SYN2010

Vowel a	Vowel b	Example	Abs. Freq.	Rel. Freq. *f*(*a*; *b*)	*M*(*a*; *b*)
r	r	SPR-RSČ	60	0.00000	0.013
é	é	Švédské	6035	0.00006	0.088
é	r	Manévr	712	0.00001	0.101
é	í	Konkrétní	26,103	0.00024	0.120
ú	í	Různých	49,824	0.00045	0.235
í	é	Bílé	62,866	0.00057	0.247
ú	é	Různé	17,885	0.00016	0.267
ú	á	Zůstává	23,845	0.00022	0.285
l	r	KLDR	336	0.00000	0.290
u	l	KDU-ČSL	10,748	0.00010	0.293
é	á	scénář	25,378	0.00023	0.295
l	ú	doplňků	1026	0.00001	0.301
é	i	problémy	88,029	0.00080	0.321
ú	ú	účtů	6734	0.00006	0.335
í	ou	nabídnout	41,539	0.00038	0.352
l	l	zmlkl	580	0.00001	0.358
ú	ou	můžou	12,814	0.00012	0.413
é	ou	prohlédnout	14,256	0.00013	0.446
a	l	padl	50,003	0.00046	0.464
l	a	vlna	17,858	0.00016	0.489
ou	r	souhrn	2833	0.00003	0.498
á	é	žádné	148,483	0.00136	0.522
é	e	téměř	193,664	0.00177	0.557
r	o	Brno	87,835	0.00080	0.563
u	a	zhruba	468,344	0.00428	0.565
u	o	tuto	504,214	0.00460	0.571
l	u	doplňuje	10,023	0.00009	0.598
ú	i	kvůli	168,373	0.00154	0.632
ou	é	dlouhé	35,653	0.00033	0.641
í	í	místní	527,600	0.00482	0.655

As mentioned in section "Data," diphthongs and the syllabic /r/ and /l/ are not included in our simplified model. The long back /ó/ is omitted, because it is quite rare and it occurs mostly in loanwords. The position of the vowel /a/ is unclear as it stands somewhere in the middle between front and back vowels. Therefore, three models were examined:

A_0 Model: /a/ and /á/ were excluded;

A_f Model: /a/ and /á/ were classified as front vowels;

A_b Model: /a/ and /á/ were classified as back vowels.

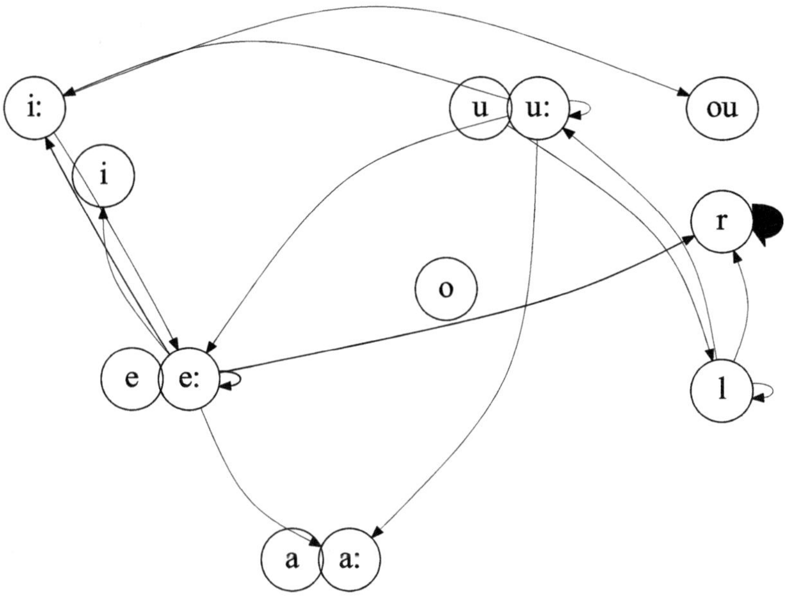

Fig. 3.4 Triangle diagram of Czech vowels—the most underrepresented vowel pairs

Table 3.7 A_0 Model results. *M* metric for vowel group pairs

		Front		Back	
SYN2010		Short	Long	Short	Long
Front	Short	0.95	1.22	0.92	1.00
	Long	0.95	0.50	1.45	1.58
Back	Short	1.07	0.88	0.98	0.89
	Long	1.21	0.25	1.25	0.35

Table 3.7 shows the results for the A_0 Model. The rows represent the first vowel, while the columns represent the second vowel in the pair (e.g, the pair "front short → front long" is 1.22 times more frequent than in the random model). Some vowel group pairs are represented almost as frequently as in the random model (e.g, front short → back long), some of them are overrepresented (e.g, front long → back short), and some of them are underrepresented (e.g, back long → front long).

Figure 3.5 reveals an interesting and unexpected cyclic pattern of Czech vowel phonotactics; this pattern is quite symmetrical. Although symmetry alone is not proof of meaningfulness, a symmetrical pattern is less complex, and thus it is reasonable to assume that it would be easier to remember. Consequently, these patterns could be utilized by a speaker more easily. The A_0 Model does not cover the whole system, as it lacks one of the most frequent vowels; nevertheless, even this incomplete model can be utilized (we will comment more on its possible usefulness in section "Explanation").

As can be seen in Fig. 3.6, the negative patterns (i.e, the list of underrepresented vowel group pairs) are less symmetrical than the positive ones, but they are much stronger. The *back* ↛ *long* pattern is especially striking. As the traditional approach to the vowel harmony in Uralic languages mainly concerns negative patterns (some vowel combinations are restricted) (Anderson, 1980), it is possible that such negative patterns are more important than positive ones.

The patterns can be also expressed more formally:

Long front → back	Long front ↛ front
Long back → short	Long back ↛ long
Short front → long front	Short front ↛ short front
Short back → short front	Short back ↛ long

Now, let us proceed to Model A_f, in which the /a/ and /á/ are classified as front vowels. Table 3.8 shows that even though the numbers are different, the overall pattern is similar, as can be observed in Figs. 3.7 and 3.8.

Now, let us proceed to Model A_b, in which /a/ and /á/ are classified as back vowels. The results are slightly different from those of the previous two models.

Table 3.9 and its graphic representation (Figs. 3.9 and 3.10) show that there is also an overall tendency towards a circular pattern. Nevertheless, some of the relations typical of A_0 and A_f are weak.

The A_b Model results suggest that it is more appropriate to classify the /a/ and /á/ vowels as front vowels, an approach which differs from the traditional model of Hungarian vowel harmony where /a/ and /á/ are classified as back vowels. A possible explanation for this phenomenon might be found in the actual pronunciation of the vowels: the Hungarian /a/ is usually classified as a back vowel (Rounds, 2001,

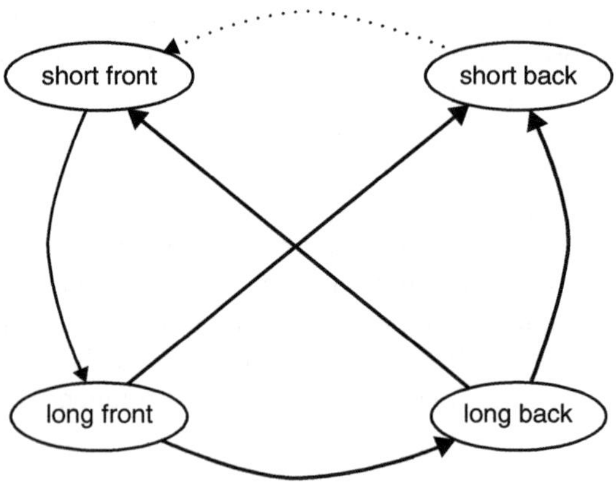

Fig. 3.5 A_0 Model results. The overrepresented vowel group pairs

Fig. 3.6 A_0 Model results. The underrepresented vowel group pairs

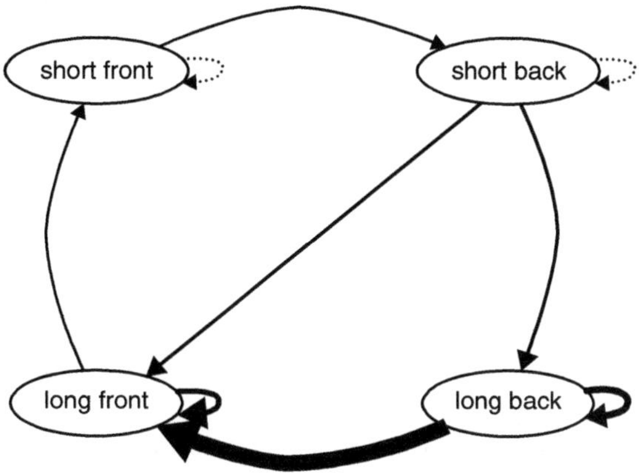

Table 3.8 A_f model results. The *M* metric for vowel group pairs

SYN2010		Front		Back	
		Short	Long	Short	Long
Front	Short	0.97	1.10	0.96	0.98
	Long	1.02	0.81	1.13	1.42
Back	Short	1.03	0.93	1.00	0.87
	Long	1.21	0.25	1.33	0.36

Fig. 3.7 A_f Model results. The overrepresented vowel group pairs

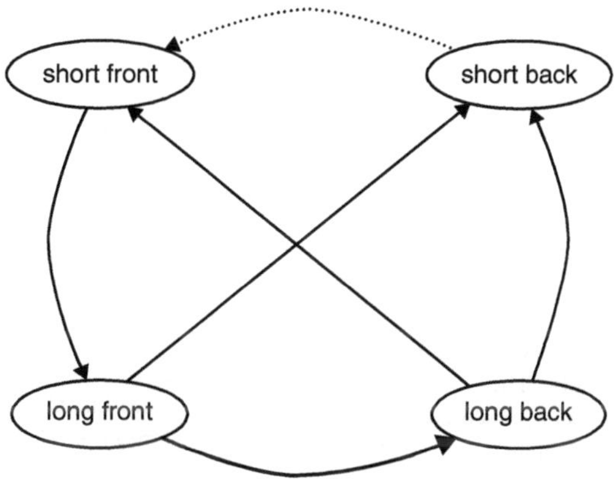

pp. 10–11), whereas the Czech one is understood to be pronounced as a central vowel (Palková, 1994, pp. 201–203). It needs to be emphasized that the /a/ and /á/ vowels are not categorizd as a front vowel for any phonetic reasons but solely for the purpose of this pattern description. It might be also appropriate to name the groups differently (e.g, *Group A* for "front" vowels and *Group B* for "back" vowels) to reduce possible confusion.

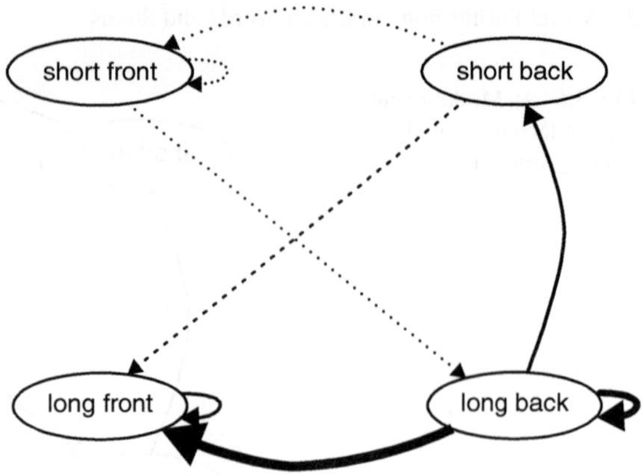

Fig. 3.8 A_f model results. The underrepresented vowel group pairs

Table 3.9 A_b model results. The *M* metric for vowel group pairs

SYN2010		Front		Back	
		Short	Long	Short	Long
Front	Short	0.95	1.20	0.96	1.00
	Long	0.88	0.46	1.39	1.12
Back	Short	1.05	0.93	0.97	1.02
	Long	1.04	0.96	1.01	0.80

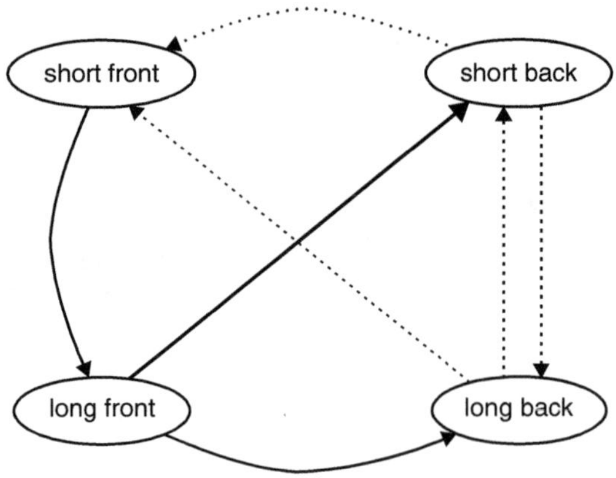

Fig. 3.9 A_b model results. The overrepresented vowel group pairs

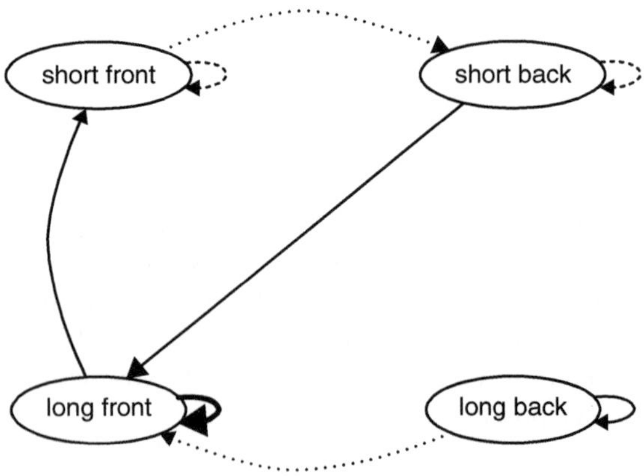

Fig. 3.10 A_b model results. The underrepresented vowel group pairs

Stems

The next question is whether or not the patterns in the Czech phonotactic system are motivated by Czech morphology: in other words, whether the patterns can also be observed internally within word stems.

Table 3.10 lists the most overrepresented vowel pairs and Fig. 3.11 shows its graphic representation. Here, too, only "native" vowels and diphthongs were taken

Table 3.10 The 30 most overrepresented vowel (or diphthong or syllabic /r/ and /l/) pairs in stems in the Czech corpus SYN2010

Vowel a	Vowel b	Example	Abs. Freq.	Rel. Freq. *f*(*a*; *b*)	*M*(*a*; *b*)
i	l	michl	313,523	0.006139	2.679
é	a	vylévan	70,414	0.001379	2.591
l	e	plzeňsk	71,878	0.001407	2.368
a	é	tragéd	206,704	0.004047	2.123
í	a	podezřívavě	572,505	0.011210	2.087
ú	l	úplně	37,635	0.000737	2.015
o	ů	potůčkov	61,486	0.001204	1.897
u	í	převažujíc	252,951	0.004953	1.871
ů	o	půldolar	366,072	0.007168	1.643
u	r	ruhrgas	80,486	0.001576	1.596
o	u	rozkulačován	1,010,445	0.019786	1.549
r	i	nepřetržitost	98,199	0.001923	1.525
u	ou	ubrous	31,089	0.000609	1.517
ou	a	poukazován	120,303	0.002356	1.420
á	a	dálkař	450,663	0.008824	1.418
a	í	bavív	684,180	0.013397	1.395
á	e	prohánějíc	820,495	0.016066	1.394
u	i	komunikativnost	596,956	0.011689	1.387
é	e	sebeméně	67,797	0.001328	1.347
o	á	prohánějíc	1,245,826	0.024395	1.321
a	ou	zastoupen	97,388	0.001907	1.311
r	e	trpělivost	136,321	0.002669	1.306
ou	í	boublík	38,414	0.000752	1.263
ou	e	zastoupen	196,328	0.003844	1.251
ú	a	úžlab	187,421	0.003670	1.245
a	i	lancashir	1,938,107	0.037950	1.242
o	r	pohr	356,105	0.006973	1.229
e	i	frajeřin	1,858,798	0.036397	1.200
i	á	vikář	492,792	0.009649	1.198
i	é	vylévan	78,841	0.001544	1.172

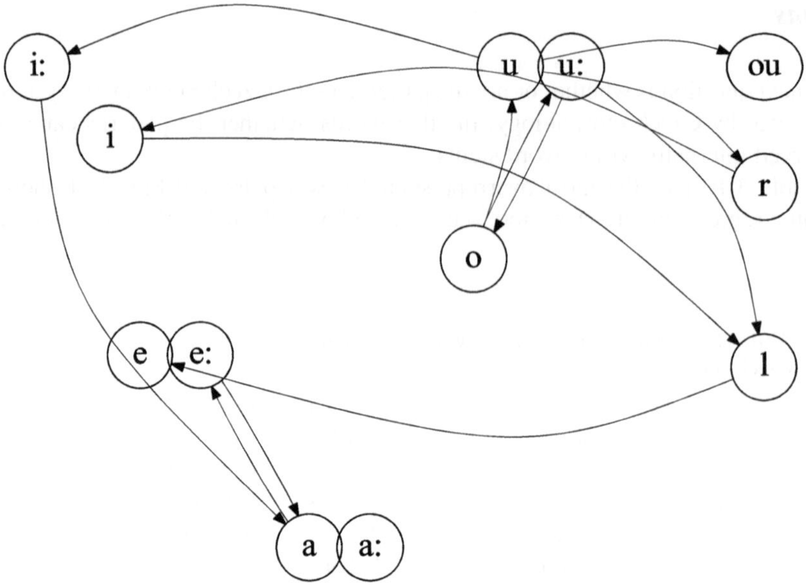

Fig. 3.11 Triangle diagram of the Czech vowels in stems—the most overrepresented vowel pairs

into account; that is, /ó/, /au/, vowels with an umlaut and other relatively rare vowel combinations were excluded.[7]

The most underrepresented vowel pairs are listed in Table 3.11.[8] The schema of the most striking tendencies is depicted in Fig. 3.12.

The most striking difference between the results for word forms (stem + ending) and the results for stems only is that there is in fact vowel harmony in the latter patterns (rather than disharmony), and that these patterns are similar to the Hungarian ones. At the same time, the patterns that hold for stems are more conspicuous than those for word forms: the *long* $\nrightarrow$ *long* pattern is almost deterministic in the A_0 and A_f Models. The results for the A_0 and A_f models are similar to each other (see Tables 3.12 and 3.13) and dissimilar to the A_b Model results (Table 3.14). The similarity is consistent with what is observed for word forms. Tables 3.12 and 3.13 along with Figs. 3.13 and 3.14 show that the front vowels do not repel other front vowels, nor do back vowels repel other back vowels, and that the main constraints relate to vowel length.

[7] The examples show that there are some errors with stem extraction, namely *ubrousek* ('napkin') is stemmed as *ubrous*, due to the alternations in the (diminutive) suffix *–ek* (e.g, obdélníček ('little rectangle nom sg')—*obdélníčku* ('little rectangle gen sg')).

[8] The ($l \rightarrow$ é), ($ú \rightarrow$ ou), ($é \rightarrow$ ú), and ($ú \rightarrow$ é) pairs are so rare within stems that there is no example for them in the corpus; the ($r \rightarrow$ r) example is a long interjection.

Table 3.11 The 30 most underrepresented vowel (or diphthong or syllabic /r/ and /l/) pairs in stems in the Czech corpus SYN2010

Vowel a	Vowel b	Example	Abs. Freq.	Rel. Freq. $f(a; b)$	$M(a; b)$
l	é		0	0.000000	0.000
ú	ou		0	0.000000	0.000
é	ú		0	0.000000	0.000
ú	é		0	0.000000	0.000
í	é	nebelvírskéh	23	0.000000	0.001
ou	é	dvoudvéřov	12	0.000000	0.002
r	r	hn[...]nchrrkch[...]chr	25	0.000000	0.003
ú	ú	úhúl	10	0.000000	0.004
é	ou	lapérous	14	0.000000	0.009
á	é	gjánéndr	332	0.000007	0.015
í	ou	štíhlounk	281	0.000006	0.019
ú	í	bůhvíkdy	1773	0.000035	0.033
l	á	plzák	578	0.000011	0.081
u	é	slunéčkov	2707	0.000053	0.101
é	l	lébl	340	0.000007	0.101
l	ou	mlsoun	92	0.000002	0.103
é	í	obdélníč	1154	0.000023	0.118
í	í	šířic	13,595	0.000266	0.138
ou	ú	dvoulůž	189	0.000004	0.149
l	r	kldr	336	0.000007	0.153
l	ú	blbůst	38	0.000001	0.155
r	ú	drnůvk	136	0.000003	0.161
ou	u	potichoučku	5007	0.000098	0.196
u	ú	nerudův	1150	0.000023	0.204
r	ou	smrťounek	669	0.000013	0.218
ou	ou	outsourcovan	1077	0.000021	0.234
é	u	vzlétnut	2109	0.000041	0.257
ú	á	díkůvzdán	16,941	0.000332	0.258
l	i	splniteln	5385	0.000105	0.287
l	u	pohlcujíc	1456	0.000029	0.294

The words examined in the previous section are shorter on average than the words examined in this section, as the stems that are explored here must be at least two syllables long. This requirement excludes many short words from the dataset. Therefore, the emergence of the vowel length patterns can be explained by the Menzerath–Altmann law. The Menzerath–Altmann law predicts that the longer the morpheme, the shorter the constituent phonemes; that is, the fewer phonemes in the morpheme, the longer the phonemes are on average (Altmann, 1980; Menzerath, 1928). In this case, phoneme length is realized as vowel quantity.

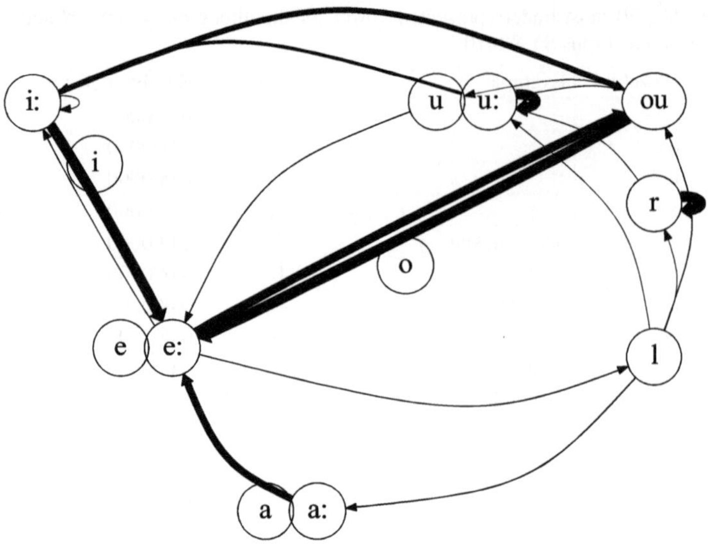

Fig. 3.12 Triangle diagram of Czech vowels in stems—the most underrepresented vowel pairs

The set of tendencies for A_0 and A_f can be summarized as follows:

Long front → short	Long front ↛ long
Long back → short back	Long back ↛ long
Short front → no preference	Short front ↛ long back
Short back → long back	Short back ↛ no dispreference

We can conclude that there is a different set of patterns for word forms than for stems. Manual stem correction is needed to draw more reliable conclusions. More precise input data are also needed to explore the phonotactics of *morphemic seams*—the vowel pairs in which the first vowel is the last vowel in the stem and the second vowel is the first vowel in the ending. These results are potentially interesting, as the Czech morphology is rich in synonymous endings for nouns and verbs, and each word is assigned its paradigm (at least to some extent) in a seemingly arbitrary manner,[9] at least from the synchronic point of view. Such a study has the potential to discover the phonotactic motivations that play out in the *word—its paradigm* assignments.

[9] There might be other patterns that affect the *word—its paradigm* assignment, both diachronically and synchronically. Their effects might be even stronger than the effects of the phenomena under consideration, but this study does not focus on them.

Table 3.12 A_0 model results. The *M* metric for vowel group pairs within stems

SYN2010—stems		Front Short	Front Long	Back Short	Back Long
Front	Short	1.02	1.00	0.97	0.60
	Long	0.97	0.15	1.24	0.49
Back	Short	0.99	1.15	0.98	1.48
	Long	0.92	0.03	1.35	0.00

Table 3.13 A_f model results. The *M* metric for vowel group pairs within stems

SYN2010—stems		Front Short	Front Long	Back Short	Back Long
Front	Short	1.00	1.04	0.98	0.68
	Long	1.11	0.36	1.06	0.68
Back	Short	0.97	1.16	0.99	1.59
	Long	1.00	0.14	1.43	0.00

Table 3.14 A_b model results. The *M* metric for vowel group pairs within stems

SYN2010—stems		Front Short	Front Long	Back Short	Back Long
Front	Short	1.01	0.94	0.98	1.06
	Long	0.79	0.12	1.42	0.65
Back	Short	1.01	1.20	0.95	1.07
	Long	0.99	0.19	1.24	0.37

Variability Across Datasets

Tables 3.15 and 3.16 represent the *M* metric values for vowel groups (A_0 Model), as in Table 3.7. The differences between the values for the SYN2010 corpus and the two other corpora (SYN2005 and SYN2015) are statistically significant but the actual difference in terms of effect size is small,[10] so that the results that we observed and described in the previous sections can be generalized to the other two corpora (Tables 3.17 and 3.18). Because there is not enough space for tables representing the

[10] As the number of the statistical units in our corpora is very large, even a small effect size causes statistically significant differences. For example, the overall number of *short front–short front* pairs in SYN2010 corpus is 14,328,194 out of all 61,503,108 pairs. The same figure for the SYN2015 is 14,243,894 out of 60,963,320 pairs. According to Fisher's test, the frequencies are significantly different ($p < 0.001$), while the real-life significance of the difference is quite low—the 95% confidence interval of the risk ratio lies between 0.9964 and 0.9977 (calculated according to Altman, 1990), which is very close to 1, i.e, the relative frequency of the specified vowel pair in the two corpora is close to being identical.

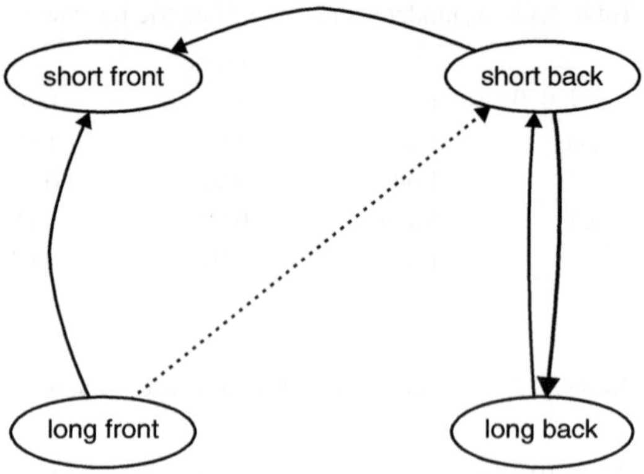

Fig. 3.13 A_f model results. The overrepresented vowel group pairs in stems

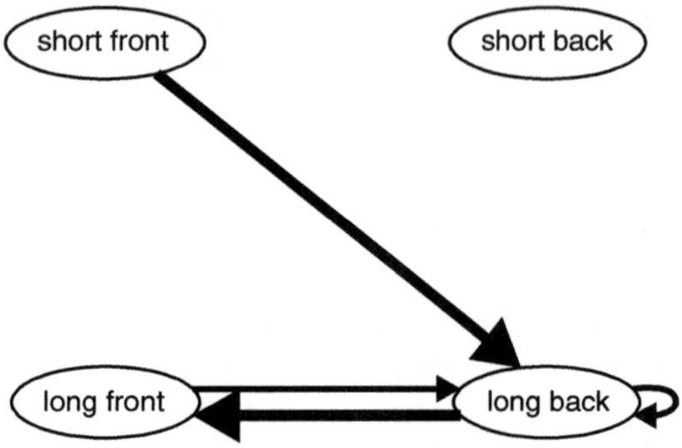

Fig. 3.14 A_f model results. The underrepresented vowel group pairs in stems

Table 3.15 A_0 model results for SYN2005. *M* metric for vowel group pairs

		Front		Back	
SYN2005		Short	Long	Short	Long
Front	Short	0.94	1.24	0.91	0.99
	Long	0.96	0.46	1.47	1.61
Back	Short	1.07	0.86	0.99	0.91
	Long	1.21	0.25	1.26	0.32

Table 3.16 A_0 model results for SYN2015. *M* metric for vowel group pairs

		Front		Back	
SYN2015		Short	Long	Short	Long
Front	Short	0.95	1.21	0.92	0.99
	Long	0.96	0.51	1.44	1.48
Back	Short	1.06	0.88	0.98	0.93
	Long	1.23	0.25	1.22	0.33

Table 3.17 A_f model results for SYN2005. *M* metric for vowel group pairs

		Front		Back	
SYN2005		Short	Long	Short	Long
Front	Short	0.97	1.12	0.95	0.98
	Long	1.03	0.80	1.12	1.39
Back	Short	1.04	0.91	1.01	0.88
	Long	1.21	0.26	1.32	0.31

Table 3.18 A_f model results for SYN2015. *M* metric for vowel group pairs

		Front		Back	
SYN2015		Short	Long	Short	Long
Front	Short	0.97	1.10	0.96	0.97
	Long	1.03	0.82	1.11	1.38
Back	Short	1.03	0.93	1.00	0.91
	Long	1.21	0.26	1.31	0.34

results for all the models and for all the corpora, we have only included the tables based on A_0 and A_f Models for words (not for stems). The rest of the tables along with the tables of individual vowel pairs (like Table 3.5) can be found at http://www.milicka.cz/kestazeni/vowels.zip.

Explanation

The rigid vowel harmony of the Hungarian phonology system can help the receiver to analyse word boundaries. But, the "sloppier" Czech vowel disharmony is less likely to play such a role. The reason for the emergence of such a structure is posited in the Shannonian Theory of Communication (MacKay, 2003, Chap. 2; Shannon, 1948). According to the theory, there must be some redundancy in the language so that the process of information transmission over a noisy channel can be successful. It is convenient to add redundancy on various levels (Milička, 2016), including the phonetic subsystem of the language.

On average, a Hungarian vowel encodes 3.12 bits of entropy, meaning that there is 6.24 bits of entropy per vowel pair.[11] When taking the phonotactic rules into account, some vowel pairs are forbidden and some are extremely probable; as a

[11] Here, we mean entropy in the Shannonian sense, i.e, $H = -\sum_{a \in A} f(a) \log_2 f(a)$, where A is set of all vowels in the language system. If the phonotactics are not taken into account, then the entropy of a vowel pair is just the doubled entropy of a single vowel.

result, on the average a Hungarian vowel bigram encodes only 5.7 bits of entropy,[12] resulting in 0.55 redundant bits per average vowel bigram.

A Czech vowel encodes 3.01 bits of entropy on average, this means 6.02 bits per vowel bigram when the phonotactics are not taken into account. In reality, the average vowel bigram resolves 5.87 bits of entropy, i.e, there are 0.15 redundant bits per average vowel bigram due to the phonotactics.

Shannon's entropy is most likely a rough approximation of the real signal processing by humans. Perception tests are therefore required in order to further verify our findings.

The Czech patterns of vowel disharmony are not as strict as the Hungarian rules of vowel harmony. The amount of redundancy is therefore lower than in Hungarian. Understanding this, we may then predict that there will be a larger amount of redundancy added to other subsystems (e.g,, the phonotactics of consonants and/or morphotactics). The most important underlying idea is that it does not matter whether the rules tend towards harmony or disharmony, as any consistent patterns can serve the same purposes. In fact, there are many "disharmony" patterns on various subsystems in various languages (cf. the Obligatory Contour Principle in the tones of tonal languages (Goldsmith, 1976; Leben, 1973) and in the consonants in Arabic roots (McCarthy, 1986)).[13]

Conclusion

We have examined the phonotactics of Czech vowels in word forms and in stems (i.e, words without endings). Following the assumption that the Czech patterns are comparable with the patterns in Hungarian and other languages with vowel harmony, we have defined four subsets of Czech vowels: short front, short back, long front, and long back. The first model was constructed by omitting the vowel /a/; only the prototypically back (/u/, /ú/, /o/) and the prototypically front (/e/, /é/, /i/, /í/) vowels were taken into account. Subsequently, we examined the position of /a/ and /á/. We have shown that the model categorizing /a/ and /á/ as front vowels yields similar results to the first model (unlike the model categorizing /a/ and /á/ as back vowels).

Both models can be seen forming some sort of circular pattern (as shown in Figs. 3.5 and 3.6): the short front vowels tend to be followed by long front vowels, long front vowels tend to be followed by back vowels, and long back vowels tend to be followed by short vowels. In contrast, there is a tendency to underrepresent pairs

[12] The entropy of the vowel pair is calculated like the entropy of a single vowel, i.e, $H = -\sum_{a \in A} \sum_{b \in A} f(a;b) \log_2 f(a;b)$, where A is set of all vowels in the language system.

[13] Admittedly, this principle belongs to the generativist linguistic framework rather than corpus or quantitative linguistics, as it was developed to describe one of the possible transformations of "deep structure" into "surface structure." But, it is nonetheless worth noting that even the generativist descriptions suggest that the phenomenon of Czech vowel disharmony is not an isolated linguistic process.

of two long back vowels, two long front vowels, and a long back vowel followed by a short back vowel.

The Czech vowel phonotactic cycle, conceptualized in this manner, is symmetrical and easy to remember. This supports the hypothesis that this pattern is not random, but that it plays a role in actual communication as a source of redundancy. The hypothesis requires further testing to verify whether speakers are (at least unconsciously) able to utilize the patterns: for example, we anticipate that it would be possible to test: (1) whether or not words that violate these patterns are misunderstood more easily than those that follow the patterns; (2) whether randomly generated pseudo-words that violate these patterns seem less acceptable to native speakers than those that follow the patterns, and whether they are harder to remember.

It is possible that the categorization of the vowels into four sets is not adequate and that better categorizations can be found. Searching for better solutions that would result in stronger patterns is left for further research.

The study opens up typological questions:

(a) Are these phonotactic constraints random, or can we find some further explanations based on language typology? This question, e.g., leads to a hypothesis that speakers of agglutinative languages might be more likely to utilize phonotactics to find word boundaries, and therefore vowel harmony might be more prevalent than vowel disharmony in these languages.
(b) Do genealogically related languages tend to share some patterns? Or, is there more of a tendency to share the patterns on an areal basis? Here, it would be worth examining Slovak which has an areal relationship with Hungarian.
(c) The constraints in Czech are less strict than the ones in Hungarian, i.e, their redundancy is lower. Is there any compensation on other levels or in other language subsystems?

Acknowledgments This study was written within the programme Progres Q08 *Czech National Corpus* implemented at the Faculty of Arts, Charles University. We would like to thank Václav Cvrček and Masako Ueda Fidler (the editors of this volume), Alžběta Růžičková, Jakub Sláma, and Sadie Gold-Shapiro for their suggestions and comments.

References

Altman, D. G. (1990). *Practical statistics for medical research*. Cleveland, OH: CRC Press.

Altmann, G. (1980). Prolegomena to Menzerath's law. In R. Grotjahn (Ed.), *Glottometrika 2* (pp. 1–10). Bochum, Germany: Brockmeyer.

Anderson, L. B. (1980). Using asymmetrical and gradient data in the study of vowel harmony. In R. M. Vago (Ed.), *Issues in vowel harmony* (pp. 271–340). Amsterdam, The Netherlands: John Benjamins.

Bičan, A. (2011). *Phonotactics of Czech*. Ph.D. thesis, Masaryk University, Brno, Czech Republic. Retrieved October 12, 2017, from https://theses.cz/id/eguqrt

Bičan, A. (2015b). Corpus-based analysis of the Czech syllable. In E. Guetiérrez Rubio (Ed.), *Beiträge der Europäischen Slavistischen Linguistik (POLYSLAV) 18* (pp. 26–36). Munich, Germany: Harrasowitz Verlag.

Bičan, A. (2015c). Fonologický lexikální korpus češtiny a slabičná struktura českého slova [Phonological Lexical Corpus of Czech Language and the Syllabic Structure of Czech Words]. *Bohemica Olomucensia, 7*(3-4), 45–59.

Bičan, A. (2015a). Distribution of vocalic quantity in Czech. *Grazer Linguistische Studien, 83*, 133–138.

Čermák, F., Doležalová-Spoustová, D., Hlaváčová, J., Hnátková, M., Jelínek, T., Kocek, J., et al. (2005). *SYN2005: žánrově vyvážený korpus psané češtiny* [*SYN 2005: Genre-Balanced Corpus of Written Czech*]. Praha, Slovakia: Ústav Českého národního korpusu FF UK Retrieved October 12, 2017, from http://www.korpus.cz

Cvrček, V., Čermáková, A., & Křen, M. (2016). Nová koncepce synchronních korpusů psané češtiny [New Conception of the Synchronic Corpora of Written Czech]. *Slovo a slovesnost, 77*(2), 83–101.

Dankovičová, J. (1999). Czech. In *Handbook of the International Phonetic Association: A guide to the use of the International Phonetic Alphabet* (pp. 70–74). Cambridge, UK: Cambridge University Press.

Goldsmith, J. (1976). *Autosegmental phonology*. Ph.D. thesis, Massachusetts Institute of Technology, Cambridge, MA.

Hnátková, M., Křen, M., Procházka, P., & Skoumalová, H. (2014). The SYN-series corpora of written Czech. *Proceedings of the ninth international conference on Language Resources and Evaluation (LREC"14)*, 160–164.

Johnson, D. C. (1980). Regular disharmony in Kirghiz. In R. M. Vago (Ed.), *Issues in vowel harmony* (pp. 89–100). Amsterdam, The Netherlands: John Benjamins.

Křen, M., Cvrček, V., Čapka, T., Čermáková, A., Hnátková, M., Chlumská, L., Jelínek, T., Kováříková, D., Petkevič, V., Procházka, P., Skoumalová, H., Škrabal, M., Truneček, P., Vondřička, P., & Zasina, A. (2016). SYN2015: Representative corpus of contemporary written Czech. *Proceedings of the tenth international conference on Language Resources and Evaluation (LREC"16)*, 2522–2528.

Křen, M., Bartoň, T., Cvrček, V., Hnátková, M.,Jelínek, T., Kocek, J., Novotná, R., Petkevič, V., Procházka, P., Schmiedtová, V., & Skoumalová, H. (2010). *SYN2010: žánrově vyvážený korpus psané češtiny* [*SYN 2010: Genre-Balanced Corpus of Written Czech*]. Praha, Slovakia: Ústav Českého národního korpusu FF UK. Retrieved October 12, 2017, from http://www.korpus.cz

Křen, M., Cvrček, V., Čapka, T., Čermáková, A., Hnátková, M., Chlumská, L., Jelínek, T., Kováříková, D., Petkevič, V., Procházka, P., Skoumalová, H., Škrabal, M., Truneček, P., Vondřička, P., & Zasina, A. J. (2015). *SYN2015: reprezentativní korpus psané češtiny* [*SYN 2015: Representative Corpus of Written Czech*]. Praha, Slovakia: Ústav Českého národního korpusu FF UK. Retrieved October 12, 2017, from http://www.korpus.cz

Kuhn, T. S. (1962). *The structure of scientific revolutions*. Chicago: University of Chicago Press.

Leben, W. R. (1973). *Suprasegmental phonology*. Ph.D. thesis, Massachusetts Institute of Technology, Cambridge, MA.

MacKay, D. J. C. (2003). *Information theory, inference and learning algorithms*. Cambridge, UK: Cambridge University Press.

McCarthy, J. J. (1986). OCP effects: Gemination and antigemination. *Linguistic Inquiry, 17*(2), 207–263.

Menzerath, P. (1928). Über einige phonetische Probleme. In *Actes du premier Congres International de Linguistes*. Leiden, Netherlands: Sijthoff.

Milička, J. (2016). *Teorie komunikace jakožto explanatorní princip přirozené víceúrovňové segmentace textů* [*The Theory of Communication as an Explanatory Principle for Natural Multilevel Text Segmentation*]. Ph.D. thesis, Charles University, Prague, Czech Republic. Retrieved October 12, 2017, from https://is.cuni.cz/webapps/zzp/detail/104810

Nguyen, N., & Fagyal, Z. (2008). Acoustic aspects of vowel harmony in French. *Journal of Phonetics, 36*(1), 1–27.

Ohala, J. J. (1994). Towards a universal, phonetically-based, theory of vowel harmony. *Third international conference on spoken language processing*, 491–494.

Oravecz, C., Váradi, T., & Sass, B. (2014). The Hungarian Gigaword Corpus. In: *Proceedings of LREC 2014*. http://www.lrec-conf.org/proceedings/lrec2014/pdf/681_Paper.pdf

Palková, Z. (1994). *Fonetika a fonologie češtiny [Phonetics and Phonology of Czech]*. Praha, Slovakia: Karolinum.

Petkevič, V. (2014). Problémy automatické morfologické disambiguace češtiny [Problems of Automated Disambiguation of Czech Morphology]. *Naše řeč, 97*, 194–207.

Poldauf, I. (1969). *Máme v češtině harmonii samohlásek? [Do We Have Vowel Harmony in Czech?]*. *Naše řeč, 52*, 201–209.

Ringen, C. O., & Kontra, M. (1989). Hungarian neutral vowels. *Lingua, 78*(2-3), 181–191.

Rounds, C. (2001). *Hungarian: An essential grammar*. Hove, UK: Psychology Press.

Shannon, C. E. (1948). A mathematical theory of communication. *Bell System Technical Journal, 27*(3), 379–423.

Suomi, K., McQueen, J. M., & Cutler, A. (1997). Vowel harmony and speech segmentation in finnish. *Journal of Memory and Language, 36*(3), 422–444.

Vago, R. M. (1976). Theoretical implications of Hungarian vowel harmony. *Linguistic Inquiry, 7*(2), 243–263.

Chapter 4
Morphological Richness of Text

Radek Čech and Miroslav Kubát

Abstract This study proposes a method for measuring the morphological richness of text. The method enables us to characterize the morphological complexity of a text (or a corpus). It is based on a computation of the difference between two measurements — the vocabulary richness of lemmas and the vocabulary richness of word forms. The greater the difference, the higher the morphological complexity of a text. The Moving Average Type Token Ratio (*MATTR*) is used for the computation of vocabulary richness. We hypothesize that the proposed indicator, known as Moving Average Morphological Richness (*MAMR*), should reflect the style of a text, and could therefore be used in stylometry. To verify this assumption, *MAMR* is applied in analyses of both genre and authorship.

Keywords Morphological richness · Vocabulary richness · Stylometry · Genre · Authorship · Czech language

Introduction

Any text can be seen as the result of miscellaneous factors. A writer (or a speaker) has many different choices to apply his or her language competence. Furthermore, it is obvious that humans use these choices intensively. Take a group of people with the same age, educational background, sex, and IQ and ask them to write a text focused on the same topic in a very specific genre; there will be just a few identical clauses (if any) and no identical paragraphs (e.g., Cvrček & Václavík, 2015; Indrisano & Squire, 2000; Pinker, 2010).[1] This well-known fact, i.e., the huge degree of variability in language use, has been recognized among linguists for many decades, and it represents a fundamental condition for any analysis of style and authorship (e.g., Juola, 2008; Kubát, 2016). There are many properties of a text that

[1] It should be pointed out that this issue is beyond the scope of this study.

R. Čech (✉) · M. Kubát
University of Ostrava, Ostrava, Czech Republic

M. Fidler, V. Cvrček (eds.), *Taming the Corpus*, Quantitative Methods in the Humanities and Social Sciences, https://doi.org/10.1007/978-3-319-98017-1_4

reflect its uniqueness, and some of these properties are more "visible" than others. For instance, vocabulary richness seems to be an intuitively comprehensible and relatively easily observable property for comparing texts; similarly, the distribution of parts of speech could also be characterized as a "visible" property. By contrast, some abstract properties based on the so-called frequency structure of a text, such as lambda structure (Popescu, Čech, & Altmann, 2011) and the writer's view (Popescu & Altmann, 2007), are less "visible."

In this study, we introduce morphological complexity as a stylometric indicator, which can be applied to classify texts; we focus particularly on genre and authorship analysis. The concept of morphological complexity is widely used in language typology, and it has been investigated many times using various measurements (cf. Baerman, Brown, & Corbett, 2015; Bane, 2008; Bentz, Ruzsics, Koplenig, & Samardžić, 2016). It has also been applied in several other fields, such as child language acquisition or second language acquisition (cf. Březina & Pallotti, 2016; Xanthos et al., 2011). The advantage of this concept lies in its intelligible interpretation and relatively simple operationalization. However, its use in stylometry faces several problems that are typical for this kind of analysis; primarily, text length impact has to be eliminated to avoid misinterpretation of the results.

This study has two aims: (1) to propose a method for measuring the morphological complexity of texts, and (2) to observe whether this method is an effective tool for stylometric research. Thus, it should be emphasized that the aim of both the genre analysis and the authorship analysis in this study is to conduct a preliminary test measurement of morphological complexity in terms of text classification. The corpus was created in accordance with the aim of this study. We do not therefore analyze these texts from a literary perspective. The method is based on a computation of the difference between two measurements — the vocabulary richness of lemmas and the vocabulary richness of word forms. The greater the difference, the higher the morphological complexity of a text. For example, let us take two sentences that both consist of 10 tokens: "I was ready to be a member of the team" (S1) and "I was ready to become a member of the team" (S2). After lemmatization, the sentences would be "I be ready to be a member of the team" (S3) and "I be ready to become a member of the team" (S4). Further, for the measurement of vocabulary richness, Type-Token Ratio (*TTR*) is used here:

$$TTR_{S1} = \frac{10}{10} = 1$$

$$TTR_{S3} = \frac{9}{10} = 0.9$$

$$TTR_{S2} = \frac{10}{10} = 1$$

$$TTR_{S4} = \frac{10}{10} = 1$$

With sentences S1 and S3, we get a morphological complexity $TTR_{S1} - TTR_{S3} = 1 - 0.9 = 0.1$; whereas with sentences S2 and S4, the result of the morphological complexity is $TTR_{S2} - TTR_{S4} = 1 - 1 = 0$. Thus, we can state that S1 has higher morphological complexity than S2.

Since the Moving Average Type-Token Ratio (Covington & McFall, 2010; Kubát & Milička, 2013) is used for the measurement of vocabulary richness, the method is named the Moving Average Morphological Richness (hereinafter *MAMR*).

Using vocabulary richness for measuring the morphological complexity of a text is not new in linguistics; Kettunen (2014) applied the Moving Average Type-Token Ratio (hereinafter *MATTR*) directly in a cross-linguistic comparison (though not as a difference computation between word forms and lemmas). He computed *MATTR* for texts in 21 languages, and the results were compared with two other methods of measuring morphological complexity. The author states that "All the three computed measures are able to order the languages quite meaningfully in a morphological complexity order that at least groups most of the languages with same kind of languages and the most and least complex languages are clearly separated" (Kettunen, 2014). However, this approach seems to be problematic, because *MATTR* represents more than just morphological richness. Perhaps Kettunen's approach is acceptable in language typology, but in our opinion it is not suitable for stylometric research.

The morphological complexity of a text seems to be the result of unconscious language behavior by the writer (or the speaker); it is hard to imagine that the author of a text consisting of perhaps thousands of words consciously distributes the proportions of particular word forms. Moreover, the distribution of word forms is strongly influenced by grammar; the author is therefore "forced" to use particular forms regardless of his or her preferences. Consequently, no one can be sure that the concept of morphological complexity is useful for determining style or authorship attribution until this is empirically proved. Thus, one goal of this study is to observe whether the *MAMR* of a text can distinguish an individual style of writing — like other stylometric indicators such as thematic concentration (Čech, 2016), vocabulary richness, or activity of text (Kubát, Matlach, & Čech, 2014; Popescu et al., 2009). A corpus of 677 Czech texts written by eight authors is used for the analysis.

This paper is structured as follows. First, the methodology is introduced (section "Methodology"). In section "Corpus," the language material is presented and analyzed. Section "Text Length" is concentred to an observation of a potential impact of text length on all indices used in the current study. Section "Results" is devoted to the results, and "Conclusion" presents the conclusions of the study.

Methodology

The method of measuring morphological richness is based on a computation of the difference between the vocabulary richness of lemmas and the vocabulary richness of word forms. As "Introduction" illustrated, the bigger the difference, the higher the morphological complexity of the text.

Another set of examples is shown below. Let us take two seven-word texts as an example:

(1a) I love her and she loves me
(2a) I love it and she loves it

We lemmatize the texts as follows:

(1b) I LOVE SHE AND SHE LOVE I
(2b) I LOVE IT AND SHE LOVE IT

Since both texts are of identical length, it is possible to use the Type-Token Ratio (*TTR*) as an indicator of vocabulary richness:

$$TTR = \frac{V}{N}$$

where *V* is the number of different words (types) in a text and *N* is the number of all words (tokens) in a text. We compute the *TTR* for each text:

$$TTR_{1a} = \frac{7}{7} = 1$$

$$TTR_{2a} = \frac{6}{7} = 0.857$$

$$TTR_{1b} = \frac{4}{7} = 0.571$$

$$TTR_{2b} = \frac{5}{7} = 0.714$$

The difference between *TTRs* based on word forms and lemmas expresses the morphological complexity of a text; specifically, for text (1) we obtain:

$$TTR_{1a} - TTR_{1b} = 1 - 0.571 = 0.429$$

and for text (2)

$$TTR_{2a} - TTR_{2b} = 0.857 - 0.714 = 0.143$$

Since 0.429 > 0.143, one can state that text (1) has higher morphological complexity.

In reality, we need to compare texts of different lengths. Thus, the Moving Average Type-Token Ratio (hereinafter *MATTR*) for measuring vocabulary richness is applied because of its independence from text length (Covington & McFall, 2010;

Kubát & Milička, 2013).[2,3] *MATTR* is defined as follows. A text is divided into overlapping subtexts of the same length (so-called "windows" with arbitrarily chosen size *L*; usually, the "window" moves forward one token at a time). Then, the type-token ratio is computed for every single subtext, and finally *MATTR* is defined as a mean of the individual values:

$$MATTR(L) = \frac{\sum_{i=1}^{N-L} V_i}{L(N-L+1)}$$

where N is the text length in tokens, L is the arbitrarily chosen length of a window ($L < N$), and V_i is the number of types in an individual window.

For example, in the following sequence of characters — *a, b, c, a, a, d, f* — the text length is 7 tokens ($N = 7$). If we choose a window size of 3 tokens ($L = 3$), we obtain 5 windows — *a, b, c|b, c, a|c, a, a|a, a, d|a, d, f* — and then we can compute the *MATTR* of the sequence as follows:

$$MATTR(L) = \frac{\sum_{i=1}^{N-L} V_i}{L(N-L+1)} = \frac{3+3+2+2+3}{3(7-3+1)} = 0.867$$

The *MAMR* of a text is defined as the difference between the *MATTR* computed in word forms and the *MATTR* computed in lemmas:

$$MAMR(L) = MATTR(L)_{wordform} - MATTR(L)_{lemma}$$

Unfortunately, the nature of the measurement does not allow us to test differences between pairs of texts statistically.[4] However, it is possible to test differences between text groups (genres, authors). In this analysis, we use the *u*-test[5]:

$$u = \frac{\left|\overline{MAMR_1} - \overline{MAMR_2}\right|}{\sqrt{\frac{s_1^2}{n_1} + \frac{s_2^2}{n_2}}}$$

[2] MATTR is a similar method to Standardized Type-Token Ratio (STTR). MATTR is based on overlapping chunks, while STTR is based on nonoverlapping chunks.

[3] Although MATTR is independent of text length, it should be mentioned that this method is problematic because of the arithmetic mean value of the chunks. For example, although two nonoverlapping text chunks (subtexts) can share the same TTR value, the inventory of types in these two chunks can be completely different. Another problem may arise when TTR on different chunks of text has a high variance. The authors of this study are aware of these problems, especially the high variance. That is why, the MWTTRD method was proposed (Kubát & Milička, 2013). Nevertheless, according to data obtained in the previous research (Kubát, 2016), the average value seems to be a reliable indicator for stylometric analyses.

[4] To put it more specifically, the problem is caused by overlapping windows.

[5] In statistics, it is usually called the *z*-test; here, we follow a convention used in quantitative linguistics.

where $\overline{MAMR_1}$ and $\overline{MAMR_2}$ are the arithmetic means of the results in each group, s_1, s_2 are standard deviations, and n_1, n_2 are the numbers of results in each group. For the significance level $\alpha = 0.05$, $u \geq 1.96$ means that the difference between the two groups is statistically significant.

For illustration, let us compare differences in *MAMR* between Karel Čapek's short stories (*Wayside Crosses* (WC), *Stories from a Pocket* (SP), *Stories from Another Pocket* (SAP), and *Painful Tales* (PT)[6]) on the one hand, and his newspaper articles (*How it is Made* (HM), *the Gardener's Year* (GY), and selected articles from The People's Newspaper (PN))[7] on the other. Using the data (texts WC, SP, SAP, PT, HM, GY, and PN), we obtain:

$$u = \frac{\left|\overline{MAMR}_{short\ stories} - \overline{MAMR}_{newspapers}\right|}{\sqrt{\frac{s^2_{short\ stories}}{n_{short\ stories}} + \frac{s^2_{newspapers}}{n_{newspapers}}}} = \frac{|0.0984 - 0.0797|}{\sqrt{\frac{0.0164^2}{71} + \frac{0.0216^2}{92}}} = 6.28$$

Since $6.28 > 1.96$, we can state that there is a significant difference between these two groups of texts (for the $\alpha = 0.05$).

Corpus

The proposed method is applied to a corpus of 677 Czech texts. For genre analysis, we decided to use texts only written by one author (Karel Čapek) in order to avoid biased results caused by different authorial styles. The texts belong to five genres: travel books (travelogues), letters, short stories, novels, and newspaper articles. However, it should be emphasized that such an analysis is limited to one particular author; we cannot generalize the findings to other authors, and the interpretation must take this fact into account. To carry out a more thorough genre analysis, texts by many authors must be investigated. The primary purpose of this study is to propose the method, and its secondary purpose is to conduct a preliminary test to discover whether *MAMR* has some potential for application in stylometric research. In other words, this article focuses on the method from the perspective of quantitative linguistics; it is not a literary genre analysis.

For the authorship analysis, novels written by eight Czech writers were chosen: Karel Čapek (1890–1938), Alois Jirásek (1851–1930), Božena Němcová (1820–1862), Vladislav Vančura (1891–1942), Bohumil Hrabal (1914–1997), Karel Poláček (1892–1945), and Svatopluk Čech (1846–1908). As in the case of the author-specific genre analysis material mentioned above (Čapek texts), this corpus

[6] The Czech original titles: *Boží muka* (WC), *Povídky z jedné kapsy* (SP), *Povídky z druhé kapsy* (SAP), and *Trapné povídky* (PT).

[7] The Czech original titles: *Jak se co dělá* (HM), *Zahradníkův rok* (GY), and *vybrané články z Lidových novin* (PN).

too is used only for preliminary testing to assess *MAMR's* potential for authorship attribution; the study does not present any literary interpretation of the results obtained.

For the purposes of this study, novels and travel books were segmented into individual chapters. Analogically, collections of short stories were segmented into individual short stories. In short, the following units were considered to be individual texts for the purposes of the present study: individual chapters of a novel or a travel book, and individual short stories, letters, and newspaper articles. The list of texts used for the genre and authorship analysis can be found in Appendix.

Text Length

Text length is a factor that influences the majority of indices used in stylometry. Needless to say, the impact of text length is undesirable, and researchers usually attempt to find some methods to eliminate it. Let us briefly mention other text size-independent methods based on *TTR*.

The idea of a moving window is not new; it is implemented in the software WordSmith (Scott, 2013) as the standardized type-token ratio (*STTR*) where the average *TTR* is based on consecutive word chunks of a text; *STTR* is based on non-overlapping windows, whereas *MATTR* uses smoothly moving windows.

Another standardized Type-Token Ratio, *zTTR*, was proposed by Cvrček and Chlumská (2015). This vocabulary richness indicator is based on comparing observed *TTR* with referential *TTR* values representing texts of identical size. The main disadvantage of *zTTR* is that it is based on a corpus which cannot be considered fully representative. The crucial question is how to select particular texts, e.g., a representative corpus of novels. There is no clear standard for selecting appropriate novels for the corpus.

Besides the aforementioned indicators, there are several other methods such as Moving Window Type-Token Ratio Distribution (*MWTTRD*) (Kubát & Milička, 2013), *R1* based on h-point (Popescu et al., 2009), a complex frequency structure indicator called lambda (Popescu et al., 2011), Yule's *K* (Yule, 1944), and Guiraud's *TTR* (Guiraud, 1954). All these methods have advantages and disadvantages; some are not fully independent of the text length, while some require specific text lengths.

The application of the "moving window" (see the *MATTR* in "Methodology") seems to be a promising method for eliminating the impact of text length. *MATTR's* advantage is in its straightforward interpretation and low computational complexity. On the other hand, this method has also some weaknesses (discussed above in this study). Nevertheless, according to data observations in the previous research (Kubát, 2016; Kubát & Milička, 2013), the *MATTR* seems to be a reliable indicator for stylometric analyses.

In this analysis, we observe the potential impact of text length on all indices used in the current study (i.e., $MATTR_{word\ form}$, $MATTR_{lemma}$, *MAMR*) (Figs. 4.1, 4.2, and 4.3). We decided to present these graphs, because text length is one of the most frequent obstacles to the use of stylometric indicators (especially, those related to

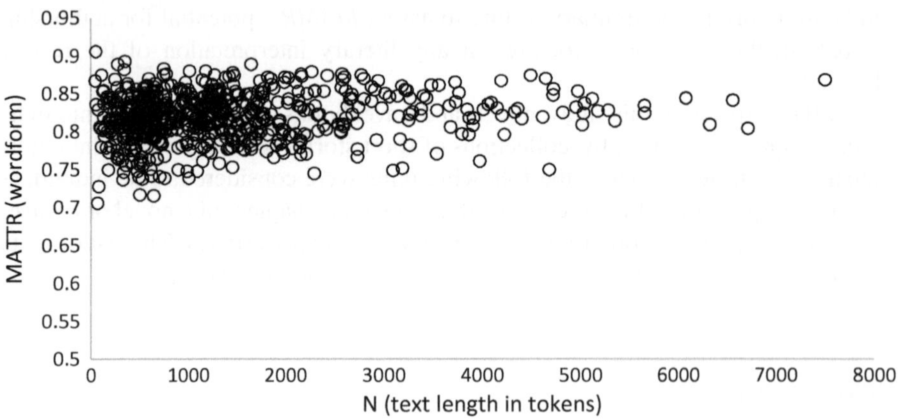

Fig. 4.1 Relationship between *MATTR* (word form) and text length in Czech texts

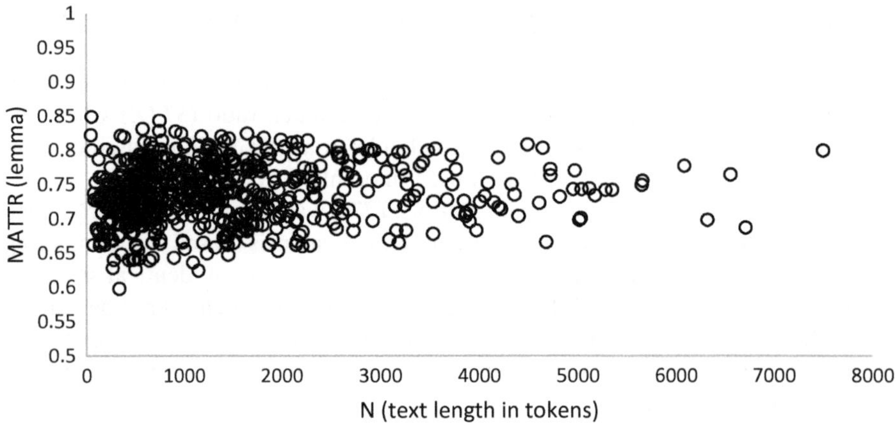

Fig. 4.2 Relationship between *MATTR* (lemma) and text length in Czech texts

vocabulary richness). In all cases, the variables are obviously independent of one another. Consequently, *MAMR* can be considered a suitable index in stylometry, at least due to its independence from text length.

Results

In stylometry, the usefulness of any method is determined by its effectiveness for a given text classification task (Juola, 2008; Kubát, 2016). In this study, we focus on two kinds of text classification: genre and authorship analysis. Our aim is to apply *MAMR* to presorted groups of texts and to observe whether significant differences appear between pairs of groups. If so, we can state that *MAMR* reflects a property of

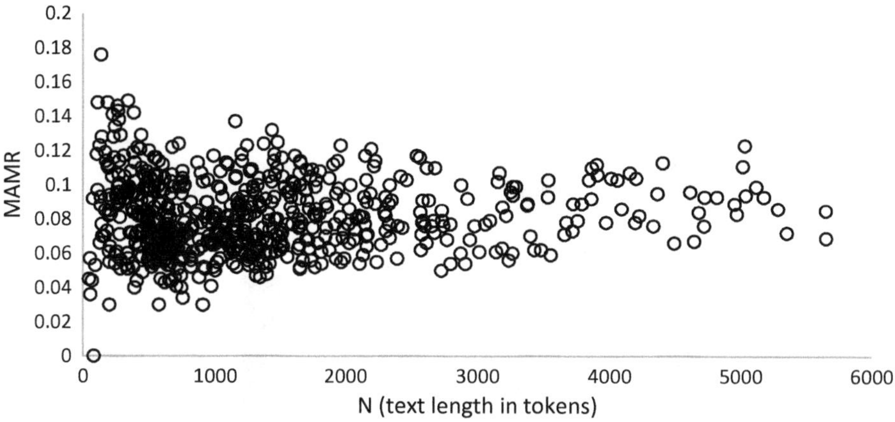

Fig. 4.3 Relationship between *MAMR* and text length in Czech texts

Table 4.1 The average *MAMR*, standard deviation (s), number of texts (n), and the adjusted p-values of u-test by genre (adjusted by the Benjamini–Hochberg–Yekutieli procedure)

		Travel books	Letters	Short stories	Novels	Newspaper articles
MAMR		0.066	0.103	0.098	0.078	0.080
s		0.017	0.020	0.016	0.016	0.022
n		132	93	71	80	92
U-test results by genre	Letters	**<0.001**				
	Short stories	**<0.001**	0.364			
	Novels	**<0.001**	**<0.001**	**<0.001**		
	Newspaper articles	**<0.001**	**<0.001**	**<0.001**	>0.999	

Bolded values denote a significant difference ($\alpha < 0.05$)

text group(s), which are strongly influenced by pragmatic factors, such as genre or authorship. In this study, the window size is set at $L = 100$.[8]

Genres

There are five genres (travel book, letter, short story, novel, and newspaper article) used for analysis in the current study. For each text, the *MAMR* is computed, and then the mean of the *MAMR* for the particular genre is determined. The results are presented in Table 4.1 and Fig. 4.4. The differences are obvious at first sight. *MAMR*

[8]The value $L = 100$ is chosen arbitrarily based on its usefulness in the previous analyses of this textual property.

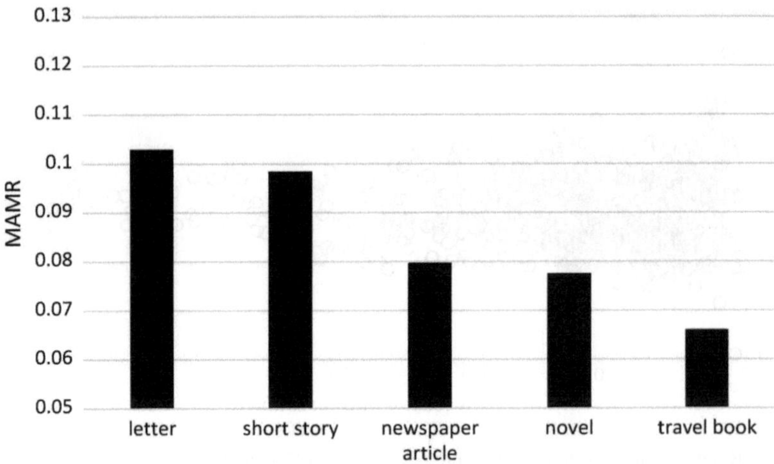

Fig. 4.4 Average *MAMR* results by genre

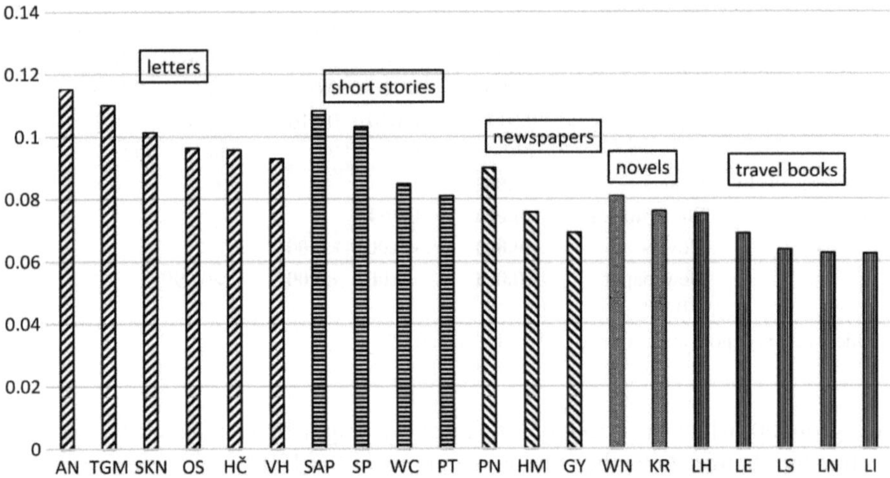

Fig. 4.5 Average *MAMR* results in Karel Čapek's books (i.e., individual novels, travel books, short story collections, etc.)

also reveals minimal differences between letters and short stories as well as between newspaper articles and novels. The observed similarities are not just "optical" (see Fig. 4.4); the results of statistical testing confirm nonsignificant differences between these pairs of groups (Table 4.1). For more details, the results of average *MAMR* for individual books are presented in Fig. 4.5.

Table 4.2 The average *MAMR*, standard deviation (s), number of texts (n), and the adjusted p-values of u-test in authorship (adjusted by the Benjamini–Hochberg–Yekutieli procedure)

	Jirásek	Němcová	Vančura	Čapek	Hrabal	Poláček	Čech
MAMR	0.078	0.103	0.065	0.078	0.087	0.074	0.067
s	0.008	0.011	0.011	0.016	0.008	0.021	0.008
n	43	19	15	80	16	74	28
Němcová	**<0.001**						
Vančura	**<0.001**	**<0.001**					
Čapek	>0.999	**<0.001**	**<0.001**				
Hrabal	**<0.001**	**<0.001**	**<0.001**	**<0.001**			
Poláček	**<0.001**	**<0.001**	**<0.001**	**<0.001**	**<0.001**		
Čech	**<0.001**	**<0.001**	**<0.001**	**<0.001**	>0.999	**<0.001**	

Bolded values denote a significant difference ($\alpha < 0.05$)

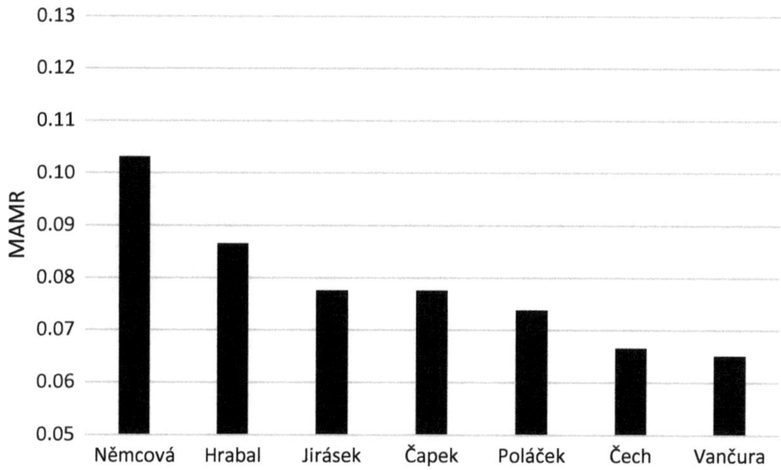

Fig. 4.6 Results of the average *MAMR* of eight Czech novelists

Authorship Analysis

For the purpose of authorship attribution, texts of one specific genre, i.e., novels, were selected. The chosen authors represent a varied spectrum of Czech writers — they were active from the middle of the nineteenth century to the second half of the twentieth century; some of them are identifiable by readers due to their specific style of writing (particularly, Vančura and Hrabal). As can be seen in Table 4.2 and Fig. 4.6, the *MAMR* results reflect significant differences between most pairs of authors.[9] Moreover, the p-values indicate great (and unexpected) differences among the particular authors. Consequently, MAMR seems to detect some important aspects of authorship attribution, at least among the novelists.

[9] Except two of them (Jirásek vs. Čapek and Čech vs. Hrabal).

Conclusion

Moving Average Morphological Richness is a method of measuring morphological complexity that offers intelligible interpretation and is, moreover, independent from text length. Given that the majority of the differences found by the study are significant (in genres 8/10 = 80%, in authorship 19/21 = 90.5%), the proposed method can be considered a promising stylometric tool (especially, for the analysis of a group of texts). In genre classification of Čapek's texts, *MAMR* is more effective than the *MATTR*, thematic concentration, activity of text, and other stylometric features (cf. Kubát, 2016). Most importantly, *MAMR's* independence from text size allows us to compare texts of different lengths.

The proposed method offers the potential to uncover some unexpected stylistic properties. These findings can inspire scholars not only in linguistics (both in quantitative and qualitative stylistics) but also in literary criticism. The next step is to conduct a deeper investigation of the differences between genres and authors involving specialists in literary studies. It should be emphasized that collaboration between quantitative and qualitative researchers is necessary in this field. Quantitative stylometry only provides some findings that should be subsequently interpreted from a qualitative point of view; otherwise, the obtained results can only be used for automatic text classification. This work is the first attempt to discuss whether *MAMR* is a suitable feature for stylometric research. Therefore, stylometric research using *MAMR* is a matter for further study.

Appendix

List of Texts Used for the Genre Analysis

Author	Genre	English title	Czech title	Tag
Karel Čapek	Travel book	*Letters from England*	*Anglické listy*	LE
		Letters from North	*Cesta na sever*	LN
		Letters from Italy	*Italské listy*	LI
		Letters from Holland	*Obrázky z Holandska*	LH
		Letters from Spain	*Výlet do Španěl*	LS
	Letter	*to Anna Nešporová*	*Anna Nešporová*	AN
		to Helena Čapková	*Helena Čapková*	HČ
		to Stanislav Kostka Neumann	*Stanislav Kostka Neumann*	SKN
		to Olga Scheinpflugová	*Olga Scheinpflugová*	OS
		to Tomáš Garrigue Masaryk	*Tomáš Garrigue Masaryk*	TGM
		to Věra Hrůzová	*Věra Hrůzová*	VH
	Short story	*Wayside Crosses*	*Boží Muka*	WC
		Stories from a Pocket	*Povídky z jedné kapsy*	SP
		Stories from Another Pocket	*Povídky z druhé kapsy*	SAP
		Painful tales	*Trapné povídky*	PT
	Novel	*Krakatit*	*Krakatit*	KR
		War with the Newts	*Válka s mloky*	WN
	Newspaper article	*How it is Made*	*Jak se co dělá*	HM
		Selected articles from The People's Newspaper	*Vybrané články z Lidových novin*	PN
		The Gardener's Year	*Zahradníkův rok*	GY

List of Texts Used for the Authorship Analysis

Author	English title	Czech title	Tag
Alois Jirásek	*Gaudeamus igitur*	*Filosofská historie*	GI
	Dog's Heads	*Psohlavci*	DH
Božena Němcová	*The Grandmother*	*Babička*	GM
	The village under mountains	*Pohorská vesnice*	VM
Vladislav Vančura	*Baker Jan Marhoul*	*Pekař Jan Marhoul*	BJM
	Last Judgement	*Poslední soud*	LJ

Author	English title	Czech title	Tag
Bohumil Hrabal	*I Served the King of England*	*Obsluhoval jsem anglického krále*	KE
	Cutting It Short	*Postřižiny*	CIS
Karel Poláček	*A House in the Suburbs*	*Dům na předměstí*	HS
	County Town	*Okresní město*	CT
Svatopluk Čech	*The Excursions of Mr. Brouček to the 15th Century*	*Nový epochální výlet pana Broučka, tentokráte do XV. století*	EC
	The Excursions of Mr. Brouček to the Moon	*Pravý výlet pana Broučka do Měsíce*	EM
Karel Čapek	*Krakatit*	*Krakatit*	KR
	War with the Newts	*Válka s mloky*	WN

References

Baerman, M., Brown, D., & Corbett, G. (Eds.). (2015). *Understanding and measuring morphological complexity*. New York: Oxford University Press.

Bane, M. (2008). Quantifying and measuring morphological complexity. In C. B. Chang & H. J. Haynie (Eds.), *Proceedings of the 26th West Coast Conference on formal linguistics* (pp. 69–76). Somerville, MA: Cascadilla Proceedings Project.

Bentz C., Ruzsics, T., Koplenig, A., Samardžić, T. (2016). Comparison between morphological complexity measures: typological data vs. language corpora. In *Proceedings of the Workshop on Computational Linguistics for Linguistic Complexity (CL4LC) at the 26th International Conference on Computational Linguistics (COLING 2016)*, Osaka.

Březina, V., Pallotti, G. (2016). Morphological complexity in written L2 texts. *Second language research,* DOI: https://doi.org/10.1177/0267658316643125.

Čech, R. (2016). *Tematická koncentrace textu v češtině* [*Thematic concentration of text in Czech*]. Praha, Czech Republic: ÚFAL.

Covington, M. A., & McFall, J. D. (2010). Cutting the Gordian knot: The moving-average type-token ratio (MATTR). *Journal of Quantitative Linguistics, 17*(2), 94–100.

Cvrček, V., & Chlumská, L. (2015). Simplification in translated Czech: A new approach to type-token ratio. *Russian Linguistics, 39*(3), 309–325.

Cvrček, V., & Václavík, J. (2015). Jednoznačnost a kontext. Kvantitativní studie [*Unambiguity and context. A quantitative study*]. *Korpus—gramatika—axiologie, 11*(2015), 28–41.

Guiraud, P. (1954). *Les catactères stitistiques du vocabulaire*. Paris, France: Presses Universitaires de France.

Indrisano, R., & Squire, J. R. (Eds.). (2000). *Perspectives on writing: Research, theory, and practice*. Newark, NJ: International Reading Association.

Juola, P. (2008). Authorship attribution. *Foundations and Trends in Information Retrieval, 1*(3), 233–334.

Kettunen, K. (2014). Can type-token ratio be used to show morphological complexity of languages? *Journal of Quantitative Linguistics, 21*(3), 223–245.

Kubát, M. (2016). *Kvantitativní analýza žánrů* [*Quantitative analysis of genres*]. Ostrava, Czech Republic: Ostravská univerzita.

Kubát, M., Matlach, V., & Čech, R. (2014). *QUITA–Quantitative index text analyzer*. Lüdensheid, Germany: RAM.

Kubát, M., & Milička, J. (2013). Vocabulary richness measure in genres. *Journal of Quantitative Linguistics, 20*(4), 339–349.

Pinker, S. (2010). *The language instinct: How the mind creates language*. New York: Harper Collins.

Popescu, I. I., & Altmann, G. (2007). Writer's view of text generation. *Glottometrics, 15*, 71–81.

Popescu, I.-I., Altmann, G., Grzybek, P., Jayaram, B. D., Köhler, R., Krupa, V., et al. (2009). *Word frequency studies*. Berlin, Germany: Mouton de Gruyter.

Popescu, I. I., Čech, R., & Altmann, G. (2011). *The lambda-structure of texts*. Lüdenscheid, Germany: RAM.

Scott, M. (2013). *WordSmith tools*. Liverpool, UK: Lexical Analysis Software.

Xanthos, A., Laaha, S., Gillis, S., Stephany, U., Aksu-Koç, A., Christofidou, A., et al. (2011). On the role of morphological richness in the early development of noun and verb inflection. *First Language, 31*(4), 461–479.

Yule, G. U. (1944). *The statistical study of literary vocabulary*. Cambridge: The University Press.

Chapter 5
A Collocation-Driven Method of Discovering Rhymes (in Czech, English, and French Poetry)

Petr Plecháč

Abstract The chapter presents a model for discovering rhymes in a corpus of poetic texts. The algorithm employs an adaptation of the usual collocation extraction technique in order to identify some common rhyme pairs in a corpus. The output is then used as a training set for simple machine learning. The method has been tested on corpora of poetry in three different languages (Czech, English, and French) with F-scores ranging from 0.9 to 0.95.

Keywords Rhyme · Versification · Morphological richness · Corpus linguistics · Machine learning

Introduction

With the current precision and availability of text-to-speech tools, the automatic detection of rhymes in a corpus of poetic texts may seem like a walk in the park. Looking for final sounds in neighboring lines which match is a straightforward task and a few lines of code are sufficient for a task of this nature. However, when inspecting the output of such algorithms, one realizes that it is not so simple; not only does it miss all the so-called imperfect rhymes but also—in the case of poetry written some centuries ago—rhymes where pronunciation has changed over time. We thus propose an algorithm which, instead of looking for precise matches of sounds, works with the probabilities of two words rhyming together derived mainly from the analyzed texts themselves.

P. Plecháč (✉)
Ustav pro ceskou literaturu, Praha, Czech Republic
e-mail: plechac@ucl.cas.cz

M. Fidler, V. Cvrček (eds.), *Taming the Corpus*, Quantitative Methods in the Humanities and Social Sciences, https://doi.org/10.1007/978-3-319-98017-1_5

Related Work

This paper builds on the work of Sravana Reddy and Kevin Knight, namely their expectation maximization algorithm for discovering rhyme schemes (Reddy & Knight 2011a, where further literature on the topic may be found). To identify rhyme schemes, Reddy and Knight use no information about pronunciation but rely rather on the fact that any large enough corpus of rhymed poetry inevitably contains repetition of rhyming pairs. The basic principle of their algorithm is as follows: At the beginning, we are given a predefined set of possible rhyme schemes for stanzas of different lengths (e.g., "aaa," "aab," "aba," … for 3-line stanzas; "aabb," "abab," "abcb," … for 4-line stanzas). The selection of the most likely schemes for particular stanzas in a corpus is then governed by: (1) the orthographic similarity of line-final words in it (defined simply as the number of characters common to both words divided by the number of characters in the shorter word) and (2) the frequency of these words' co-occurrence within the entire corpus.

As orthographic similarity is only taken into account with the initial estimation of the parameters, the algorithm relies mostly on reoccurrences of rhyme pairs. One may thus expect it to perform much better with minimally inflected languages (such as English) than with highly inflected ones (such as Czech). This is based on a simple assumption—further probed in "Training Set"—that the more often grammatical suffixes are used in language, the more possible rhyme pairs a poet can use and the less the same rhyme pairs will reoccur in a corpus. Very roughly speaking, when a Czech poet wants to rhyme the word *básník* '*poet*,' he is free to combine it with any other word of the same inflectional paradigm, as long as they use both, in the dative case for example (e.g., *básník-ovi—Štěpán-ovi* 'to [the] poet—to Štěpán').

The significant weak point of Reddy and Knight's model, however, lies in the predefined sets of schemes from which the algorithm picks up the most likely one. These sets were originally generated from the gold standard of English and French corpora (all schemes found there) against which the authors test the performance of their algorithm. The selection is thus done from a very limited number of possible schemes and the success rates reported by Reddy and Knight may thus be considered biased to a large extent.

Let us illustrate this with some examples. Generally, there are five schemes which a 3-line stanza may follow: "aaa," "aab," "aba," "abb," and "abc," but only the first three of these are actually present in Reddy and Knight's set as "abb" and "abc" never occurs either in the English or French corpus. This simply increases the chances of the algorithm guessing the correct scheme. And, the longer the stanzas are, the smaller portion of all possible schemes the set contains. For 4-line stanzas, there are only 8 schemes out of a possible 15; for 6-line stanzas, there are only 32 out of 203 and this trend intensifies. The main pitfall comes with poems that are structured into long irregular strophes rather than stanzas or where there is no such structuring at all. Let us take an example from the English corpus of Reddy and Knight: *L'Allegro* by John Milton. There is no stanzaic division in the text, hence all 172 lines are considered to form a single stanza. As there is no other 172-line stanza found in the English or French corpus, the algorithm cannot possibly go wrong—the selection is made from a set containing only one scheme, the correct one. As a matter of fact, 16% of lines in the English corpus and 29% of lines in the French corpus come from such stanzas where the algorithm generates a singleton.

In addition, with the sets generated this way the application of the algorithm to other corpora is problematic; it would most probably encounter correct stanza schemes unknown to the algorithm, e.g., "abb." What Reddy and Knight (2011a, p. 81) suggest in this case is to generate all possible schemes for a stanza of a particular length instead of using the predefined sets. But, this is far beyond the capabilities of contemporary machines. The number of possible schemes of n-line stanzas is equivalent to the number of ways a set of n distinct elements can be partitioned into nonempty subsets, the so-called Bell numbers (cf. Gardner 1978). And, these numbers grow extremely fast. While for a 3-line stanza there are (as already mentioned) just $B_3 = 5$ possible schemes, for an 8-line stanza there are $B_8 = 4140$ possible schemes, for a 20-line stanza it is a number consisting of 14 digits, and for the longest stanza analyzed by Reddy and Knight (220 lines) it is a 291-digit number. Even though many schemes may be excluded as unperceivable and rather coincidental than intentional, for example, a 220-line stanza where only the first and last line rhyme, the number would be still too large.

In what follows, we propose an algorithm which: (1) looks for rhymes themselves instead of parsing whole stanza schemes, (2) takes advantage of the recurring nature of rhyme employing an adaptation of the usual methods of corpus linguistics, and (3) aims to solve the problem of insufficient repetitions in highly inflected languages by focusing on phonetic components of particular rhyme pairs instead of words themselves. We will demonstrate that through this one may discover a vast majority of rhymes in three different languages with very high precision.

Data

We test our algorithm on three corpora of poetry—Czech, English, and French. The Czech data comes from the Corpus of Czech verse (Plecháč & Kolár 2015) and contains around 2.5 million of verse lines. The English corpus (~90 thousand lines) and French corpus (~25 thousand lines) come from the aforementioned study of Reddy and Knight.[1] Each corpus has been phonetically transcribed. In Czech, this has been done by means of the system KVĚTA (Plecháč 2016), in English and French by means of MaryTTS (2017). Further details on the corpora are provided in Table 5.1. In all three corpora, the rhyme pairs are annotated. In Czech, this was done with the help of a (very simple) script, the output of which has been manually

[1] According to the authors, the English corpus comes originally from the study of Sonderegger (2011) and the French comes from the ARTFL (2009) project.

Table 5.1 Corpora details

	Czech	English	French
Number of lines	2,727,632	93,030	26,543
Number of authors	296	32	9
Time span	18th–20th century	16th–20th century	16th–17th century
Grouping of data to subcorpora	Decade when author was born (1740–1890)	100-year interval when author was born (1450–1550 to 1850–1950)	100-year interval when author was born (1450–1550, 1550–1650)

checked in detail. In English and French, the complete annotation was done manually by the authors. These annotations are taken as the gold standard against which the output of our algorithm is tested.

Method

We initially employ an adaptation of the usual collocation extraction technique in order to identify some common rhyme pairs in each corpus. The output is then phonetically transcribed and used as a training set for simple machine learning.

Training Set

The algorithm first reduces each poem in a corpus to a string consisting of its line-final words, for example:

> Dalekoť jeho sen, umrlý jako stín,
> obraz co bílých měst u vody stopen klín,
> takť jako zemřelých myšlenka poslední,
> tak jako jméno jich, pradávných bojů hluk,
> dávná severní zář, vyhaslé světlo s ní,
> zbortěné harfy tón, ztrhané strůny zvuk[2]
> …
> (K. H. Mácha)

gives:

> stín klín poslední hluk ní zvuk

These strings are then treated as being regular texts in which the algorithm looks for collocations. The logic behind this is simple: if some pair of words co-occur more

[2] "Far is that lost dream now, a shadow no more found,/Like visions of white towns, deep in the waters drowned,/The last indignant thoughts of the defeated dead,/Their unremembered names, the clamour of old fights,/The worn-out northern lights after their gleam is fled,/The untuned harp, whose strings distil no more delights." (translation: Edith Pargeter)

Table 5.2 Precision and recall of rhyme pairs extracted on the basis of word-pairs' *T*-score

	Czech	English	French
Precision	0.90	0.96	0.995
Recall	0.18	0.15	0.03

often than would be expected by chance, there is a high probability that it is due to the fact that they rhyme and may thus be used to build a training set:

1. For each pair of different words *A* and *B* which co-occur in all the strings of line-final words at least *m* times in a span of *s* words,[3] count the number of such co-occurrences *f(AB)* and the overall frequencies *f(A)* and *f(B)*.
2. Calculate *T*-score[4] of these word-pairs:

$$T(\mathrm{AB}) = \frac{f(\mathrm{AB}) - \frac{f(A)f(B)}{N}}{\sqrt{f(\mathrm{AB})}} \tag{5.1}$$

where *N* is the size of a corpus measured by the number of lines.

3. If $T(A,B) > \alpha$, add pair *A*, *B* to the training set.[5]

When comparing the output against the gold standard, we obtain very high precision and (as expected) pretty low recall (Table 5.2). As this is not the final output, but just a training set for further processing, we may consider the results satisfactory.

Yet, there is another thing worth noting. The fact that in the French corpus we were able to capture only a very limited portion of rhymes (recall = 0.03) may be easily explained by its small size—in such a corpus only a few rhyme pairs occur repeatedly. On the other hand, the Czech corpus is more than 25 times larger than the English one, but the recall for both is almost the same. This brings us back to the hypothesis mentioned in "Related Work," namely, that in highly inflected languages particular words have more possible rhyme counterparts and therefore rhyme pairs do not reoccur as often as in minimally inflected ones.

[3] Here, we use the experimental values: $m = 4$, $s = 5$.

[4] In regular collocation extraction, there are two most frequently used measures: *T*-score and MI-score. The first one derives from a statistical hypothesis testing (Student's *t*-test) and aims thus to calculate the confidence with which we can assert that the difference from the expected frequency is not random; it gives no information on the strength of such an association. MI-score on the other hand directly measures the strength of the association but gives no information on what the probability is that it was caused by chance. The practical consequences are *T*-scores being sensitive to the co-occurrence of high-frequency grammatical words (the more the evidence, the more confidence), while MI-scores seem to overestimate the co-occurrences of words with low frequencies. As we are interested in distinguishing the significant co-occurrences from random ones and not in their ranking from strongest to weakest, *T*-score seems to be the optimal choice here.

[5] Here, we use $\alpha = 3.078$.

Table 5.3 Rhyme-type/rhyme-token ratio

	Czech	English	French
Mean (n = 1000)	[0.9784, 0.9826]	[0.9199, 0.9295]	[0.9562, 0.9644]
St.dev (n = 1000)	[0.0028, 0.0062]	[0.0043, 0.0099]	[0.0037, 0.0080]
Mean (n = 10,000)	0.8885	0.6881	0.8052
St.dev (n = 10,000)	0.0040	0.0029	0.0033

To test this hypothesis, we adopt another indicator common in the field of corpus linguistics—the type token ratio (TTR). We measure the richness of rhyme repertory as the number of unique rhyme pairs (rhyme-types) divided by the total number of rhyme pairs (rhyme-token). As TTR is generally strongly affected by corpus size, we have performed two experiments with random samples of the same size for all three languages.

First, we have measured TTR in 10 random samples (sampling without replacement) of 1000 rhyme-pairs apiece. Next, we calculated the arithmetic mean and standard deviation of the 10 values obtained. This process was then repeated 10 times. The results (provided in Table 5.3 in the form of *min* and *max* values) seem to support our hypothesis. Highly inflected Czech exhibits noticeably higher values of TTR than minimally inflected English, while moderately inflected French takes place in between. Low standard deviation values show that TTR is rather constant across samples.

In order to test this on larger data, we performed another experiment, where 10,000 random samples (sampling with replacement) were taken from each corpus in 10,000 iterations. The mean and standard deviation of TTRs from each iteration (Table 5.3) once again indicate that the richness of rhyme repertory of a language is affected by the extent to which it is inflected: the more inflected the language, the richer its rhyme repertory and the less the same rhyme pairs reoccur.

Learning

With the training set built, the algorithm learns the rhyme probabilities between particular vowels (syllable peaks) and consonant clusters.

Each line-final word in a corpus is represented as a set of relevant phonetic positions. For Czech and English, we generate relevant sounds in the following ways: (1) cut off all sounds before the peak of the last stressed syllable (if there is one), (2) if the remaining string is longer than two syllables, cut off all sounds before the peak of the penultimate syllable, and (3) cut off all consonants from the beginning of a string:

Czech	zapadlý → [ˈzapadli:] → adli:
English	rhyme → [ˈrAIm] → AIm

In the French corpus, we unfortunately cannot rely on stress placement. Due to a bug in MaryTTS's[6] lexicon source file, stress placement was incorrectly assigned to initial syllables (see example below). We thus disregard it and treat all sounds starting at the peak of the *penultimate* syllable as relevant (or the final syllable in the case of monosyllabic words):

French	commancer → [' kOma~se] → a~se

These strings are then split into substrings consisting of syllable peaks and consonant clusters (across syllable boundaries) and their order is inverted:

Czech	adli: → $\{\varnothing\}_1$ $\{\text{i:}\}_2$ $\{\text{dl}\}_3$ $\{\text{a}\}_4$
English	AIm → $\{\text{m}\}_1$ $\{\text{AI}\}_2$
French	a~se → $\{\varnothing\}_1$ $\{\text{e}\}_2$ $\{\text{s}\}_3$ $\{\text{@\textasciitilde}\}_4$

(∅ representing null consonant cluster)

Each line-final word in a corpus is thus ultimately represented by a set of 2–4 substrings.

The probability that two words in a corpus rhyme is calculated in the following ways:

1. Let *A* and *B* be two line-final words, a_i be the *i*-th phonetic substring of *A*, and b_i be the *i*-th phonetic substring of *B*.
2. Let $f_T(a_i,b_i)$ be the relative frequency of pairs in the training set where substrings a_i and b_i meet at *i*-th position, $f_C(a_i)$ be the relative frequency of line-final words in an entire corpus having substring a_i at *i*-th position, and $f_C(b_i)$ be the relative frequency of line-final words in an entire corpus having substring b_i at *i*-th position.
3. Let $p_i(a_i,b_i)$ be the probability that *A* and *B* rhyme together based on their substrings a_i and b_i: $p_i(a_i,b_i) = f_T(a_i,b_i)/(f_T(a_i,b_i) + f_C(a_i)\, f_C(b_i))$. In order not to eliminate rhymes, some component of which is not present in a training set, we assign in such cases a high probability (0.9) to pairs formed by identical substrings a_i and b_i and a minimal probability (0.0001) to those where a_i and b_i are different:

$$p_i\left(a_i,b_i\right)=\begin{cases}\dfrac{f_T\left(a_i,b_i\right)}{f_T\left(a_i,b_i\right)+f_C\left(a_i\right)f_C\left(b_i\right)}, & \text{if } f_T\left(a_i,b_i\right)>0\\[2ex] 0.9, \text{ if } f_T\left(a_i,b_i\right)=0 \text{ and } a_i,b_i \text{ are the same}\\[2ex] 0.9, \text{ if } f_T\left(a_i,b_i\right)=0 \text{ and } a_i,b_i \text{ are the same}\end{cases} \quad (5.2)$$

[6] See issue #323 at MaryTTS (2017). It has been fixed later on.

4. Let *P(A,B)* be the probability that *A* and *B* rhyme together based on all relevant substrings. If all the relevant substrings in *A* and *B* are identical, we have no reason to doubt that they rhyme together. In other cases, *P(A,B)* is calculated from partial probabilities:

$$P(A,B)=\begin{cases}1, \text{ if all substrings from } 1 \text{ to } m \text{ are the same}\\ \dfrac{\prod_{i=1}^{m} p(a_i,b_i)}{\prod_{i=1}^{m} p(a_i,b_i)+\prod_{i=1}^{m} 1-p(a_i,b_i)}, \text{ otherwise}\end{cases} \quad (5.3)$$

where m is the number of substrings in shorter of two sets.

Based on these probabilities, the algorithm marks each two lines which occur within a span of s lines as rhyme pairs (the same as with collocations, section "Training Set"), if their line-final words are different and *P(A,B)* of which was found to be >0.95. The output of such tagging is then taken as a new training set and new learning and tagging are performed. These iterations go on until the training set and tagging output are found to be equal.

As a safety net for rhyme pairs, the pronunciation of which has changed over time, for example:

	Original (Crystal 2007)	Contemporary
if thy soul check thee that I come so near	NE:r	NI:r
and will thy soul knows is admitted there	DE:r	
(Shakespeare)		

we also introduce a probability based on their orthography, namely their final character-trigrams:

1. Let g_A, g_B be the final character-trigrams of words *A* and *B*, respectively.
2. Let $f_T(g_A,g_B)$ be the relative frequency of pairs in a training set where g_A and g_B meet, $f_C(g_A)$ be the relative frequency of line-final words ending with g_A in entire corpus, and $f_C(g_B)$ be the relative frequency of line-final words ending with g_B in entire corpus.
3. Let $P_G(A,B)$ be the probability that *A* and *B* rhyme together based on their final trigrams:

$$P_G(A,B)=\begin{cases}1, \text{ if } g_A, g_B \text{ are the same}\\ \dfrac{f_T(g_A,g_B)}{f_T(g_A,g_B)+f_C(g_A)\ f_C(g_B)}, \text{ otherwise}\end{cases} \quad (5.4)$$

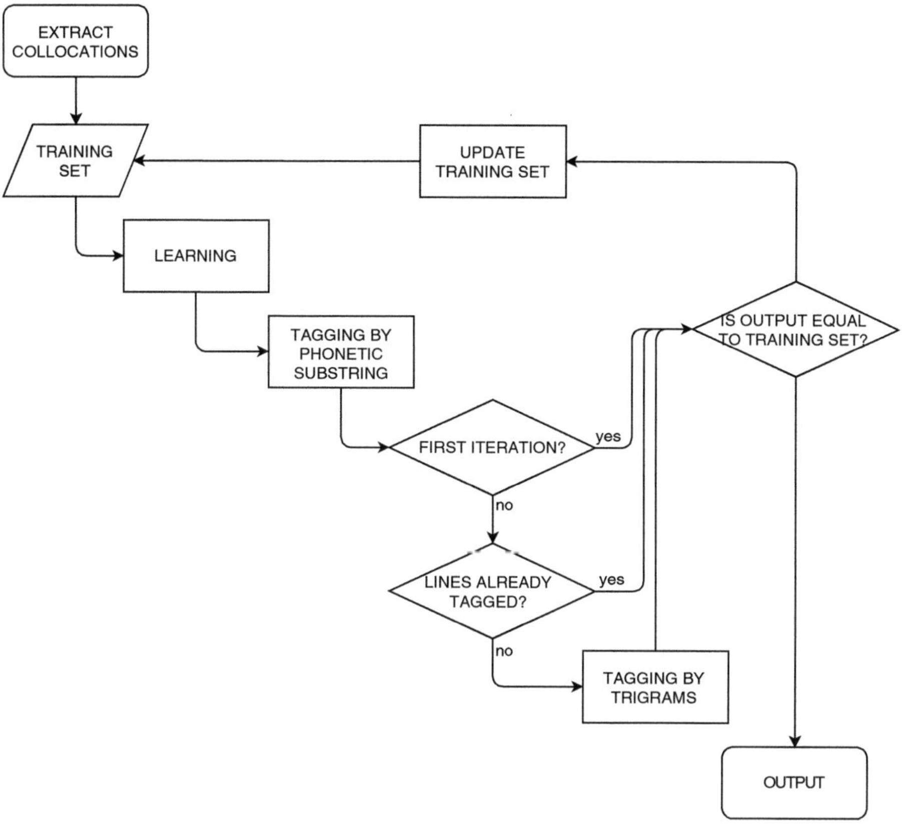

Fig. 5.1 Algorithm scheme

The idea behind this is that some other words may have preserved the original pronunciation of a given trigram and may thus be found in a training set (e.g., *wear, pear, swear* in this case).

As tagging based on orthography is of course much less reliable than that based on phonetic substrings, we mark pairs of lines as rhyme pairs according to trigrams ($P_G(A,B) > 0.95$) only in the case that none of them have been tagged as rhyming with another according to the substrings. In addition, we do not apply tagging in the first learning/tagging iteration (Fig. 5.1).

Results

We measure the algorithm's precision by the number of rhyme pairs in the intersection of the output and gold standard divided by the number of all pairs in the output. Recall is measured by the number of rhyme pairs in the intersection divided by the number of all pairs in the gold standard.

Doing that we:

1. Disregard (for obvious reasons) those pairs in the gold standard (if any) that consist of two identical words;
2. Disregard rhymes spanning different stanzas both in the output of the algorithm and in the gold standard. This is due to these rhymes being tagged according to repetitions of the stanza schemes rather than to actual rhymes in gold standard files, and we do not want to punish the algorithm for decisions that are generally correct, for example:

	Gold standard	Algorithm results
"Sisters and brothers, little maid,	a	a
"How many may you be?"	b	b
"How many? seven in all," she said,	a	a
And wondering looked at me.	b	b
"And where are they, I pray you tell?"	c	c
She answered, "Seven are we,	d	b
"And two of us at Conway dwell,	c	c
"And two are gone to sea.	d	b
(Wordsworth)		

In Table 5.4, we provide F-scores, that is:

$$F = \frac{2 \cdot \text{precision} \cdot \text{recall}}{\text{precision} + \text{recall}} \tag{5.5}$$

of our algorithm (collocation-driven) for the entire corpora of Czech, English, and French poetry and for their particular subcorpora. We also distinguish between the results of the algorithm trained on an entire corpus and trained on a given subcorpus only.

For the sake of comparison, we also report the F-scores of Reddy and Knight's original expectation maximization algorithm. As the authors use different measurements (average precision and recall of particular lines, cf. Reddy & Knight, 2011a, p. 79), we provide the values obtained from running their code (Reddy & Knight, 2011b)[7] on English and French with a slightly modified evaluation function. Recall

[7]We have used the stanza-independent EM model with θ initialized by orthographic similarity (Reddy & Knight, 2011a, p. 79), the original F-score of which is reported in Table 5.2, column "ortho. init." at ibid.: 81.

Table 5.4 F-score of particular algorithms

		Collocation-driven		Expectation maximization		
		Training on entire corpus	Training on particular subcorpora	Training on entire corpus	Training on particular subcorpora	Rule-based
English	All	0.92		0.84		0.80
	1450	0.87	0.84	0.86	0.85	0.67
	1550	0.91	0.91	0.87	0.87	0.77
	1650	0.92	0.91	0.96	0.95	0.81
	1750	0.92	0.92	0.73	0.69	0.82
	1850	0.93	0.93	0.78	0.77	0.84
French	All	0.90		0.72		0.39
	1450	0.90	0.88	0.69	0.68	0.45
	1550	0.91	0.90	0.74	0.74	0.31
		Collocation-driven		Expectation maximization		Rule-based
		Training on entire corpus	Training on particular subcorpora	Stanzas ≤20 lines	Known schemes only	
Czech	All	0.95		–		0.71
	1740	0.83	0.74	0.63	0.91	0.74
	1750	0.91	0.87	0.74	0.82	0.82
	1760	0.92	0.86	0.60	0.65	0.83
	1770	0.97	0.96	0.75	0.82	0.92
	1780	0.94	0.90	0.78	0.89	0.87
	1790	0.95	0.90	0.68	0.72	0.83
	1800	0.94	0.92	0.63	0.71	0.82
	1810	0.94	0.92	0.62	0.72	0.79
	1820	0.95	0.93	0.76	0.80	0.77
	1830	0.97	0.96	0.71	0.79	0.76
	1840	0.95	0.94	0.61	0.70	0.73
	1850	0.96	0.96	0.70	0.80	0.67
	1860	0.95	0.95	0.69	0.75	0.66
	1870	0.94	0.94	0.68	0.75	0.64
	1880	0.93	0.92	0.66	0.78	0.61
	1890	0.89	0.79	0.48	0.60	0.61

that these values may be considered biased due to the fact that the sets of possible schemes are generated from the corpora themselves (Section "Related Work").

This also causes problems with application to the Czech corpus. First of all, there are many stanzas in the corpus of a length which does not occur in the English or in French corpus and therefore the algorithm has nothing to select from. For this reason, we have evaluated the algorithm only with stanzas of a length which is common also in the original English and French corpora (≤20 lines). In addition, we have added one very essential type of schemes not originally included in the predefined sets since they do not occur in the original corpora—the schemes in question where no lines rhyme at all (i.e., "ab," "abc," "abcd,"...). F-scores of the algorithm with these settings are provided in column 3. However, there are still many stanzas in the Czech corpus with a scheme that is unknown to the algorithm—in most subcorpora this varies between 5% and 20%. In order to obtain the values comparable to the English and French, we also provide the F-scores of stanzas with known schemes only (column 4). Both aforementioned columns provide the evaluation of the algorithm trained on a given subcorpus only.[8]

Finally, we provide the F-score of the simple rule-based algorithm mentioned in the introduction: lines are tagged as rhymed if they co-occur in a span of *s* lines within one stanza and their relevant phonetic substrings are precisely the same.

Apart from the F-scores (harmonic mean of precision and recall) in Table 5.4, we also provide a graphical representation of precision and recall themselves in Fig. 5.2.

Table 5.4 shows that the performance of the collocation-driven algorithm is generally very good—in all three corpora the overall F-score ranges from 0.90 to 0.95. The weakest performance occurs where pronunciation differs significantly from the contemporary (en-1450), where rhyming conventions have not really been established yet (cs-1740), or where one may expect many modernist experiments with imperfect rhymes (cs-1890). The differences between training on an entire corpus and training on particular subcorpora are of some importance, mainly with small subcorpora; in most cases, they are negligible.

Comparing the results of the expectation maximization algorithm across particular corpora and subcorpora support our initial assumption only to a certain extent. Generally, the best performance occurs with the minimally inflected English language, but highly inflected Czech seems to work slightly better than moderately inflected French despite our expectations; this may perhaps be due to the differences in the size of the corpora. What is important is that the collocation-driven algorithm outperforms that of the expectation maximization with only two exceptions: en-1650 (here, however, 29% of lines comes from the stanza picked by the expectation maximization algorithm as a singleton) and cs-1740 (if only known schemes are taken into account).[9]

The collocation-driven algorithm in all cases also outperforms the rule-based one. As the latter may be considered overspecified (cf. Introduction), it is no surprise that it has a very high precision and a poor recall (Fig. 5.2).[10]

[8] As Reddy and Knight (2011b) point out, their algorithm has a very high demand on internal memory. To train the algorithm on an entire corpus as large as the Czech corpus would require a machine with several terabytes of RAM. Keeping the data on a hard drive instead of RAM would, on the other hand, lead to several months of computational time per evaluation of each subcorpus.

[9] The most appropriate comparison would be that of where the expectation maximization algorithm works with all the possible schemes of stanzas of a given length. Such an approach—as already mentioned—is far beyond the capabilities of contemporary machines in general. We were thus only able to process two small subcorpora this way with short stanzas only: cs-1740 and cs-1750, getting the F-scores 0.61 and 0.75, respectively.

[10] Extremely low recall for French is due to the abovementioned inaccurate setting of relevant substrings (section "Learning"). Notice also that the precision for Czech constantly decreases starting with authors born in the beginning of the 19th century. This may be attributed to the fact that after the national-revival period rhyme pairs where vowel lengths match go out of fashion (cf. Jakobson 1923/1995, pp. 204–211).

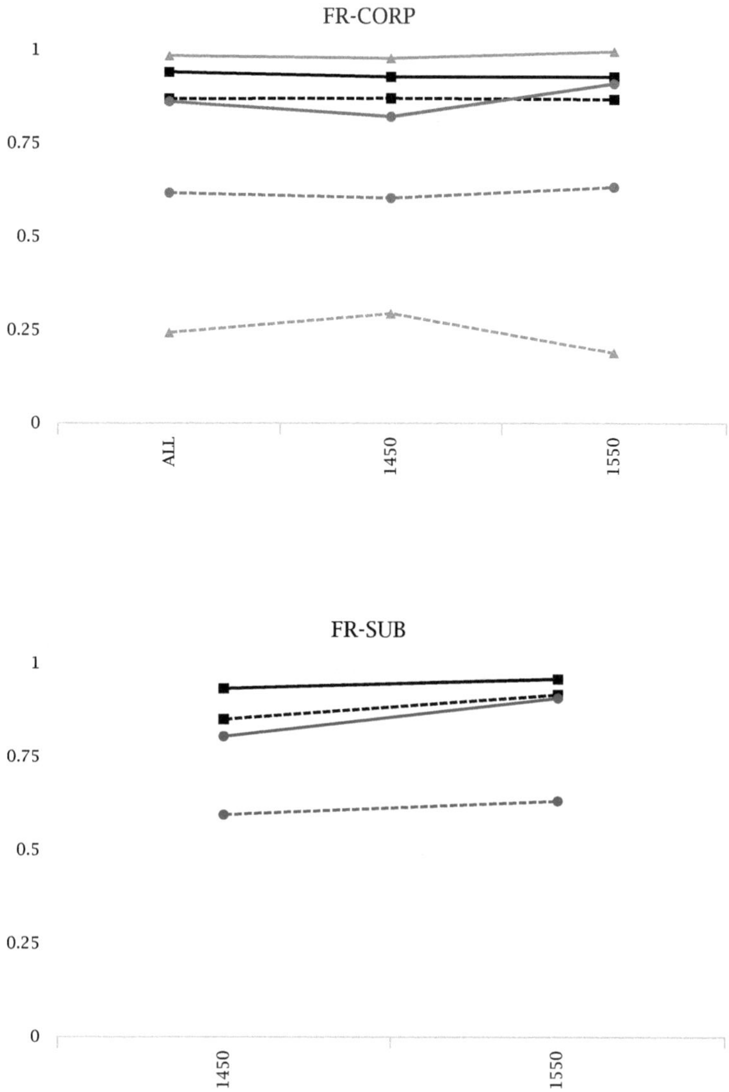

Fig. 5.2 Precision (full line) and recall (dashed) of particular algorithms: collocation-driven (CD: "filled square"), expectation maximization (EM: "filled circle"), EM with known stanza schemes only (open circle), and rule-based (RB: filled triangle). CORP: CD and EM trained on entire corpus + RB, SUB: CD and EM trained on particular subcorpora

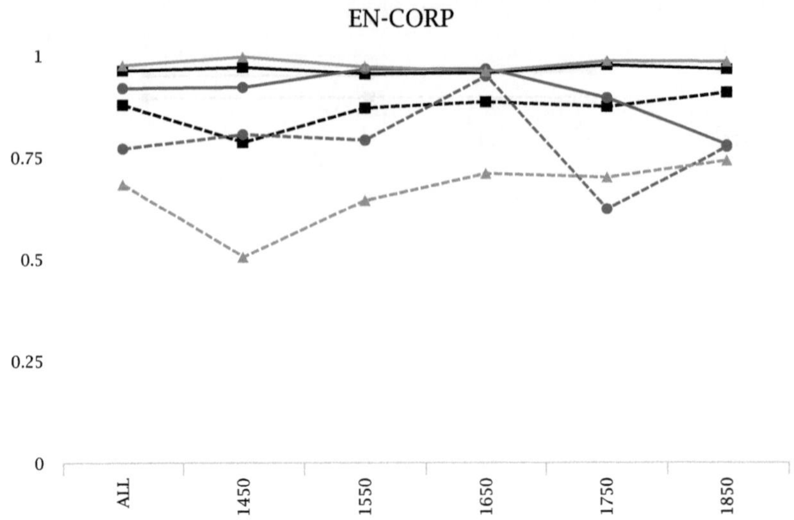

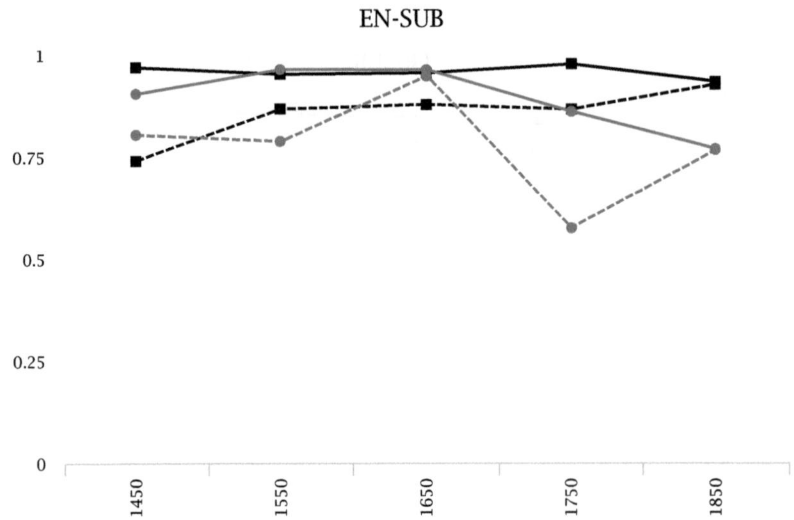

Fig. 5.2 (continued)

Conclusions and Future Work

The collocation-driven algorithm that we have proposed here yields very good results. As expressed by the value of *recall*, we were able to discover more than 95% of all the rhymes in the Czech corpus (recall = 0.9571) and more than 85% in the English and French (recall = 0.8763 & 0.8668, respectively). In less than 7% of

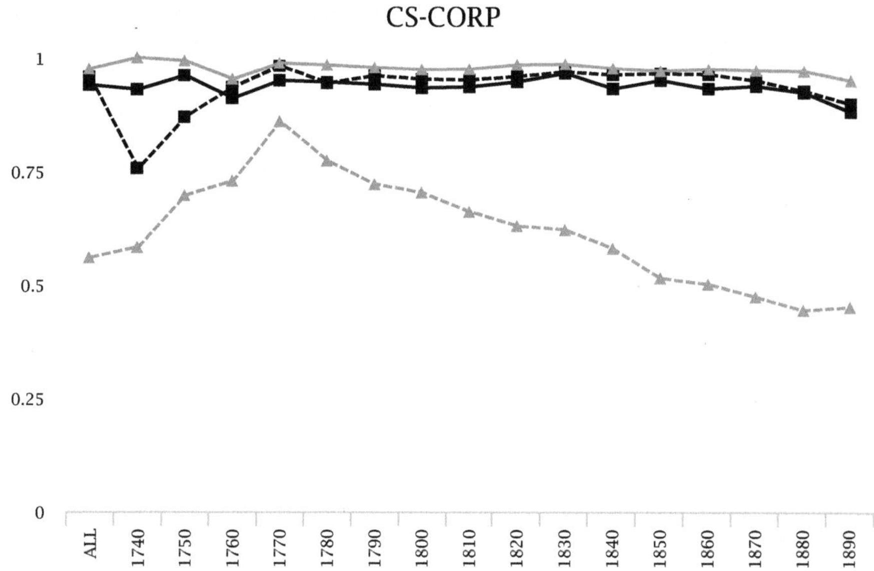

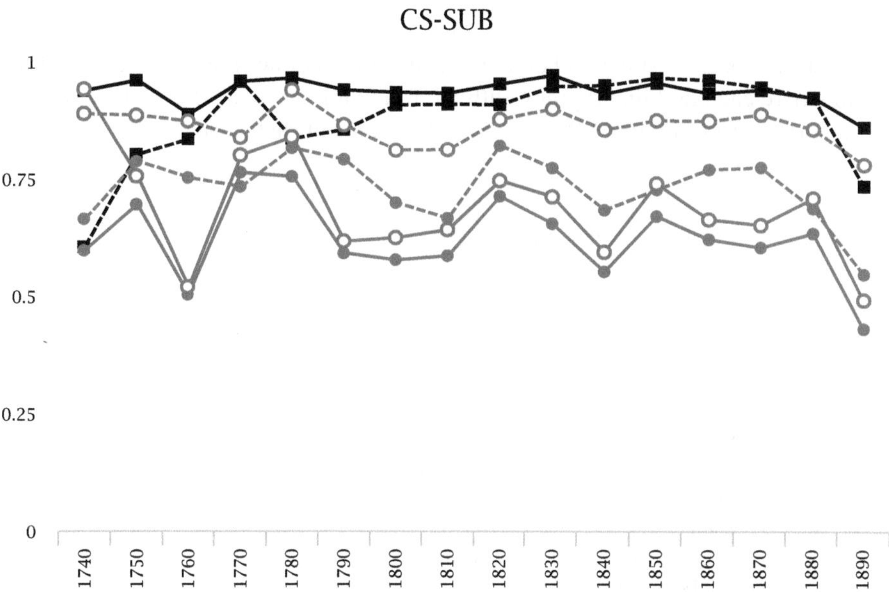

Fig. 5.2 (continued)

cases in all three corpora, the pairs marked by the algorithm as rhymes were contaminated by pairs which actually do not rhyme. In other words, the value of *precision* is higher than 93% in all the corpora (namely, 0.9393 for Czech, 0.9606 for English, and 0.9379 for French). Performance with particular subcorpora varies to some extent and seems to be affected by different factors, that is, the size of the subcorpus, age of the texts analyzed, and the frequency of imperfect rhymes. In most cases, however, it may be considered satisfactory. Yet, there is still room for improvement.

The precision may possibly be slightly improved if relevant substrings were not limited by word boundaries. The example below shows the situation where only one sound remains from the unstressed monosyllable ([I]) which leads to the incorrect decision that all lines in quatrain rhyme with each other. This obviously would not happen if relevant substring were starting on penultimate ([ajsI]).

Tys jediná teď, která ze vší touhy	['to_uh\I]	→	[o_uh\I]
a mladých snů mých v duši zůstala jsi	[jsI]	→	[I]
v ten život smutný, bolestný a dlouhý	['dlo_uh\i:]	→	[o_uh\i:]
a šťastný jenom zábleskem tvé krásy	['kra:sI]	→	[a:sI]
(J. Kvapil)			

Gold standard: abab
Output: aaaa
Translation: You're the only one now that—from all the desire/and juvenile dreams of mine—remains in my soul/in this sad, painful and long life/to which nothing but a glimmer of your beauty brings happiness

There is also the question of whether to somehow consider repeating rhyme patterns (not necessarily stanza schemes). The example below shows a piece of a long poem where each odd line rhymes with the following even one. Should we prevent our algorithm from finding other occasional rhymes in such cases?

	Gold standard	Output
Nor art, nor nature's hand can ease my grief;	a	a
Nothing but death, the wretch's last relief:	a	a
Then farewell youth, and all the joys that dwell,	b	b
With youth and life, and life itself farewell!	b	b
But why, alas! do mortal men in vain	c	c
Of fortune, fate, or Providence complain?	c	c
God gives us what he knows our wants require,	d	d
And better things than those which we desire:	d	d
Some pray for riches; riches they obtain;	e	c
But, watch'd by robbers, for their wealth are slain	e	c
(Dryden)		

The final choice would most probably depend on the research question: whether one is primarily interested in the distribution of rhymes in stanzas, that is, whether one aims to discover all the realizations of fixed forms such as sonnets or terza rima; or, whether one is interested in the rhymes themselves, to build a rhyming dictionary.

Acknowledgments *Funding*: This work was supported by the Czech Science Foundation, project GA17-01723S ("Stylometric Analysis of Poetic Texts") and the research institution 68378068. *Data and source code*: available at http://github.com/versotym/rhymeTagger/.

References

ARTFL: American and French research on the Treasury of the French Language. (2009). Centre National de la Recherche Scientifique/University of Chicago. http://artfl-project.uchicago.edu/content/artfl-frantext. Accessed 1 Mar 2017.

Crystal, D. (2007). *Original pronunciation transcriptions of Shakespeare's Sonnets*. http://www.davidcrystal.com/books-and-articles/shakespeare. Accessed 1 Mar 2017.

Gardner, M. (1978). The bells: Versatile numbers that can count partitions of a set, primes and even rhymes. *Scientific American, 238*, 24–30.

Jakobson, R. (1923/1995). Základy českého verše [Foundations of Czech Verse]. In M. Červenka (Ed.), *Poetická funkce [Poetic Function]* (pp. 157–248). Jinočany, Czech Republic: H&H.

MaryTTS: An open source, multilingual text-to-speech synthesis system. (2017). GitHub. http://github.com/marytts/marytts. Accessed 1 Mar 2017.

Plecháč, P. (2016). Czech verse processing system KVĚTA: Phonetic and metrical components. *Glottotheory, 7*, 159–174. https://doi.org/10.1515/glot-2016-0013

Plecháč, P., & Kolár, R. (2015). The corpus of Czech verse. *Studia Metrica et Poetica, 2*, 107–118. https://doi.org/10.12697/smp.2015.2.1.05

Reddy, S., & Knight, K.. (2011b). *Unsupervised discovery of rhyme schemes*. The code. GitHub. https://github.com/sravanareddy/rhymediscovery. Accessed 1 Mar 2017.

Reddy, S., & Knight, K. (2011a). Unsupervised discovery of rhyme schemes. In *Proceedings of the 49th Annual Meeting of the Association for Computational Linguistics* (pp. 77–82). Portland, OR: ACL.

Sonderegger, M. (2011). Applications of graph theory to an English rhyming corpus. *Computer Speech and Language, 25*, 655–678.

Part II
Not Only "Lost" in Translation

Chapter 6
Prominent POS-Grams and *n*-Grams in Translated Czech in the Mirror of the English Source Texts

Lucie Chlumská

Abstract The most typical or prominent POS-grams, i.e., sequences of parts of speech or possibly other grammatical categories, can reveal a lot about the character of a text, especially with regard to its dynamics (reflected in the dominance of nominal or verbal constructions) or lexical density (the accumulation of lexical words as opposed to grammatical word sequences).

In the study of translated Czech, previous research has shown that the POS-grams salient in translated texts differ from those in comparable non-translated Czech texts: they include more verbal combinations and pronouns. Their concrete realizations, e.g., the most frequent *n*-grams (sequences of *n* words) in given combinations, have indicated a possible interference effect based on the most represented source language: English.

This study builds on the previous POS-gram and *n*-gram research on translated Czech and strives to describe and interpret the prominent POS-grams in translated Czech in the light of their corresponding English source texts, using a parallel corpus (namely, the English–Czech part of the InterCorp corpus). As a theoretical basis for description, hypotheses about translation universals are discussed. The results of the analysis indicate that some of the presumably universal translation tendencies can certainly be traced in Czech translations; however, translators' choices tend to be the result of a combination of factors rather than a single reason (such as explicitation or normalization). The study also comments on the specificities of cross-linguistic comparison based on POS-grams and *n*-grams in two typologically different languages.

Keywords Language of translation · POS-grams · *n*-grams · Parallel corpus · Interference

L. Chlumská (✉)
Institute of the Czech National Corpus, Charles University, Prague, Czech Republic

M. Fidler, V. Cvrček (eds.), *Taming the Corpus*, Quantitative Methods in the Humanities and Social Sciences, https://doi.org/10.1007/978-3-319-98017-1_6

Introduction

Translations from foreign languages seem to form an integral part of any culture with a written tradition, and are all the more important in small countries where the amount of locally published books cannot be compared to foreign production. This is precisely the case of the Czech environment. Translated literature has always played a crucial role in Czech culture, although the translation landscape has been dominated by different source languages and cultures at various points in history. Translations had different functions in different periods of Czech history: during the national revival from the late eighteenth century to the mid-nineteenth century, they were supposed to compensate for the lack of local production (especially, in certain literary genres) and prove that the Czech language could compete with prominent foreign languages and express the same rich linguistic variety. Nowadays, with Czech having established itself as a fully fledged literary language, the reasons for the publication of translated literature are far more prosaic, motivated mostly by the demand for popular foreign authors.

Translations into Czech

When we look at the general publication statistics in the Czech Republic regularly issued by the National Library (Fig. 6.1), we can see that translations of non-periodical publications (i.e., books including fiction, nonfiction, popular, and academic

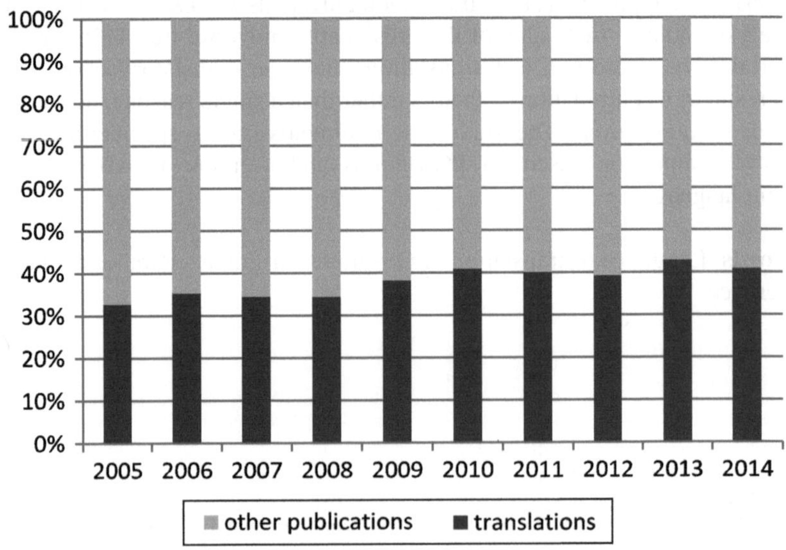

Fig. 6.1 Proportion of translations in Czech non-periodical publications

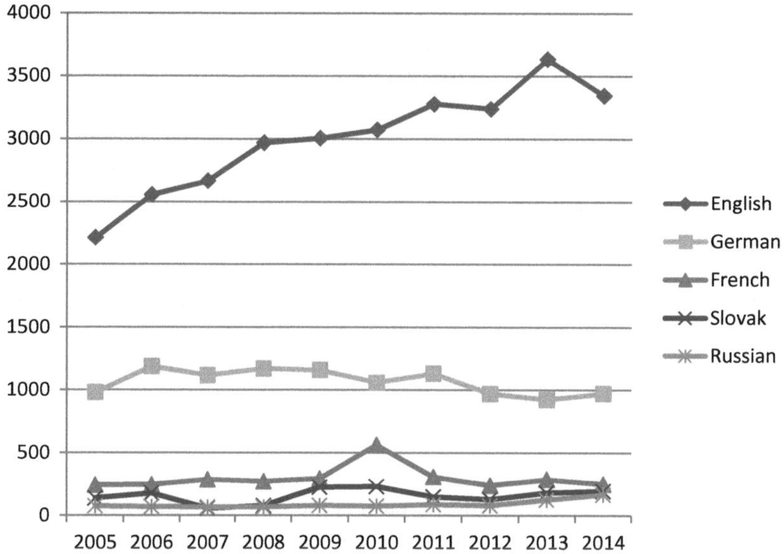

Fig. 6.2 Most frequently translated languages into Czech, 2005–2014

literature) account for approximately one third of all published books in the country and the proportion seems to be on the rise (from 33% in 2005 to 41% in 2014[1]).

For many years now, the most frequently translated language into Czech has been English, covering more than half of all translated books (Fig. 6.2). For example, in 2014, 3344 of a total of 6355 foreign-language books were translated from English, with German in second place (971 books) and French in third (249). The top ten most translated languages have not changed much in recent years; they include English, German, French, Slovak, Russian, Spanish, Polish, Italian, and Swedish. Norwegian and Japanese have made occasional stints in the top ten, which usually reflected sudden surges in popularity of certain authors or genres (e.g., detective stories from Scandinavia).

Why and How to Study Translated Czech

It seems to be a generally recognized fact that the reception of texts influences our linguistic perception and possibly even our production. In other words, what we read and consume in terms of texts affects our view of language and our own linguistic performance. Given that on average every third book published in Czech is a translation, we should ask whether "translated Czech" (and by extension, the

[1] These statistics tend to be published with a delay; the newest available data at the start of 2017 were from 2014 (see http://www.nkp.cz/sluzby/sluzby-pro/sluzby-pro-vydavatele/vykazy).

language of translation in general) has certain specific qualities that distinguish it from common, non-translated written production. If this is so, it might have a distinctive impact on the way Czech is perceived and used (including further implications for language research in terms of corpus design and its representativeness), which gives us a good reason to analyze the language of translation both in comparison to local, non-translated production and from the viewpoint of the original source texts and their possible effects.

Different perspectives on translations have led to the fact that terminology used in translation studies may seem rather misleading, depending on the context and the type of research: e.g., "originals" sometimes refer to the source texts that are translated into the target language, sometimes to "non-translations," i.e., texts that did not undergo any translation process at all and were written directly in the target language (as opposed to translations that were translated into it). To clarify these ambiguities, the following summary defines how these terms are used in this particular study:

source = source language (text, culture, etc.) is the one translated *from*
target = target language (text, culture, etc.) is the one translated *into*
translations = texts translated from a source language into a target language
originals = source texts of individual translations (included and studied in multilingual parallel corpora)
non-translations = texts written in the target language that were not translated from any source language (included and studied in monolingual comparable corpora)

The particular orientation on the target text and on the linguistic properties of translations, instead of a predominant focus on the correspondences between a source text and its translation, is typical for the field of corpus-based translation studies, a fruitful combination of descriptive translation studies and the methodology and data of corpus linguistics.

Corpus-Based Approach to Translations

The Birth of Corpus-Based Translation Studies

Before the advent of text corpora as a basis for translation research in the 1990s, translation studies experienced an important shift at the end of the 1970s, transitioning from a normative and prescriptive approach to translation to a more empirical and descriptive perspective. This trend was reflected in several translation schools of that period, especially in the polysystem theory formulated by Itamar Even-Zohár (1979) and in Gideon Toury's laws of translation (1980, 1995).

The polysystem theory had a crucial impact on the modern development of translation studies, since it brought the target text and target culture into the center of attention and regarded translations as a distinctive system of their own. Translated text was no longer perceived as a mere derivative of the original writing, inherently flawed or deficient compared to the source text; to the contrary, it became an independent entity with its own qualities, worth analyzing in its own right or in comparison to other (non-translated) texts in the target culture.

In Toury's attempt to devise a general theory of translation (1995) based on the descriptive approach, we can also see the origins of the idea that translated language possesses specific features and follows certain rules that can be researched and described (Toury calls them "laws of translation"). In her seminal paper, Mona Baker (1993) called such features "translation universals" and inspired many translation scholars to search for them in different languages.

With the massive democratization of computers and electronic text corpora (incl. parallel corpora) in the late 1990s, new avenues for translation research opened up, enabling scholars to test the translation universals hypotheses on authentic large-scale translation data. The combination of a descriptive approach with empirical research based on large quantities of texts and a quantitative perspective (enabled by the corpus linguistics methodology) proved to be very efficient in analyzing the language of translation and became one of the leading trends in modern translation studies.

Language of Translation and Translation Universals

As suggested before, the idea that the language of translation is a sort of unique code with its own characteristic features goes back to the pre-corpus era; Frawley (1984, p. 257) calls it "a third code" and argues that "[...] since the translation truly has a dual lineage, it emerges as a code in its own right, setting its own standards and structural presuppositions and entailments, though they are necessarily derivative of the matrix information and target parameters."

Attempts to describe specificities of translated language have also led to the term "translationese," originally coined by Martin Gellerstam (1986). He defined "translationese" as fingerprints left in the translation by the source language; nowadays, we would consider such features a result of interference or source language effect instead (Granger, 2013), whereas "translationese" has a generally pejorative meaning, referring to those features that appear unnatural or inappropriate in the translated text, usually due to the translator's incompetence or infelicitous solutions.

The most prolific concept in corpus-based translation studies is the notion of *translation universals*. Baker defined these as "features which typically occur in translated text rather than original utterances and which are not the result of interference from specific linguistic systems" (Baker, 1993, p. 243). It is clearly stated in this initial definition that these universal features are in no way connected to the particular systems of the languages involved in the translation, unlike interference which consists in using specific source language features in the target text (usually with an undesirable effect).

Originally, Baker identified six possible translation universals based on other scholars' research (1993, pp. 243–245), which she later trimmed down to four (1996, pp. 176–7):

1. *simplification* [...] the idea that translators subconsciously simplify the language or message or both;
2. *explicitation* [...] the tendency to spell things out in translation, including, in its simplest form, the practice of adding background information;
3. *normalization* or conservatism [...] the tendency to conform to patterns; and practices that are typical of the target language, even to the point of exaggerating them;
4. *levelling-out* (later called *convergence*) [...] the tendency of translated text to gravitate around the center of any continuum rather than to move towards the fringes.

Since these hypotheses were based on "small-scale studies and casual observation" (Baker, 1993, p. 243) and the general idea of universality seems to be rather controversial, the list immediately triggered many questions and criticisms. House (2008, pp. 11–12) summarizes the main objections to the concept, including the issues of strong language-pair specificity, directionality, and genre-specificity (i.e., that the features of translated language may differ depending on the particular language pair, direction of translation, or genre) that contradict the assumed universality of these features. Other scholars have criticized the vagueness of the formulations (Becher, 2010, p. 8) or the lack of rigorous methodology (De Sutter, Goethals, Leuschner, & Vandepitte, 2012).

After more than twenty years of translation universals research, new translation hypotheses have been formulated ("the unique items hypothesis" by Tirkkonen-Condit, 2002, 2004 or "the gravitational pull hypothesis" by Halverson, 2003) and the old ones have been tested on additional languages (cf. Mauranen, 2000 on Finnish, Xiao, 2010 on Chinese, or Grabowski, 2012 on Polish). Currently, translation scholars tend to agree on the fact that translated language does indeed possess specific features; however, these are not at all universal in terms of occurring in every translation to/from every language. The tendency now is to call them "translation properties" (Neumann, 2014) or "features of translated language" rather than universals, as they appear to a different degree in various genres and languages. However, the term "translation universals" usually remains in use when a researcher wants to refer to the original hypotheses by Baker. Last but not least, there are many different methods to analyze these features.

Two Main Perspectives on the Features of Translated Language

To compare translated texts and their source texts with the aim of identifying the so-called s-universals (features connected to source texts, see Chesterman, 2004), parallel corpora (i.e., corpora of mutually aligned translations and their originals) are needed. On the other hand, to compare translations with non-translated production in the target language, in order to identify the so-called t-universals (features reflecting translator's work with the target language), a monolingual comparable corpus is necessary, consisting of translations and comparable non-translated texts written originally in the target language. The best option enabling researchers to look at both types of features at the same time is a balanced bidirectional parallel corpus (or reciprocal corpus, see Zanettin, 2011, p. 21), such as the Norwegian–English Parallel Corpus[2]. These are, however, very difficult to design and build since translations to and from a foreign language are usually not available in the same amounts and/or text types (due to many reasons, including the status of the language in terms of its prominence, general demand for certain text types in a given culture, etc.). That is why translation features with respect to the source and target language tend to be examined separately.

This is precisely the case of the research on translated Czech: as a first step, a complex quantitative study was conducted using a large monolingual comparable corpus (Chlumská, 2017); as the second phase of the research, this case study focuses on prominent word and part-of-speech combinations in translations using an English–Czech parallel corpus (see below). First, I briefly summarize the results of the initial study in order to provide the necessary background information for the present investigation.

Previous Research on Translated Czech

Even though translated literature accounts for more than a third of all publications in the Czech Republic (see above), Czech in translations has not been systematically analyzed from a quantitative point of view until recently (Chlumská, 2017). To describe the properties of translated Czech compared to domestic production (i.e., features that distinguish translations from non-translated texts), Jerome, a new monolingual comparable corpus, first had to be designed and built (Chlumská, 2013), including both fiction and nonfiction texts.[3]

The main advantage of the *Jerome corpus* is its large size: 85,065,312 tokens, incl. punctuation, in 1526 texts. It was designed to be as heterogeneous as possible, e.g., no author or translator was included more than three times. Publication date was also an important factor; newer publications (max. 25 years old) were preferred. In terms of source languages in the translated part of the corpus, the design reflects reality—translations from English predominate. This can be considered both an advantage (the corpus provides an authentic sample of translations that Czech readers encounter) and a disadvantage (the prevalence of one source language

[2] See https://www.hf.uio.no/ilos/english/services/omc/enpc/.

[3] Since journalistic texts tend to be written directly in the target language or loosely adapted (rather than translated) from foreign resources, it is hard to track translations in newspapers and magazines. They were therefore excluded from the corpus.

may affect the results of research into language-specific phenomena such as interference).

The research reported by Chlumská (2017) was inspired by the aforementioned theory of translation universals and focused mainly on simplification, convergence, and general frequency characteristics, including parts-of-speech distribution and *n*-gram analysis. The findings corroborated the hypothesis that translated Czech, as reflected in the Jerome corpus, differs from non-translated Czech in terms of its higher degree of simplification (lower lexical richness and density, shorter sentences, and higher readability), convergence (translations tend to be more similar to each other than non-translations), and distinct lexical patterning (some word combinations in Czech are prominent only in translations). The differences, however, are not as striking as expected, especially when compared to the distinction between fiction and nonfiction; the latter proved to be more prominent and recognizable based on the tests that were carried out. This particular outcome confirmed the role of genre specificity in translation research and the need to analyze different text types separately.

One of the analyses showed that Czech translations tend to contain slightly more verbs and fewer nouns (in number of tokens) than non-translated Czech texts (Chlumská, 2017, p. 58), which is also reflected in the part of speech sequences (POS-grams) typical for translations: these are more verb-based and pronoun-based, unlike POS-grams in non-translations, which include more nouns (Chlumská, 2017, p. 72). However, since the monolingual comparable corpora do not include source texts (only translations and comparable non-translations), it was impossible to move beyond description and explain the differences observed in translated language.

POS-grams, and particularly their concrete realizations, *n*-grams (word sequences of length *n*), seem to be highly dependent on the topic of the text and thus potentially highly influenced by their source texts (as the topic of translation copies the topic of the original). Given that most of the translations in the Jerome corpus come from English, a look into the English–Czech parallel corpus may provide us with additional insights and possible explanations for these phenomena.

Methodology and Data

Multi-Word Combinations and POS-Grams in Cross-Linguistic Studies

Meaning in language often tends to be expressed by multi-word combinations rather than in isolated words. This is particularly visible in translations where meaning is what is primarily being translated, together with style. Using multi-word combinations as a point of departure for cross-linguistic studies (whether translation, contrastive, or a combination of both) therefore seems to be a logical step, advocated by many linguists and translation scholars (e.g., Baker, 2004; Chlumská, 2016; Ebeling, Ebeling, & Hasselgård, 2013; Mauranen, 2000).

In order to describe recurrent multi-word units in language, many different terms have been used so far. Biber, Conrad, Finegan, Leech, and Johansson (1999) identified a number of recurrent 4–6-g that occur commonly in different register types and called them "lexical bundles." For an *n*-gram to qualify as a "lexical bundle," it needs to occur within a certain frequency threshold and in a minimum number of texts, depending on the length of the given *n*-gram. Another commonly used term for repeating *n*-grams is "cluster." "Cluster" is a more general term for a recurring sequence of words; it is now commonly used in particular in corpus stylistics (Mahlberg, 2012). Both Mauranen (2000) and Ebeling et al. (2013) use the generic term "word combinations" in their research, which can encompass various types of multi-word units, including collocations, phraseological units, and other lexical patterns. Since this term seems to be less theoretically loaded than the others, it is employed for describing specific *n*-grams in this study as well.

In cross-linguistic studies, *n*-gram analysis has been used both to compare translated and non-translated language and to look at languages in contrast. Baker (2004) used *n*-grams of multiple lengths to compare translations and non-translations; in cross-linguistic contrastive studies, Forchini and Murphy (2008) analyzed 4-gram in Italian and English, Cortes (2008) analyzed 4-gram in English and Spanish, Ebeling and Ebeling (2013) analyzed *n*-grams in English and Norwegian, and Granger (2014) and Granger and Lefer (2013) used *n*-gram methodology for a comparison of English and French.

Extracting *n*-grams from corpora seems rather straightforward; however, several important issues arise in their analysis and comparison. First, what is a suitable *n*-gram length to look at? This is especially important in the contrastive perspective, since it has been shown (Čermáková & Chlumská, 2016; Granger, 2014) that the lengths of *n*-grams in typologically different languages, such as Czech and English, do not always correspond and thus are not directly comparable (e.g., 4:4 as in EN: *from side to side*—CZ: *ze strany na stranu,* but also 4:1 as in EN: *for the first time*—CZ: *poprvé*). Inflectional languages tend to express more within a single word than analytical languages such as English, and this fact needs to be taken into account in analysis (see below).

Second, how should the right *n*-grams be selected for analysis? Gries (2008, p. 4) identifies several criteria for the identification of a "pattern," including a statistical criterion ("frequency of co-occurrence is larger than expected on the basis of chance"); however, as Ebeling et al. (2013, p. 179) point out, the frequency parameter may not be the most important in cross-linguistic or translation studies—it is the semantics of the combination that matters most. In the past, the following types of *n*-grams were analyzed: text-structuring discourse markers (e.g., *on the other hand, when it comes to*) and metatextual expressions (e.g., *in other words, that is to say*) as in Baker (2004), phraseological units in Ebeling et al. (2013), and place expressions in Čermáková and Chlumská (2017).

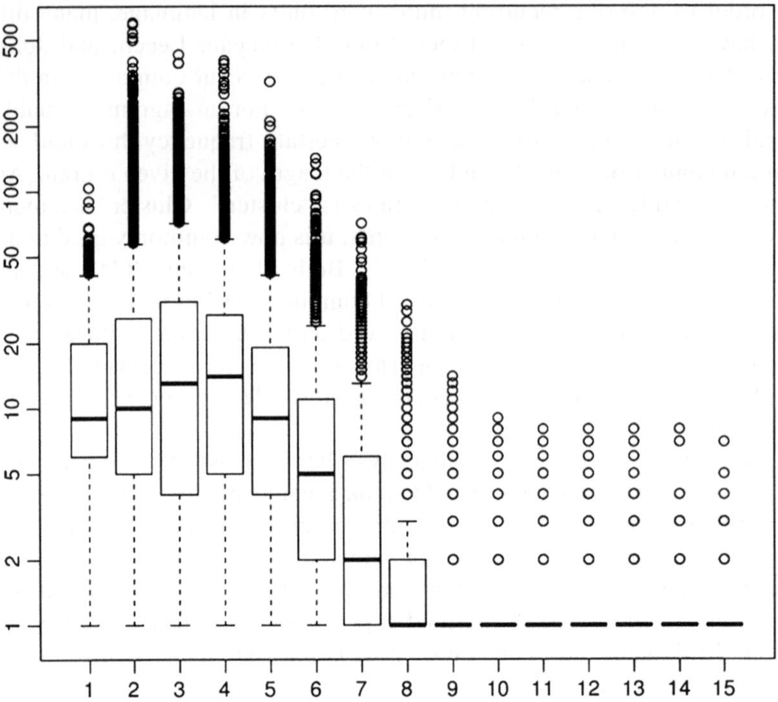

Fig. 6.3 The relation between *n*-gram length (X axis) and number of different realizations (Y axis)

Data

As a starting point for this study, three POS-grams and their most frequent realizations in the form of 4-gram (word forms) were selected for further analysis based on previous Jerome corpus research (Chlumská, 2017, p. 72). These were identified as structures that are used significantly more often in translations than in non-translated texts (as confirmed by statistical significance tests and the DIN effect size estimator[4]).

The length of four subsequently following units (both for POS-grams and *n*-grams) was selected based on research pertaining to Czech context disambiguation (Cvrček & Václavík, 2015) as a structure that tends to have the greatest number of different realizations in Czech texts. Figure 6.3 shows the relation between the

[4]DIN, or difference index, is a statistical measure estimating how exclusive a specific linguistic structure is to a given text or corpus by comparing its rate of occurrence to a reference text or corpus (Fidler & Cvrček, 2015). DIN can reach values up to 100 (for exclusive use in the target text/corpus) or −100 (for exclusive use in the reference text/corpus).

Table 6.1 POS-grams prominent in Czech translations (Jerome corpus, fiction only)

	Non-translations		Translations		
POS-grams	Rank	ipm[a]	Rank	ipm	DIN
J–V–P–V[b]	45	968.72	30	1197.64	10.57
P–R–P–V	14	1577.46	11	1904.80	9.40
J–V–P–N	54	917.44	35	1095.45	8.84

[a]Instances per million
[b]J = conjunction, V = verb, P = pronoun, R = preposition, and N = noun

length of an *n*-gram and the number of different realizations in the SYN2010[5] corpus. If we take a single lemma (number 1 on the x-axis), its variability in terms of different word forms is around 9 (as shown by the median of the first boxplot). The highest variability can be observed in 4-gram (sequences of 4 lemmas) that reach up to 15 different word forms. It can thus be assumed that a 4-gram structure is long enough to show combinatorial tendencies while not being so long as to occur too infrequently in the corpus.

POS-grams were searched for within sentence boundaries and uninterrupted by any punctuation, such as commas or dashes. The following parts of speech were identified in the prominent POS-grams (in translations) as shown below: J = conjunction, V = verb, P = pronoun, R = preposition, and N = noun. These POS-grams are not the most frequent combinations in Czech data (cf. their rank), but they show the greatest difference (albeit not a dramatic one, given their relatively low DIN values) in use in translations compared to non-translations; this is why, they deserve special attention. Table 6.1 shows that these POS structures include mostly verbs and pronouns.

These combinations, represented by their most prominent realizations, were then searched for in the InterCorp parallel corpus, namely in its English (source language) and Czech (target language) subcorpora. Only original English and American fiction and their Czech translations were selected for the study.[6] The English–Czech subcorpus featured 95 books by 75 different authors (with a maximum of three books by a single author), with a total size of 11,124,921 tokens in the English part and 10,526,005 tokens in the corresponding Czech translated part.

Analysis of Prominent POS-Grams in Translated Czech

What do these parallel data tell us about the most frequent word and part-of-speech combinations in translated Czech? Thanks to the greatest advantage of a parallel corpus, i.e., the alignment of segments (usually sentences) to each other between source and target, it is quite easy to identify translation counterparts. These can then

[5] A representative corpus of contemporary Czech, consisting of approx. 100 million text words (for more information see http://wiki.korpus.cz/doku.php/en:cnk:syn2010).

[6] Unfortunately, there are not enough data for nonfiction at the present moment.

Table 6.2 Proportion of most frequent realizations by pattern

Pattern	Absolute frequency of the pattern (tokens)	No. of different realizations (types)	No. of hapax legomena	No. of realizations occurring more than once/their total frequency in corpus	Proportion of the analyzed realizations within non-hapaxes (%)
J–V–P–V	12,277	9681	8684	997/3593	8.4
P–R–P–V	19,947	15,200	13,140	2060/6807	8.4
J–V–P–N	11,354	10,711	10,324	387/1030	9.1

Table 6.3 English counterparts of Czech structure *jako*^{J} *by*^{V} *to*^{P} + *být*^{V} ('as if it' + be)

English structure	No. of occurrences of *jako by to* + *být* ('as if it' + be)	Relative frequency in %
as if	155	51.5
like	57	18.9
as though	46	15.3
seem	22	7.3
Other (lexical) phrase	21	7.0

reveal a lot not only about the translation itself, but also about the languages in question and their specific natures.

Each of the following subsections focuses on one of the prominent POS-patterns (see Table 6.1): for each pattern, the most frequent realization (including its variations, where applicable) was analyzed in detail in terms of its source text counterparts. Table 6.2 summarizes the occurrence of different realizations within the pattern in order to provide a broader picture. As we can see, most of the different realizations are hapax legomena, occurring only once in the corpus. Out of the remaining types that occur at least twice, only the most frequent word combination was selected for a more detailed analysis, covering around 9% of instances.

Conjunction–Verb–Pronoun–Verb (J–V–P–V)

The most common realizations of this 4-gram structure are variations on the following word combinations: *jako*^{J} *by*^{V} *to*^{P} *byla/bylo/byl/byly/byli*^{V} ('as if it was/were'), *jako*^{J} *by*^{V} *to*^{P} + lexical verb ('as if it' + lexical verb), and *že*^{J} *by*^{V} *to*^{P} + lexical verb ('that it would' + lexical verb).

The most frequent word combination chosen for analysis, *jako*^{J} *by*^{V} *to*^{P} + *být*^{V} ('as if it' + be), occurs 302 times in the parallel corpus and has more than one English counterpart (see Table 6.3). Predominantly, it is a mirror translation of a phrase including *as if* (in 51.5% of occurrences); however, a synonymous structure with *as though* is far less frequent (only 15.3%). Slightly more often, the Czech word combination is used as a translation of English *like* (see examples 1–3):

1. EN: (...) he slopped down wine, beer, and whisky *like* water.
   CS: (...) lil do sebe víno, pivo, whisku, *jako*^{J} *by*^{V} *to*^{P} *byla*^{V} voda.
2. EN: (...) he opened the eastward window and let the wind rush in *like* a wild cleansing force.
   CS: (...) otevřel východní okno a vpustil dovnitř vítr, *jako*^{J} *by*^{V} *to*^{P} *byla*^{V} nějaká divoká očišťující síla.
3. EN: Zora used both hands to lift up a massive carton of juice, high and away from her body, *like* a cup she'd won.
   CS: Zora oběma rukama zvedla velkou krabici džusu, vysoko a daleko před tělem, *jako*^{J} *by*^{V} *to*^{P} *byl*^{V} pohár pro vítěze.

What we also find in the English originals is a construction with the verb *seem*, which does not have a direct counterpart in Czech. Although this construction could also be literally translated as *vypadat*/*připadat*^{V} ('look like') or *zdát*^{V} *se*^{P} ('appear'), a periphrastic structure was used (*jako*^{J} *by*^{V} *to*^{P} *byl*^{V}), sometimes in combination with the aforementioned lexical verb (*připadat* as in example 6).

4. EN: Mina opened her eyes; but she did not *seem* the same woman.
   CS: Mina otevřela oči, ale *jako*^{J} *by*^{V} *to*^{P} *byl*^{V} někdo úplně jiný.
5. EN: But Chloe *seemed* not to care.
   CS: Ale Chloe *jako*^{J} *by*^{V} *to*^{P} *bylo*^{V} jedno.
6. EN: (...) the exploration of Rama already seemed part of another life.
   CS: (...) že zkoumali Ramu, to jim připadalo^{V}, *jako*^{J} *by*^{V} *to*^{P} *bylo*^{V} kdysi dávno.

Among other lexical phrases in the source language are conditional clauses (example 7), attributive expressions (8 with a great deal of license in its translation) or simple constructions with *as* (9).

7. EN: It's spelled out in fragile proteins, but *it could be* carved in stone, or tempered steel.
   CS: Je to podrobně objasněno v křehkých proteinech, *jako*^{J} *by*^{V} *to*^{P} *bylo*^{V} navždy vytesáno do kamene nebo vyryto do kalené oceli.
8. EN: Her voice had a *pent-up harshness* (...).
   CS: Hlas měla chraptivý od běhu, *jako*^{J} *by*^{V} *to*^{P} *byl*^{V} *nůž* (...)
9. EN: She'd wave her pointer over the map and say, *as* a sort of afterthought.
   CS: Mávla ukazovátkem nad mapou a řekla, *jako*^{J} *by*^{V} *to*^{P} *byl*^{V} nějaký dodatečný nápad.

Having examined the parallel concordances, we can identify two possible reasons why *jako*^{J} *by*^{V} *to*^{P} + *být*^{V}, as the representative of J–V–P–V, occurs more often in translations than non-translated texts. First, it is one of the functional translation equivalents of phrases with the verb *seem,* which are very commonly used in English, but have no direct and/or frequent counterpart in Czech (that could be found in non-translations). Second, as an equivalent of English *like*, it supports the idea of explicitation (Baker, 1996), i.e., translators' tendency to "spell out both the form and the contents of the original" (in other words, use a longer phrase than necessary or express directly a covert meaning), as the simple Czech unigram *jako* would be a sufficient equivalent to the 4-gram in most cases.

Pronoun–Preposition–Pronoun–Verb (P–R–P–V)

This POS-gram is the most frequent of the three selected combinations; according to the Jerome corpus study, it is the eleventh in the list of most frequent POS-grams in translations (and 14th in non-translated Czech texts). When we look at the concrete realizations, one structure stands out: *se*^{P} *na*^{R} *ni/něj*^{P} *podíval/a*^{V} ('he/she looked at him/her') and similar word combinations, such as *se*^{P} *na*^{R} *ni/něj*^{P} *usmál/a*^{V} ('he/she smiled at him/her'), and *se*^{P} *k*^{R} *ní/němu*^{P} *otočil/a*^{V} ('he/she turned to him/her'). What all these word combinations have in common is that they begin with the pronoun particle *se* predominantly used with inherently reflexive verbs (*reflexives tantum*), such as *podívat*^{V} *se*^{P} ('look at'). The reflexive pronoun *se* (or *si* in certain verbs) is one of the enclitics, i.e., particles that need to occupy a specific spot in the Czech sentence: the second place after the first word (and all its modifying words, including an embedded clause). These initial words vary (and due to their greater variability, they do not occur in the *n*-gram), but the enclitics always stand in the second position; it is in fact the only rigid rule in the relatively free Czech word order.

When we look at the corresponding structures of the *se*^{P} *na*^{R} + pronoun + *podívat*^{V} *n*-gram ('look(ed) at' + pronoun) in the parallel corpus, we get the results summarized in Table 6.4.

Out of 574 occurrences of this n-gram, more than a half (335) are straightforward translations of phrases with English *look at* (or *have a look at*). However, the remaining 42% of occurrences include different verbs of seeing (examples 10–12) or other lexical phrases bordering on phraseological units (examples 13–16).

Table 6.4 English counterparts of Czech structure *se*^{P} *na*^{R} + pronoun + *podívat*^{V} ('look(ed) at' + pronoun)

English structure	No. of occurrences	Relative frequency in %
look at	335	58.4
see	81	14.1
glance	24	4.2
stare	18	3.1
watch	11	1.9
glare	6	1.0
gaze	5	0.9
Other verb or phrase	87	15.2

10. EN: He *glanced at me* sidelong and laughed.
    CS: Po očku *se*^{P} *na*^{R} *mě*^{P} *podíval*^{V} a zasmál se.
11. EN: (...) he stumbled over to *peer at himself* in the glass of his wife's dressing table.
    CS: Vyklopýtal z postele, aby *se*^{P} *na*^{R} *sebe*^{P} *podíval*^{V} v zrcadle na toaletce své ženy.
12. EN: She *focuses hard on him*, to get the one-word answer.
    CS: Soustředěně *se*^{P} *na*^{R} *něj*^{P} *podívá*^{V}, hledá jednoslovnou odpověď.

In the following examples, the phrase *se*^{P} *na*^{R} + pronoun + *podívat*^{V} has a rather figurative meaning; it does not refer to a direct act of seeing, but rather to the shifted meaning of *seeing to something* in the sense of checking something (examples 13 and 14). In some cases, the translator uses this phrase in Czech without having any support in the original—in example 15, there are other options to express the minimalistic statement ("Well, well"), with a similarly repetitive construction like *Ale, ale* (literally "But, but"). The translator, however, chose to be more explicit and idiomatic. In the last example 16, the meaning of considering an alternative is expressed in both the original and the translation, which uses the idiom *podívat se na něco z jiné strany* ('to look at sth from a different angle').

13. EN: He's going to *run a thorough computer check.*
    CS: Důkladně *se*^{P} *na*^{R} *něho*^{P} *podívá*^{V} do počítače.
14. EN: Well, I was anxious about the dear child in the night, and *went into her room.*
    CS: Víte, dělala jsem si v noci o to drahé dítě starosti a šla jsem *se*^{P} *na*^{R} *ni*^{P} *podívat*^{V}.
15. EN: "*Well, well,*" he said.
    CS: "A to *se*^{P} *na*^{R} *to*^{P} *podívejme*^{V}," zabručel.
16. EN: "*Let me give you a scenario.*"
    CS: Zkus *se*^{P} *na*^{R} *to*^{P} *podívat*^{V} z jiné strany.

What can we derive from the evidence in the source texts in this particular example? The phrase *se*^{P} *na*^{R} + pronoun + *podívat*^{V} seems to be rather universal in Czech, covering different meanings from mere looking at something, checking something, to a range of idiomatic meanings. The trend to use a more neutral, general word instead of a specific expression, i.e., an equivalent of *look at* instead of an equivalent of *gaze*, *glare*, or *stare,* may suggest translators' tendency to normalization, i.e., choosing the most frequent and prototypical expression from the range of synonyms in order to make the translation look "normal" in the target culture so that it does not stand out from the set of similar texts. This may, however, result in a "more normal" text than non-translated Czech texts in fact are. The explanation why this POS-gram P–R–P–V (with its dominating n-gram) occurs more in translation can therefore lie in this subconscious tendency of translators to create a typical, unobtrusive text with more frequent words as opposed to choosing a more appropriate yet rarer expression.

Conjunction–Verb–Pronoun–Noun (J–V–P–N)

When we look at the concrete realizations of this POS-gram in the parallel corpus, we can again spot one prominent word combination: *že*^{J} *je*^{V} *to*^{P} *pravda*^{N} ('that it is true') and its variations *jestli/pokud je to pravda* ('if it is true') and *ale je to pravda* ('but it is true'). Unlike the previous *n*-grams in this study, these combinations with conjunction + *je to pravda* (conjunction + 'it is true') do not correspond to a large variety of expressions in the originals; on the contrary, they tend to be literal translations of the mirror phrase conjunction + *it is true* (with several exceptions such as *it is the truth* or *he/she is right*), see Table 6.5 below.

Out of a total of 92 occurrences of conjunction + *je to pravda* in the corpus, 65 include the phrase *it is/was/were true* in the original, 12 contain the word *truth*, and 3 the word *right* (examples 17–19).

17. EN: Well, *it's true.*
    CS: *Vždyť*^{J} *je*^{V} *to*^{P} *pravda*^{N}.
18. EN: I knew the *truth* of it then, sir.
    CS: Tehdá jsem poznal, *že*^{J} *je*^{V} *to*^{P} *pravda*^{N}.
19. EN: You know *that's right*, don't look at me like that!
    CS: Však ty víš, *že*^{J} *je*^{V} *to*^{P} *pravda*^{N}, jen se na mě tak nedívej!

The remaining 15 cases are mostly translations of an English question tag (examples 20–21) or a short, condensed clause with *so* (examples 22–23).

20. EN: She looks just like her mother, *doesn't she*?
    CS: Vypadá zrovna jako její matka, *že*^{J} *je*^{V} *to*^{P} *pravda*^{N}?
21. EN: (...) and you go back every day because of the way he looks at you, *don't you*?
    CS: (...) vracíš se tam každý den kvůli tomu, jak se na tebe dívá, *že*^{J} *je*^{V} *to*^{P} *pravda*^{N}...?
22. EN: *If so*, how did it reproduce?
    CS: *Pokud*^{J} *je*^{V} *to*^{P} *pravda*^{N}, jak se tedy rozmnožovali?
23. EN: *If this is so*, then I cannot say how sorry I am.
    CS: *Pokud*^{J} *je*^{V} *to*^{P} *pravda*^{N}, ani vypovědět nemůžu, jak je mi to líto.

Table 6.5 English counterparts of Czech structure conjunction + *je*^{V} *to*^{P} *pravda*^{N} (conjunction + 'it is true')

English structure	No. of occurrences	Relative frequency in %
it is/was/were true	65	70.7
Phrase containing *truth*	11	11.9
if… so	4	4.3
Phrase containing *right*	3	3.3
Question tag	2	2.2
Other	7	7.6

The fact that translators tend to choose the most similar translation equivalent (*je to pravda*), even though there are other frequent options in Czech, such as *je to tak* ('it is so'), *pravda* ('true'), or even a one-word counterpart to the question tag *že* ('right'), suggests an interference effect, i.e., a tendency to follow the structure of the original phrase and use the most similar counterpart in terms of form. This may not be necessarily wrong or inappropriate but it may affect the lexical richness of the text, as there might be other options in the target language than the exact mirror of the original phrase. It also points to the aforementioned tendency towards explicitation as the chosen phrase *že*^{J} *je*^{V} *to*^{P} *pravda*^{N} is longer and more explicit than other natural possibilities (such as simple *že* or *je to tak*).

Conclusion

As we can see from the parallel corpus analysis, there is no one reason for the different distribution of selected POS-grams and *n*-grams in translated Czech; on the contrary, each example showed slightly different tendencies and revealed traces of different translation universals (or properties) in the texts, including explicitation (using a longer phrase than necessary), normalization (using typical and frequent lexemes instead of a range of synonyms), but also direct interference from English (copying the form and contents of the original phrase).

The idea to begin with part-of-speech and word combinations in the translation properties research has proved to be valid as this is certainly a useful starting point for analysis, especially in the parallel corpus where the translation counterparts of multi-word units can reveal a lot about the process of translation and about the languages in question and their typological specificities. It may seem that the POS-grams represent general structures (with parts-of-speech as broad categories), but in reality it is usually one or two specific *n*-grams or their variations that stand behind the higher frequency of the whole POS-gram. A detailed look into the source texts can reveal the reasons for the use of the particular word combination.

With inflectional languages such as Czech, POS-grams and their concrete realizations can point not only to common structures but also to constraints in the otherwise free word order (cf. the fixed position of enclitics, such as *se*). Concerning the issue of the n-gram length, a look into the parallel concordances confirmed that a Czech 4-gram does not always correspond to a similar structure in English (see section "Multi-Word Combinations and POS-Grams in Cross-Linguistic Studies"), e.g., a single word *like* can be translated as a 4-gram *jako by to* + *být* ('as if it' + be). This asymmetry must be taken into account in contrastive studies that wish to compare similar structures in morphologically different languages.

The theory of translation properties provides many avenues for further research. This case study focused on translations from English to Czech, as English is the most prolific source language in the Czech context; however, a look at other typologically different languages (such as French or Finnish) in comparison with Czech might bring further insights. Using a reciprocal corpus (containing the same amount of texts translated from and to Czech) may also provide researchers with more possibilities, such as a "reverse look" starting with prominent English phrases translated from Czech. Such a view may reveal possible regularities in the use of certain phrases and constructions in translation, regardless of directionality.

References

Baker, M. (1993). Corpus linguistics and translation studies: Implications and applications. In M. Baker, G. Francis, & E. Tognini-Bonelli (Eds.), *Text and technology: In honour of John Sinclair* (pp. 233–250). Amsterdam, The Netherlands: John Benjamins.

Baker, M. (1996). Corpus-based translation studies: The challenges that lie ahead. In H. Somers (Ed.), *Terminology, LSP and translation: Studies in language engineering in honour of Juan C. Sager* (pp. 175–186). Amsterdam, The Netherlands: John Benjamins.

Baker, M. (2004). A corpus-based view of similarity and difference in translation. *International Journal of Corpus Linguistics, 9*(2), 167–193.

Becher, V. (2010). Abandoning the notion of "translation-inherent" explicitation. Against a dogma of translation studies. *Across Languages and Cultures, 11*(1), 1–28.

Biber, D., Conrad, S., Finegan, E., Leech, G., & Johansson, S. (1999). *Longman grammar of spoken and written English*. Harlow, England: Longman.

Chesterman, A. (2004). Hypotheses about translation universals. In G. Hansen, K. Malmkjær, & D. Gile (Eds.), *Claims, changes and challenges in translation studies. Selected contributions from the EST Congress Copenhagen 2001* (pp. 1–14). Amsterdam, The Netherlands: John Benjamins.

Chlumská, L. (2013). *JEROME: jednojazyčný srovnatelný korpus pro výzkum překladové češtiny* [*JEROME: a Monolingual Comparable Corpus for the Research of Translated Czech*]. Institute of the Czech National Corpus, Faculty of Arts, Charles University, Prague. Available at WWW: http://www.korpus.cz. http://www.korpus.cz.

Chlumská, L. (2016). (Ne)typické slovní kombinace v českých překladech a možnosti jejich zkoumání. [(Non)typical word combinations in Czech translations and avenues for their research]. In A. Čermáková, L. Chlumská, & M. Malá (Eds.), *Jazykové paralely* [*Linguistic Parallels*] (pp. 235–266). Prague, Czech Republic: NLN.

Chlumská, L. (2017). *Překladová čeština a její charakteristiky* [*Translated Czech and its Characteristics*]. Prague, Czech Republic: NLN.

Cortes, V. (2008). A comparative analysis of lexical bundles in academic history writing in English and Spanish. *Corpora, 3*(1), 43–57.

Cvrček, V., & Václavík, J. (2015). Jednoznačnost a kontext. Kvantitativní studie. [Unambiguity and context. A Quantitative study]. *Korpus, gramatika, axiologie, 11*, 28–41.

Čermáková, A., & Chlumská, L. (2016). Jazyk dětské literatury: kontrastivní srovnání angličtiny a češtiny [The language of children's literature: A contrastive comparison of English and Czech]. In A. Čermáková, L. Chlumská, & M. Malá (Eds.), *Jazykové paralely* [*Linguistic Parallels*] (pp. 162–183). Prague, Czech Republic: NLN.

Čermáková, A., & Chlumská, L. (2017). Expressing 'place' in children's literature: Testing the limits of the n-gram method in contrastive linguistics. In T. Egan & H. Dirdal (Eds.), *Cross-linguistic correspondences. From lexis to genre* (pp. 75–95). Amsterdam, The Netherlands: John Benjamins.

De Sutter, G., Goethals, P., Leuschner, T., & Vandepitte, S. (2012). Towards methodologically more rigorous corpus-based translation studies. *Across Languages and Cultures, 13*(2), 137–143.

Ebeling, J., & Ebeling, S. O. (2013). *Patterns in contrast*. Amsterdam, The Netherlands: John Benjamins.

Ebeling, J., Ebeling, S. O., & Hasselgård, H. (2013). Using recurrent word-combinations to explore cross-linguistic differences. In K. Aijmer & B. Altenberg (Eds.), *Advances in corpus-based contrastive linguistics* (pp. 177–200). Amsterdam, The Netherlands: John Benjamins.
Even-Zohár, I. (1979). Polysystem theory. *Poetics Today, 1*(1-2), 287–310.
Fidler, M., & Cvrček, V. (2015). A data-driven analysis of reader viewpoints: Reconstructing the historical reader using keyword analysis. *Journal of Slavic Linguistics, 23*, 197–239.
Forchini, P., & Murphy, A. (2008). N-grams in comparable specialized corpora. Perspectives on phraseology, translation, and pedagogy. *International Journal of Corpus Linguistics, 13*(3), 351–367.
Frawley, W. (1984). Prolegomenon to a theory of translation. In *Translation: Literary, linguistic and philosophical perspectives*. Newark, NJ: University of Delaware Press.
Gellerstam, M. (1986). Translationese in Swedish novels translated from English. In L. Wollin & H. Lindquist (Eds.), *Translation studies in Scandinavia* (pp. 88–95). Lund, Sweden: CWK Gleerup.
Grabowski, L. (2012). On translation universals in selected contemporary Polish literary translations. *Studies in Polish Linguistics, 7*(1), 165–183 Xiao 2010.
Granger, S. (2013). Tracking the third code: A cross-linguistic corpus-driven approach to discourse markers. Conference paper at *ICLC 7 – UCCTS 3*, 11–13 July 2013, Gent, Belgium.
Granger, S. (2014). A lexical bundle approach to comparing languages: Stems in English and French. *Languages in Contrast, 14*(1), 58–72.
Granger, S., & Lefer, M.-A. (2013). In K. Aijmer & B. Altenberg (Eds.), *Advances in corpus-based contrastive linguistics: Studies in honour of Stig Johansson*. Amsterdam, The Netherlands: John Benjamins.
Gries, S. (2008). Phraseology and linguistic theory: A brief survey. In S. Granger & F. Meunier (Eds.), *Phraseology: An interdisciplinary perspective* (pp. 3–25). Amsterdam, The Netherlands: John Benjamins.
Halverson, S. (2003). The cognitive basis of translation universals. *Target, International Journal of Translation Studies, 15*(2), 197–241.
House, J. (2008). Beyond intervention: Universals in translation? *trans-kom: Zeitschrift für Translationswissenschaft und Fachkommunikation, 1*(1), 6–19.
Mahlberg, M. (2012). *Corpus stylistics and Dickens's fiction* (Vol. 14). New York, NY: Routledge.
Mauranen, A. (2000). Strange strings in translated language. A Study on corpora. In M. Olohan (Ed.), *Intercultural faultlines. Research models in translation studies 1: Textual and cognitive aspects* (pp. 119–141). Manchester, England: St. Jerome Publishing.
Neumann, S. (2014). Beyond translation properties: The contribution of corpus studies to empirical translation theory. Plenary talk at the *UCCTS 4*, Lancaster, UK, 25 July 2014.
Tirkkonen-Condit, S. (2002). Translationese – a myth or an empirical fact? A study into the linguistic identifiability of translated language. *Target, 14*(2), 207–220.
Tirkkonen-Condit, S. (2004). Unique items? over- or under-represented in translated language? In A. Mauranen & P. Kujamäki (Eds.), *Translation universals - Do they exist?* (pp. 177–185). Amsterdam, The Netherlands: John Benjamins.
Toury, G. (1980). *In search of a theory of translation*. Tel Aviv, Israel: The Porter Institute for Poetics and Semiotics.
Toury, G. (1995). *Descriptive translation studies - and beyond*. Amsterdam, The Netherlands: John Benjamins.
Xiao, R. (2010). How different is translated Chinese from native Chinese? *International Journal of Corpus Linguistics, 15*(1), 5–35.
Zanettin, F. (2011). Translation and corpus design. *SYNAPS – A Journal of professional Communication, 26*, 14–23.

Chapter 7
Revolution with a "Human" Face: A Corpus Approach to the Semantics of Czech *Lidskost*

David S. Danaher

Abstract This contribution uses corpus tools to examine the meaning of a Czech word, the abstract noun *lidskost*, and some of its related forms. *Lidskost* is usually translated as "humanity," "humanness," or "humaneness," but it has cultural and political import in the Czech(oslovak) context that these English terms lack. It is, for example, associated with the work of the seventeenth-century Czech pedagogue and philosopher Jan Amos Comenius as well as with the humanistic ethos of T. G. Masaryk, the president of the first Czechoslovak Republic (1918–1938), and also with the 1968 Prague Spring movement and the Velvet Revolution that followed two decades later. I first present a semantic-discourse portrait of the word within its larger semantic field, and then investigate English translation equivalents. With this baseline established, I then analyze, in its original Czech as well as in English translation, a *lidskost*-oriented text from the 1980s written by Václav Havel, which provides a map of *lidskost* as simultaneously a personal and sociopolitical principle, one that can adequately serve as a rallying cry for revolutionary moments in Czech(oslovak) history, if not also beyond.

Keywords Czech Language · Language of translation · Parallel corpus · Corpus-based approach · Discourse analysis · Vocabulary richness

Introduction

Politics has famously been described as a battle over word meanings. In contemporary America, words like "government," "marriage," "family," and countless others have served as cultural and political battle-zones: by controlling the cultural discourse surrounding key terms, political movements more easily advance their ideological agendas. While politics and culture cannot be reduced to language, language

D. S. Danaher (✉)
University of Wisconsin-Madison, Madison, WI, USA
e-mail: dsdanaher@wisc.edu

M. Fidler, V. Cvrček (eds.), *Taming the Corpus*, Quantitative Methods in the Humanities and Social Sciences, https://doi.org/10.1007/978-3-319-98017-1_7

is nonetheless a central component of political, cultural, and also personal identity.[1]

Using a corpus approach to semantic analysis, this study seeks to examine the meaning of *lidskost*, a key political and cultural term in the twentieth-century Czech(oslovak) history that is usually translated as "humanity," "humanness," or "humaneness." My goal here is threefold: (1) to provide a semantic portrait of *lidskost* (and its related forms) in order to better understand how it has acquired socio-political import in the Czech context, (2) to investigate the limitations of English translations of the word and its related forms, and (3) to suggest, through comparison of a key *lidskost*-oriented Czech text with its English translation, that its import may not be limited to the East Central European context.

Prague Spring (1968) and the Velvet Revolution (1989)

Lidskost is strongly associated with at least one revolutionary moment in the twentieth-century Czech(oslovak) history, that is, the Velvet Revolution in 1989 that resulted in the overthrow of the totalitarian regime. It is also secondarily and indirectly associated with another, namely the Prague Spring reformist movement in the late 1960s.

Although not an official slogan of the late-1960s reformist movement, the phrase *Socialismus s lidskou tváří* ('Socialism with a human face') has nonetheless come to represent the process of democratization and political liberalization that was intended to restore faith in the ideals of socialism.[2] This process was nominally led by Alexander Dubček and his supporters in the presidium of the Communist Party. The reformist movement was, however, short-lived: the Soviet Union grew nervous at the implications of reforming the socialist system in one of the bloc's countries and invaded Czechoslovakia on August 21 of the same year, putting an end to the project. Czechoslovakian 'Socialism with a human face' is usually viewed as a key episode in postwar European politics, one that strongly influenced the 1980s initiatives of *glasnost* and *perestroika* in the USSR, which ultimately precipitated the fall of the Soviet regime. When asked in 1987 what the difference was between the Prague Spring and the Soviet reforms, the Soviet leader Mikhail Gorbachev's spokesperson Gennadiy Gerasimov famously replied: "Nineteen years" (Rosenberg, 1996, p. 21).

Given this history, it is not surprising that *lidskost* resurfaced in Czechoslovakia of the late 1980s as the central principle of 1989s Velvet Revolution (Krapfl, 2013). "Humanness" was "the revolution's central ideal, to which all others were logically subordinate" (Krapfl, 2013, p. 100). Czechs and Slovaks "did not reject the Communist regime because it was socialist, but because it was unresponsively bureaucratic and 'inhumane'" (Krapfl, 2013, p. 7). In his study of revolutionary discourse in Czechoslovakia, Krapfl further claims that *lidskost* as a core value was

[1] In his book *Using Corpora in Discourse Analysis*, Baker notes that while language is not the only way that discourse is constructed, nonetheless "we can carry out analyses of language in texts in order to uncover traces of discourses" (Baker, 2007, p. 5).

[2] For a detailed analysis of Prague Spring, see Williams (1997).

the central new idea of 1989: "In no other modern revolution... has [this] idea been so elevated and consciously defended" (Krapfl, 2013, p. 108).

The Semantic Field of Lidskost

Lidskost exists in a rich semantic field of related Czech words, which is one factor that complicates its translation into English. I will consider only part of this field here, namely, the nouns *lidstvo* ('humanity') and *lidství* ('humanity'), the adjective *lidský* ('human[e]'), which is by far the most frequent representative of the field in the Czech National Corpus (CNC), and the adverb *lidsky* ('humanely'). In addition, I will examine the antonym *nelidskost* (*nelidský*, *nelidsky*) and one other word with the root *lid-* (*lidé* 'people'). I am consciously leaving out of this analysis a host of other words with *lid-* as a root (e.g., *lidový* 'people's') as well as the Czech words *humanita* (noun) and *humánní* (adjective), which are obviously international cognate forms.[3]

English Translations

As evident above, the primary pathway for English translation of words in the *lidskost* semantic field is via words with the root "human." In his study of *lidskost* as a core value, for example, Krapfl mainly resorts to "humanness," sometimes "humaneness." This pathway accurately renders the etymological source (the root *lid-* means "human" or "people") but fails to convey the cultural grounding and semantic nuances of many of the terms. Words in the *lidskost* field can prove challenging to translate, and several pieces of anecdotal evidence indicate what is at stake in trying to translate *lidskost* and related terms in certain contexts.

The first piece of evidence relates to the adjective *lidský*, usually translated as "human" or "humane," and concerns an international linguistics conference in Prague that I attended a number of years ago. At the closing dinner for the event, one of our kind hosts, a native Czech who spoke English, pronounced a toast in the latter language: "This was not only a scholarly experience for us, but also a human one." Although the speaker's intention here is clear, the use of "human" in this context simply does not work, perhaps because the word activates more of the denotative meaning ("human" as opposed "non-human").[4] The source sentence in Czech would likely have been *Nebyl to pro nás jen vědecký zážitek, ale i zážitek lidský*, and

[3] *Humanita* as a lemma is represented by 163 forms in SYN2015, and the adjective *humánní* has 298 (which includes negated forms).

[4] There was a cynical joke about the slogan *Socialismus s lidskou tváří* that also turned on the denotative ("human") versus connotative ("humane") divide. The word *socialismus* was replaced with *alkohol*, which was a reference to Stará myslivecká, a popular herbal liquor with the face of a hunter on the bottle's label. According to the joke, this represented the real meaning of the political slogan. The joke implies a simultaneous awareness of both senses of the Czech adjective, and it is bitterly funny precisely because of the semantic ambiguity.

in Czech this is a completely normal use of the adjective *lidský*. The situation becomes, however, even more complex when we consider another possible translation: instead of "human experience," the speaker could have chosen "humane experience," which might be expected to work better given that "humane" profiles connotative aspects of meaning. This, of course, also fails, at least in part because of the stylistic constraints on the use of "humane," but also perhaps because of the close connection between "humane" and its antonym "inhumane" (see below for a discussion of this in connection to *nelidskost*). To assert that a conference was a "humane" experience might then imply that it was notable for the lack of suffering that it caused its participants, which certainly does not convey the meaning of the Czech source phrase.[5]

The second piece of evidence concerns *lidskost* and *lidství* in the translation of an abstract of a Czech university thesis on pedagogy, which I happened to come across on the internet. The Czech words and their translations are underlined in these excerpts:

> Diplomová práce "Lidskost v komunikaci učitele se žáky na prvním stupni základní školy" se zaměřuje na způsoby komunikace učitele se žáky na prvním stupni základní školy v souvislosti s výchovou k lidskosti. Výchově k lidství se zabývají úvodní kapitoly teoretické části a poukazují na její význam. Ve spojitosti se Komenského antropologií naznačují, jak velkou roli má při vzdělávání výchova k lidskosti. Další kapitola pojednává o způsobech komunikace, kterými učitel svou lidskost projevuje, nebo naopak neprojevuje.
> The thesis 'Humanity in Pedagogical Communication in Primary School' is focused on ways of pedagogical communication in primary school in connection with humanity education. The thesis is divided into two parts. The theoretical part deals with education for humanity and points to its importance. In relation to Comenius's anthropology, it indicates the crucial role of education for humanity in the learning process. The next chapter presents the ways teachers express their humanity in pedagogical communication.[6]

The question here is what exactly should a translator do with *lidskost* (or *lidství*) in reference to pedagogy and specifically in the phrase *výchova k lidskosti*, which is rendered in this translation as "education for humanity." Answering that question requires understanding how the term is grounded in Czech intellectual and cultural history: as Krapfl notes, *lidskost* as an idea harks back to the Judeo-Christian tradition, but it found especially fertile soil in the twentieth-century Czechoslovakia (Krapfl, 2013, p. 108). I will return to this point below and mention the possible pathways for translation in light of the corpus analysis.

---

[5] To convey the sense that the speaker wishes to convey here, we might avoid "human(e)" altogether and say something like "This was not just a scholarly experience for all of us, but a personal one as well."

[6] This is obviously not a translation that has been checked by a native speaker of English, and I have cleaned up certain aspects of it, such as the use of English articles, for readability while leaving the translation of *lidskost*-related terms as I found them. I discuss an alternate translation of the phrase *výchova k lidskosti* below.

A Corpus Approach to Investigating the Semantics of Lidskost *and Related Words*

Krapfl has written that *lidskost* is a concept "that one intuitively appreciates but that cannot be precisely defined, and this indeterminacy was part of its appeal" (Krapfl, 2013, p. 100). While a corpus approach to semantic analysis of *lidskost* will not eliminate all indeterminacy of meaning, it will enable us to create a more precise semantic portrait, especially in contrast to the translation of the word (and related terms) into English. In what follows, I will use the CNC and the analytic tools that it provides to bring us closer to understanding the revolutionary import of the term.[7]

Specifically, I will analyze and compare *lidstvo*, *lidství*, *lidskost*, *lidský*, and *lidsky* using Treq and KonText, the former of which makes use of the InterCorp corpus to provide a database of Czech–English translation equivalents and the latter of which investigates usage in a chosen corpus with access to a concordance.[8] Contemporary collocations with *lidskost* in the corpus SYN2015 will also be examined, and using the SyD tool I will map usage of the term over the course of time.[9] Given that Danaher (2010) argues that *lidskost* and related terms are words in the core vocabulary of the dissident playwright and post-1989 politician Václav Havel, I will also examine, partly through use of the CNC's KWords tool, one of his texts from the mid-1980s, *Politika a svědomí* ("Politics and Conscience").[10] As I will show, this essay can serve as an exemplary locus for information about the semantic potential inherent in *lidskost*, and comparison of the original Czech text with its English translation helps us understand the value of the various pathways for translation. Results of a hand-analyzed corpus of additional texts written by Havel will provide further evidence for his semantic expansion of the term, which will serve to clarify how and why *lidskost* may function as a politically charged, if not revolutionary, ideal.

[7] Danaher (2010) is a first-pass analysis of *lidskost* that relies on a hand-analyzed corpus of literary texts but makes use of neither the CNC nor the tools it provides.

[8] For Treq, see Vavřín and Rosen (2015) as well as Škrabal and Vavřín (2017). For InterCorp, see *Český národní korpus—InterCorp* 2017; InterCorp is a parallel corpus containing over 30 languages and 1.46 billion words.

[9] For SYN2015, see Křen et al. (2015, 2016) and Cvrček, Čermáková, and Křen (2016); SYN2015 is a 100-million-word balanced representative corpus consisting of texts mainly from 2010 to 2014. For SyD, see Cvrček and Vondřička (2011a, 2011b). SyD covers the period from the thirteenth century to 2009.

[10] For KWords, see Cvrček and Vondřička (2013).

The Semantics of *Lidstvo*, *Lidství*, and *Lidskost*

Czech has three words that may be rendered into English by the word "humanity." Corpus analysis clarifies how these words differ in usage and also thereby elucidates the special semantic case of *lidskost*. In this section, I will briefly discuss *lidstvo* and *lidství*, and then flesh out usage of *lidskost* in some detail. At the outset, we should note the relative frequency of each lemma in the SYN2015 corpus: a search on *lidstvo* yields 3392 instances, *lidství* yields 352, and *lidskost* 492.

Lidstvo

Lidstvo is the most straightforward of the three terms for "humanity" in Czech: its meaning is exclusively denotational. Analysis via Treq yields 1971 examples with the following distribution of translation equivalents[11] (Table 7.1).

Most of the examples given as "human" actually fall under "human race"; there are also errors in mapping the original word with the appropriate translation, which accounts for many of the instances that fall under the category of "Other."[12]

The overall picture is, however, clear: *lidstvo* denotes the collective of "humanity" in the sense of "mankind" or the "human race." Perhaps not surprisingly, the word was strongly represented in science-fictional texts (where *lidstvo* is opposed, implicitly or explicitly, to an alien race) and philosophical texts. Two example sentences taken from KonText illustrate the general usage:

(1) *Proboha, lidstvo, vždyť je to přece jen čtyři světelné roky!*
"For heaven's sake, mankind, it's only four light-years away, you know!"

(2) *Já jsem jenom chtěl říct, že stejně tak věřím v budoucnost lidstva, v pokrok a v to všechno.*
"I only wanted to say that I also believe in the future of humanity, in progress and all that."

Table 7.1 Translation equivalents for *lidstvo* (via Treq)

"mankind": 37.8%
"humanity": 33.8%
"human": 14.1%
"humankind": 5.6%
"man": 3.6%
"people":0.9%
"world": 0.9%
"(human) race": 0.6%
Other: 2.7%

[11] This term and all others discussed in this study were searched as lemmas.

[12] Errors of this sort exist for all Treq searches discussed in this study and are due to the fact that alignment between texts is automatized without follow-up manual correction.

It should be noted that entries in bilingual dictionaries support the corpus analysis. Fronek (2000, p. 402), for example, gives "mankind, humankind, humanity, the human race, the human species" as the primary equivalent for *lidstvo* with the secondary meaning being *davy* ("crowds" of people), as in the phrase *v obchodech bylo plno lidstva* ("the shops were [terribly] crowded, packed").

Lidství

Lidství is the least frequent of the three words with only 86 examples in Treq. The range of translations indicates a more nuanced semantic picture than with *lidstvo* (Table 7.2).

While translation via "humanity" still predominates, it would be a mistake to assume that *lidství* denotes a *lidstvo* collective. Instead, it is oriented toward qualities that define "humanness." The examples with "human" as a translation make this clear: in none of these instances, do we have "human race," but rather we find "human nature," "human consciousness," and "being human." In one case with "human," a Czech genitive noun phrase (in the phrase *hodnoty lidství*) is rendered into English as a direct modifier ("human values"). The genre of source texts is, perhaps not surprisingly, similar but not identical to examples with *lidstvo*: philosophical and science-fictional texts as well as some religious texts.

Four examples, each with a different translation equivalent, illustrate the range of usage:

(3) *Ta bolest je součástí lidství.*
"The pain is part of being human."

(4) *Pronásledovali kočovné lidi, lidi na prahu lidství, kteří ještě nevěděli o síle zrna a tedy byli odsouzeni ke kočovnému životu.*
"They had pursued nomadic people, on the threshold of humanity, still ignorant of the power of the seed, and therefore condemned to a life of wandering."

(5) *A zdá se mi, že má-li se změnit k lepšímu svět, musí se cosi změnit především v lidském vědomí, v samotném lidství dnešního člověka.*
"It seems to me that if the world is to change for the better it must start with a change in human consciousness, in the very humanness of modern man."

(6) *Při všem lidství, přesně to jsem udělal.*
"In all humility, that's exactly what I did."

Table 7.2 Translation equivalents for *lidství* (via Treq)

"humanity": 80.2%
"human": 9.3%
"humanness": 3.5%
"humankind": 1.2%
"humility": 1.2%
Other: 4.7%

The first example gives us one case where "human" is the designated Treq translation equivalent, but the actual equivalent corresponding to Czech *lidství* is the whole phrase "being human." The second example, from a science-fiction text, points to the ambiguity of the word "humanity" in English: in Czech, *lidstvo* denotes humanity as a species, while *lidství* focuses more on that which makes humans human, that is, on "human nature" in one way or another. More specifically here, we have reference to a distinction between the more primitive hunter–gatherer stage of human cultural evolution and the more advanced agricultural stage that obviously allows for the fuller development of "humanness." The third example is taken from a text by Václav Havel, and the translation via "humanness" alerts us to Havel's emphasis on the challenges of "being human" in the modern world; we will return to these challenges as Havel understands them shortly. The final example is an isolated instance of translation equivalency via "humility," which again represents an aspect of what it means to "be human" in a more or less concrete way.

A final point with regard to the meaning of *lidství* is that bilingual dictionaries tend not to differentiate it as separate in meaning from *lidskost*: Fronek, for example, has "v. lidskost" as the entry for *lidství* (2000, p. 402). We have already seen this conflation at work in the university thesis on "education for humanity," which has *lidství* instead of *lidskost* in one of the contexts. I make no claim about whether *lidství* and *lidskost* are, in fact, synonyms; my focus in this study lies elsewhere. I do note, however, that the former is marginal compared to latter in terms of frequency and also, as we will see in the discussion of *lidskost* below, stylistically constrained.

Lidskost

In this section, I discuss in some detail the semantics of *lidskost*, which also necessitates analysis of the related adjective (*lidský*) and adverb (*lidsky*) as well as the negated form *nelidskost*. My focus here is on the special semantic status of *lidskost*, one that we have already seen hints of in the meaning of *lidství* and one that will both clarify why the concept has acquired sociopolitical import for Czechs and Slovaks and also refine our understanding of that import. I intend for this analysis to be more strategic than exhaustive: much more could be done in terms of corpus analysis to flesh out the meaning of *lidskost* and related words.

Specifically, my analysis here will be limited to the following: historical mapping of the use of *lidskost* throughout the twentieth century with brief commentary on the cultural and intellectual grounding of the term; Treq and KonText data for translation equivalents with discussion of key examples; SYN2015 concordance data to determine collocational candidates with some detailed discussion of the data; selected Treq and KonText data for the adjective and adverb; selected Treq data for *nelidskost*.

It is worth noting at the outset how Czech–English bilingual dictionaries translate these words because the entries convey more or less in a nutshell the results of the corpus analysis. Fronek (2000, p. 401), for example, translates *lidskost* as "humanity, humaneness" and exemplifies typical usage with the phrase *zločiny proti lidskosti* ("crimes against humanity"). For the adjective *lidský*, he gives "human" as the primary meaning, followed by "humane" (Fronek, 2000, p. 402). For the adverb *lidsky*, he provides "humanely, decently" and gives the example phrase *jednat s kým lidsky*, which he translates as "to treat sb humanely" (Fronek, 2000, p. 401); a variant of the Fronek dictionary provides another example phrase, *chovat se lidsky*, which translates as to "behave like a civilized person." These entries once again illustrate the ambiguity of English "humanity" and "human," and the corpus data discussed below will serve to expand our understanding of *lidskost* (*lidský*, *lidsky*) in intriguing ways that reinforce the limitations of English with regard to this particular semantic field.

Historical Data for *Lidskost*

Historical usage of the lemma *lidskost* prior to and over the course of the industrial era (1850 to present) is captured in the three graphs below (Graphs 7.1, 7.2, and 7.3):

The graphs indicate that the starting point in using the term is the seventeenth century. Then, we note a gradual increase in usage from 1850 onward with peaks of usage in the 1920s and 1930s, corresponding to the interwar First Czechoslovak Republic, then again through the 1960s with a high point in the late part of that decade, corresponding to the culmination of the Prague Spring movement. We see a peak in usage yet again at the end of the 1980s with the Velvet Revolution, which confirms Krapfl's claim.

To make better sense of this graph, we need to understand that *lidskost* is a concept with strong grounding in the Czech intellectual and cultural tradition. Briefly stated, the concept is initially associated with the Czech philosopher, educator, and theologian John Amos Comenius (1592–1670), whose pedagogical goal was to "humanize" education in order to cultivate a "new humanism" that would set the

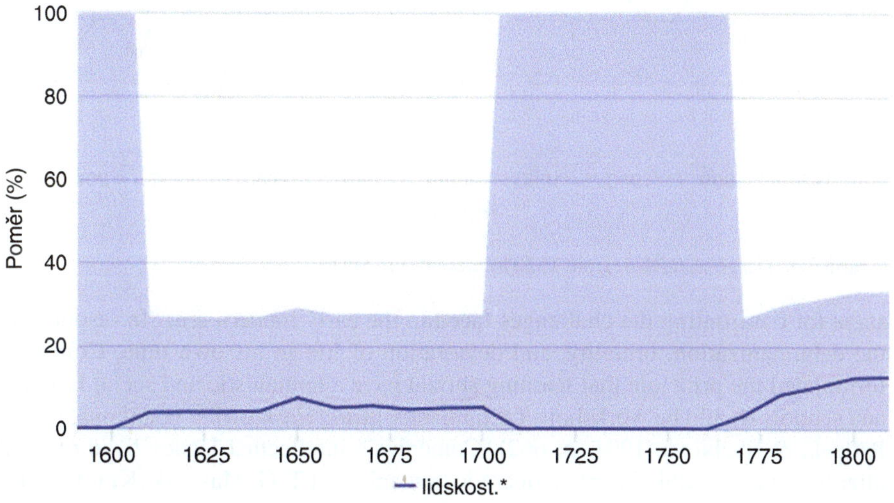

Graph 7.1 Usage of *lidskost* from 1600 to 1800 (via SyD)

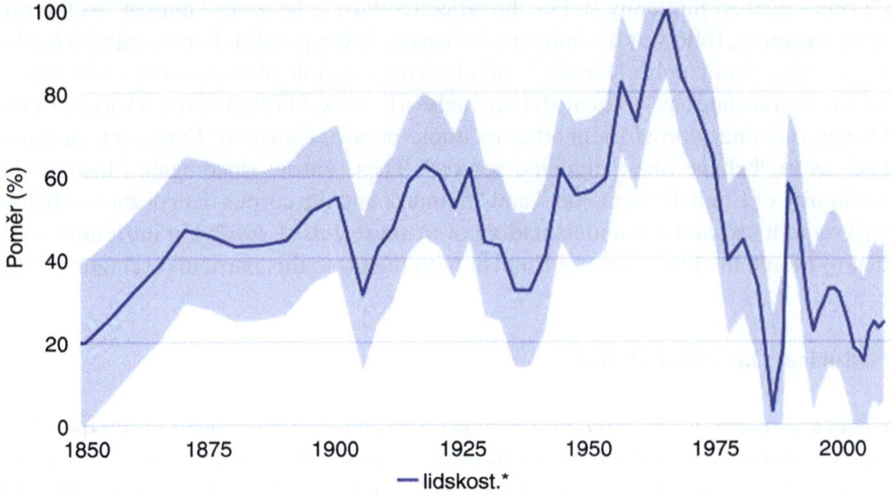

Graph 7.2 Usage of *lidskost* in the modern industrial era (via SyD)

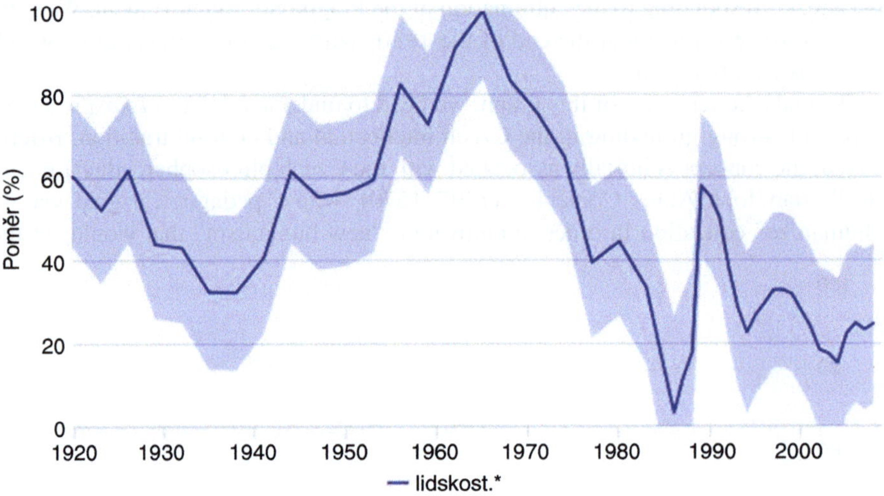

Graph 7.3 Usage of *lidskost* from 1920 to present (via SyD)

stage for confronting the challenges faced in the early modern era: "In response to the dehumanization, brutality, and devastation of life in his own time, Comenius formulated the principle that learning should have a humanistic and social function and schools should be workshops for humanity [*dílna lidskosti*]"[13] (Čapková, Bacík, Pařízek, & Skalková, 1991, p. 662). Comenius's intellectual legacy lived on well after his death, notably in the democratic humanism of T. G. Masaryk (Krapfl, 2013,

[13] The translation here is mine.

p. 108), president of the First Republic (1918–1936), which explains the usage peak during this period and also likely the fall in usage after the Communist take-over in 1948 since the Communist regime would have acted to deemphasize First Republic ideals. The phrase "Socialism with a human face" can be understood to invoke, consciously or not, Comenius's and Masaryk's legacies, and this phrase, as we noted earlier, became associated with the reformist movement in the 1960s. Comenius also influenced the twentieth-century Czech philosopher Jan Patočka (1907–1977), who was an original spokesperson for Charter 77 and whose thought and, ultimately, personal sacrifice had an enormous impact on Czech(oslovak) intellectual dissidents in the 1960s, 1970s, and 1980s.[14] The return of *lidskost* as a guiding principle in the 1989 revolution and its peak in usage in that same year makes sense, then, given this history.

Treq and KonText Data for *Lidskost*

There are 616 instances of *lidskost* in the Treq database. Treq data demonstrate that "humanity" is by far the most common translation equivalent for *lidskost*, just as it is for *lidství*, although not in the denotational sense that we see for *lidstvo*, where "humanity" is the second most frequent pathway (Table 7.3).

Contexts with the path-of-least-resistance "humanity" are the least interesting ones for our purposes, but contexts with "human" prove much more so. As we saw previously, the "human" examples are mostly phrases with "human" as adjective followed by a noun: for example, "human touch," "human self," and "human nature." Four other instances with "human" are the following:

(7) *Chybí ti lidskost.*
"The human parts of you are missing."
(8) *Nepředstírej, že máš v sobě lidskost, Annie.*
"Don't pretend you're a human being, Annie."
(9) *Má v sobě i lidskost.*
"Some part of him's human."
(10) *To z tebe mluví tvoje lidskost.*
"Such a human thing to say."

One striking thing about these examples, and many of the intriguing isolated examples discussed below, is that they occur in the genre of film subtitles. Presumably, the spoken context encourages the translator to choose a more creative option than the more prototypical but formal variant "humanity," and this may well partly account for the fact that *lidskost* has a higher number of isolated (or "other") translation equivalents (10.3%) than either *lidství* (4.7%) or *lidstvo* (2.7%).

[14] The aging Patočka died as a result of stress brought on by a lengthy interrogation conducted by the secret police as a result of his leading role in the Charter 77 movement. For more on Charter 77 and its role in the Czechoslovak culture of dissent that would lead to the Velvet Revolution, see Bolton (2012). Note that my goal here is not to trace in exhaustive detail of the cultural history of *lidskost*, which is a topic for another study.

Table 7.3 Translation equivalents for *lidskost* (via Treq)

"humanity": 82.5%
"human": 7.1%
Isolated examples: 10.3%

As we saw with earlier data, many of these isolated examples are inaccurate mappings between the Czech word and its translation in the English context.

A number of the isolated examples demonstrate more creative translation pathways, and these include the following:

(11) *Svět na nás útočí, využívá naši pýchu, naši chamtivost a jeho kostelem je světská lidskost.*
"The world is us, use our pride, our greed… secular humanism is his church."[15]
(12) *Zlé domy nenávidí naši laskavost, naši lidskost.*
"Bad houses hate our warmth, our humanness."
(13) *Lidskost přijmout moje místo ve vesmíru.*
"The humility of accepting my place in the universe."
(14) *apel na lidskost*
"an appeal for humaneness"
(15) *Někdy si, Otto, myslím, že máš moc víry v lidskost.*
"Sometimes, Otto, I think you have too much faith in people."
(16) *Polož to… přiblížil tento problem s lidskostí a oddaností.*
"Get off the phone… to address this problem with compassion and commitment."[16]
(17) *Navrhuji, abychom soutěžili… se ctí a lidskostí.*
"May I suggest we compete with honor and civility."

These more creative pathways suggest the special meaning of *lidskost* that cannot be conveyed by English "humanity," which is more formal and less personal, a conclusion that is only strengthened in the data for the adjective and adverb (see below).

SYN2015 Collocational Data for *Lidskost*

In addition to Treq analysis for translation equivalents, I conducted a concordance analysis on *lidskost* as a lemma in the SYN2015 corpus and developed a candidate list for collocates.[17] According to Baker, a concordance analysis "elucidates *semantic preference*," that is, it indicates a possible relationship between a given lemma

[15] There are obvious errors in the English transcription here, which nonetheless do not invalidate the *lidskost*–"humanism" connection.

[16] The Czech context here seems to contain an error, which, as above, does not invalidate the *lidskost* translation pathway.

[17] I used a range of −/+3 words and eliminated punctuation, pronouns, and conjunctions. I then refined the list of collocational candidates by eliminating words that were clearly in a more functional and less productively semantic relationship.

and a set of semantically related words (Baker, 2007, p. 86).[18] Baker goes on to note that when two words frequently collocate, "there is evidence that the discourses surrounding them are particularly powerful—the strength of the collocation implies that these are two concepts which have been linked in the minds of people" (Baker, 2007, p. 114). Given 496 examples of the lemma in SYN2015, the following words appear as potentially significant collocational candidates[19] (Table 7.4).

Table 7.4 Collocational candidates for the lemma lidskost (via SYN2015)

	Frequency	logDice score
zločin ('crime')	63	8.662
slušnost ('decency')	7	7.513
humanita ('humanity')	3	7.221
mravnost ('morality')	3	7.040
genocida ('genocide')	3	6.952
statečnost ('bravery')	3	6.635
špetka ('hint, trace')	5	6.491
empatie ('empathy')	3	6.486
laskavost ('kindness')	3	5.891
lekce ('lesson')	4	5.860
překračovat ('to exceed')	3	5.848
proti ('against')	78	5.598
postrádat ('to lack')	4	5.476
definice ('definition')	3	4.867
spravedlnost ('justice')	4	4.758
obyčejný ('ordinary')	7	4.714
úcta ('respect')	3	4.703
odsoudit ('to condemn')	3	4.669
zásada ('principle')	5	4.501
prostý ('simple')	4	4.440
víra ('faith')	5	4.237
projev ('display')	5	3.999
mír ('peace')	3	3.946
hranice ('limit')	8	3.871
obecný ('general')	4	3.867
láska ('love')	9	3.776
projevit ('to display')	3	3.725

[18] Baker gives the helpful example that the word "rising" in the British National Corpus co-occurs with "incomes, prices, wages, earnings…" (Baker, 2007, p. 86).

[19] I used a lemma search for potential collocates, and I have also sorted the words by their logDice value, since the overall frequencies are relatively low and logDice, unlike the MI-score, is not prone to overrating the collocational strength of words with low frequency.

One result that seems immediately clear is the collocational strength of the first item on the list (*zločin*), which tends to co-occur with the other most frequent item (*proti*): indeed, Fronek has already indicated that the phrase *zločin(y) proti lidskosti* ("crime[s] against humanity") is a fixed phrase with a high degree of typicality.[20]

The collocational candidate ranked in second place is Czech *slušnost*, which can be translated as interpersonal "decency, politeness, courtesy." Three examples of the relationship between *slušnost* and *lidskost* include the following[21]:

(18) *Lékaři jsou tu, domnívám se, velmi kvalitní, ale k pacientům lidsky nepřístupní. Jako bychom s léty strávenými v totalitě ztratili slušnost, lidskost, pochopení.*
'The doctors here are, I suppose, very qualified, but they don't interact with their patients in a human way. It's as if we've lost our decency, humanity, and understanding after all those years we spent living under a totalitarian regime.'

(19) *Jako tolik našich krajanů chováme i my upřímnou náklonnost k Holand'anům, nebot' si slušnost a lidskost zachovali i v době, kdy v Evropě obě tyto vlastnosti právě nebyly příliš v kursu.*
'Like many of our fellow countrymen, we too have a sincere liking for the Dutch. They somehow managed to preserve decency and humanity at a time when neither of these qualities was much in evidence in Europe.'

(20) *Je to skvělý den pro tisk a malé vítězství pro slušnost a lidskost.*
'It's a great day for the press and a small victory for decency and humanity.'

This is the strongest collocate of all candidates that occur outside of the scope of the fixed phrase.

Another candidate on the list, *hranice* ("limits"), occurs five times in the phrase *hranice lidskosti* ("limits of *lidskost*"), and repeatedly with another ranked collocate, the verb *překračovat/překročit* ("to cross, overstep, go beyond"). One example is the following:

(21) *Na mysli mám ty nelítostné vraždy, které překračují hranice lidskosti, a to znovu and znovu.*
'I have in mind those merciless killings that exceed the limits of human decency, and do so again and again.'

The assumption here seems to be that there is an expectation of interpersonal *lidskost*, but only up to a certain point or limit: certain behaviors may exceed that limit.

Other candidates also help paint a portrait of the usage of *lidskost* in specific contexts. Several examples are below:

(22) *Cena Arnošta Lustiga se uděluje od roku 2012 osobnostem, které v životě prokázaly odvahu, statečnost, lidskost a spravedlnost.*
'Since 2012, the Arnošt Lustig Prize has been awarded to individuals who have demonstrated courage, bravery, humanity and justice.'

(23) *Ta poslední otázka by mohla být komplikována pro X..., který sice má vzdělání, ale chybí mu osobnostní dispozice jako je empatie, lidskost.*
'The last question may be complicated for X..., who, while educated, also lacks personality traits like empathy and civility.'[22]

---

[20] This is also probably the reason that the Czech translation of the popular game "Cards Against Humanity" is *Karty proti lidskosti* (see http://protilidskosti.cz/karty/).

[21] Translations here and below are mine.

[22] One could naturally argue about the best translation in this context for *lidskost*.

(24) *A vy takový názor nesdílíte? Denně stojíte v pitevně a sledujete, jak vám přivážejí oběti vražd... Chcete mi tvrdit, že to nikdy neotřese vaší vírou v lidskost?*
'And you don't share that opinion? Every day you're in the autopsy room and see them bringing in murder victims... You want to tell me that this never shakes your faith in humanity?'

(25) *Vaše svědomí a smysl pro čest vás musí vést k tomu, abyste jednali s národy na okupovaných územích v duchu spravedlnosti, lidskosti a širokého nadhledu.*
'Your conscience and sense of honor leads you to negotiate with nations in the occupied regions in a spirit of justice and humanity with a view to the long term.'

(26) *Každodenních projevů lidskosti, lásky v praxi je v kteroukoli denní dobu dost a bývá velmi často anonymní.*
'Everyday manifestations of human decency and love in action are ample on any given day and very often remain anonymous.'

Semantically, similar collocations to those on the list above include the following: *humanita* ('humanity'), *mravnost* ('morality'), *laskavost* ('kindness'), *úcta* ('respect'), *zásada* ('principle'), and *mír* ('peace'). Weaker collocates that appear further down the list and are not represented in Table 7.4 include *snášenlivost* ('tolerance'), *ohleduplnost* ('considerateness, thoughtfulness'), *morální výtříbenost* ('moral refinement'), *skromnost* ('modesty'), *pokora* ('humility'), *férové chování* ('sense of fair play'), *zodpovědnost* ('responsibility'), and *soucit* ('sympathy'). In addition, there was one example of an antonym to *lidskost* in the concordance, which was the phrase *zvířecí instinkt* ('animal instinct'). Taken together, these data hint strongly that *lidskost* is associated with positive values or moral principles in both large and small spheres of human activity.

The data also indicates that *lidskost* is a normal, ordinary value that is expected to be displayed or expressed (note the noun *projev* and the verb *projevit* as well as the collocational adjectives *obecný* and *obyčejný*). A lack of *lidskost* is something that might also be highlighted (note the verb *prostrádat*), and a miserly measure of *lidskost* (note the collocate *špetka*) is to be lamented.

One collocate is also *lekce* ('lessons'), which occurs several times in the phrase *lekce z lidskosti* ('lessons in *lidskost*') with specific reference to the work of Comenius. Another collocate is *definice* ('definition'), which is used several times to suggest that the meaning of the concept is subject to discussion.

Although the data is limited, the cumulative picture points clearly in one direction: *lidskost* is a value that human beings are expected to have, albeit within certain limits. It is unambiguously associated with other positive values. While it has grounding in Czech cultural history, its exact meaning is subject to debate. It is a value that can be noble but is also often prosaically everyday: we expect it to be displayed and lament the lack of it when it is not. Our conduct should be guided by it because we are morally higher on the scale of being than mere animals: *lidskost* is, in short, that which makes humans authentically human.

Table 7.5 Translation equivalents for *lidský* and *lidsky* (via Treq)

Adjective	Adverb
"human": 93.5%	"human": 39%
"man": 1.4%	"humanly": 18.6%
"people('s)": 1.4%	"humanely": 16.9%
"humane": 0.2%	"humane": 6.8%
"public": 0.2%	"decent": 5.1%
"civil": 0.1%	

The Adjective *lidský* and the Adverb *lidsky*

In SYN2015, the lemma for the adjective *lidský* is by far the most represented of all the terms in the semantic field with over 26,000 hits (which includes negated forms); the adverb yields 535 hits, also including negated forms. In the Treq database, we have 26,985 hits for the adjectival lemma (again including negated examples) and a mere 59 for the adverb (also including negated examples). Treq yields the following translation pathways for adjective and adverb[23] (Table 7.5).

We see once again that the dominant translation is the path-of-least resistance "human." For our purposes, the more interesting examples are those that go beyond "human": these non-prototypical pathways for translation amplify or extend our understanding of the special semantics of *lidskost*.

One non-prototypical pathway for translating the adjectival form highlights the reading of "people('s)" that we saw in just one example with *lidskost*. Hundreds of examples in the corpus equate *lidský* and "people('s)," thereby avoiding the less personal and more formal translation pathway via "human." Contexts here include: *lidské životy* ("people's lives"), *lidské příbytky* ("people's homes"), *lidské tváře* ("people's faces"), *lidské hlavy* ("people's heads"), *lidské bytosti* (literally, "human creatures," but rendered in translation merely as "people"), *lidské úsudky* ("people's judgments"), and *lidské sny* ("people's dreams"). Two full-sentence examples of this are the following:

(27) *Takhle třískat kapitál z lidských citů.*
"Trading on people's emotions like that."
(28) *A bylo slyšet mnoho lidských hlasů.*
"And there was the noise of many people talking."

It should be added that in colloquial Czech the adjective itself can also function as a noun in the meaning of "a person," and there is one example of this in InterCorp.[24] We might conclude, then, that use of the adjective reinforces the everydayness of the concept: it belongs not merely to the technical, formal realm of science ("the human species") or philosophical thought ("crimes against humanity") but also, and perhaps even primarily, to the realm of everyday life ("people's emotions"). It is a concept relevant both to individual lives and at the same time to humanity as a collective.

[23] To simplify the picture, I have not recorded translations for negated forms.

[24] This is identical to the way in which the singular adjectives *ženská* ("woman's, female") and *mužský* ("man's, male") may colloquially function as nouns meaning "a woman" and "a man."

Another adjectival tendency is translation via the word "public," particularly with the phrase *lidské zdraví* ("public health"). This is not a strong tendency but is perhaps also illustrative of an expansion from the everyday interpersonal realm of closely related individuals to a larger sociocultural collective (at least as far as "health" is concerned).

Contextual examples with the adverb focus on manner. One tendency that we see, anticipated in Fronek's dictionary entry, is translation via "humanely" and "decent(ly)," and one isolated example is translation as "sympathetic"[25]:

(29) *lidsky důstojná práce*
"decent work"
(30) *Chceme se chovat lidsky.*
"We all want to do the decent thing."
(31) *Pohřbi je lidsky.*
"Give them a decent burial."
(32) *To by vypadal víc lidsky.*
"That would really make him sympathetic."

The first example is repeated in the corpus as a standard translation for an EU workplace regulation, and the last example here is again from the genre of film subtitles, which seems to give, if not require, the translator to take more liberty with the translation than might be appropriate in other genres.

The Antonym *Nelidskost*

Of the three Czech words for "humanity," only *lidskost* can be negated.[26] In Treq, there are sixteen examples of *nelidskost* with 13 rendered as "inhumanity," 2 as "cruelty," and 1 as "barbarity." This fact along with readings of many of the contexts in which *lidskost* is typically used points to the possibility that *lidskost* is at least partly defined against a background possibility of *nelidskost*, which may also be true for English "humane" (against the background of that which is "inhumane"). The presence of the fixed phrase *zločiny proti lidskosti* ("crimes against humanity") lends further support to this hypothesis.

Summary

While more work could be done to analyze usage of words in this semantic field, particularly with regard to the adjective *lidský*, and while frequency constraints in the corpus limit the strength of conclusions to be drawn, the data discussed

[25] Note that in all of these examples, Czech grammar requires an adverb while the English translation has an adjective.

[26] Google offers up the possibility of *nelidství*, infrequent at best and seemingly limited to academic writing, but this word is not present in the CNC.

above—anecdotal evidence, data from bilingual dictionaries, Treq analysis, and collocational analysis from SYN2015—nonetheless paint a more or less clear picture with regard to several key points. These are:

1. Czech has three words that can be translated into English as "humanity," but these words differ in meaning: the Czech semantic field of *lid-* words is more nuanced and complex than the English field of "human"-related words. *Lidstvo* is denotational "humanity," while *lidství* and *lidskost* connote "humanness." These last two terms seem to differ primarily with regard to frequency and style: the former is more marginal and limited to bookish contexts. In addition, only *lidskost* can be negated, which leads us to conclude that this word for "humanity" has a special status: it is understood against the background of falling short of realizing, in one way or another, one's full or authentic "humanness." Collocational data with *lidskost* help us understand this special status even more, given that the word is associated with violations of authentic "humanness" and a series of unambiguously positive ideals and values.
2. While "humanity" and "human" represent prototypical pathways for translation of the Czech words, certain contexts (if not certain genres) encourage non-prototypical translations. At least sometimes, then, translators seem to question the semantic equivalency of the Czech words via forms of the word "human." In this regard, evidence from film subtitles is particularly compelling: in spoken dialogue, translators eschew the impersonal, formal "human" and choose words or constructions that connote everyday friendless and basic decency. Put another way, English "human" and "humanity" seem unnecessarily technical in contexts where *lidskost*, *lidský*, and *lidsky* often do not, and translators must either use nonstandard words with the root "human" (e.g., "humanness") or go outside of the "human" semantic field in order to adequately communicate the sense of the Czech words.
3. These translation challenges derive at least in part from the fact that *lidskost*, unlike "humanity," is a concept that spans stylistic registers. Its usage and meaning span various human "circles of home," much like Comenius's pedagogical model was intended to cultivate human development of individuals within their larger sociocultural setting.[27] *Lidskost* is simultaneously a prosaic, everyday concept as well as a noble, philosophical one. The adjective *lidský* and the adverb *lidsky*, for example, occur in contexts that depict everyday interpersonal relationships ("to behave in a *lidský* manner") as well as concepts related to international law (*lidská práva* or "human rights"). Czechs assume *lidskost* in interpersonal relationships (although there are limits to this), which then allows for the possibility of generalizing these authentic manifestations of everyday "humanness" to larger circles of home (i.e., to sociocultural and sociopolitical spheres of human existence).
4. The Czech word *lidskost* has cultural and intellectual grounding in the Czech context in a way that "humanity" does not in the English world.

[27] For a discussion of the concept of "circles of home" in the thought of Václav Havel, see Danaher (2015), p. 285ff.

This final consideration, in combination with the three points above, facilitates a return to the question posed earlier in this paper, which is how exactly to translate the phrase associated with Comenius *výchova k lidskosti.* I asked two Czech–English bilinguals, one a native speaker of Czech who has lived in the USA for years and who works as college-level ESL instructor and the other a native speaker of English who is a professional literary translator from Czech into English.[28] Both gave, unprompted by me, two responses. The Czech native said either "education in humaneness" or, secondarily, "education as a way to nurture being human"; the English native speaker first gave the conventional "education for humanity" but then added that "education on how to be human" might be a better rendering. Both second responses echo translations we see in the CNC from film subtitles and point to the idea that *lidskost* is oriented toward process, which is also perhaps why the adjectival form is so dominant in the corpus data: it is, in other words, less of a technical, objective fact than it is a lived-through, describable experience.

Václav Havel's "Politics and Conscience"

The notion that *lidskost* may be oriented toward the process of "being human" (or more accurately "being *lidský*") certainly moves us closer to understanding its use as a revolutionary ideal, but there is still more to the story. To finish telling the tale and to export the political potential of *lidskost* from the heart of East Central Europe to the whole modern world, we turn to a text written by Havel in 1984. "Politics and Conscience" was a speech written for the University of Toulouse, which had bestowed on Havel an honorary doctorate. Given his status as a dissident, Havel could not travel abroad to receive the award, and he was represented at the ceremony by his friend Tom Stoppard, the celebrated British playwright. In this section, I will compare the original Czech text and its English translation using the KWords tool in the CNC to look at both keywords and thematic concentrations, which will set the stage for interpretative analysis.[29] In the course of the essay, Havel provides a map of *lidskost* as simultaneously a personal and sociopolitical principle, one that could adequately serve as a rallying cry for the 1989 revolution in Czechoslovakia, if not also beyond.

One thing to note with regard to instances of *lidskost* in Havel's text(s) is that he primarily (and prolifically) uses the adjective *lidský*, which puts him fully in accord with the usage data in the CNC.

[28] I am grateful to Lidka Mikulášová and Alex Zucker for their help. I am also grateful to another Czech–English translator, Lisette Saint-Germain, for a discussion of these translation challenges.

[29] The original Czech text appears in Havel (1999) (volume 4). The translation by Erazim Kohák and Roger Scruton is cited as Havel (1984) and appears in the collection of essays in Havel 1991. I am aware that the reference corpora used in this analysis, SYN2015 and Totalita for the Czech text and the British National Corpus for the English translation, are not directly comparable, but this is inevitable in analyzing texts in two different languages.

Table 7.6 KWords analysis of *Politika a svědomí* (Totalita as reference corpus)

KWs: *lidský* and *lidství*				
TCs: *světa* ('world') and *jen* ('only')				
KW ranking				
Rank	Form	DIN	Text freq	Ref freq
18	*lidství* (noun)	99.45	7	40
77	*lidskou* (adj)	89.51	3	342
81	*lidské* (adj)	88.52	12	1505
KW links				
lidství: *objektivity* 'objectivity' (1); *vlastní* 'one's own' (1)				
lidskou: none				
lidské: *svědomí* 'conscience' (1); *světu* 'world' (1); *smysl* 'meaning' (1); *osobní* 'personal' (1)				

KWords Analysis of the Czech Text

In subjecting the Czech text to KWords analysis, I looked at keywords (KWs) against the background of two different reference corpora, Totalita (a 12-million-word corpus of journalistic and propagandistic texts from the 1950s through the 1970s in former socialist Czechoslovakia) and SYN2015, and thematic concentrations (TCs).[30] Both analyses yielded more or less the same results with regard to the status of *lidskost*-related words as KWs and TCs, although with small differences in KW ranking and remarkably large differences in KW links. The data in graph form appears below (KWs here are limited to *lidskost*-related words)[31] (Tables 7.6 and 7.7).

The frequency of words in each reference corpus is more or less the same when adjustments are made for the comparative size of each corpus.

The startling difference is, however, in the KW links: these are much more prominent when keyword analysis is carried out in comparison with the SYN2015 corpus, which may indicate that contemporary readers would process Havel's arguments regarding *lidskost* in a more nuanced and complex manner.[32] More importantly,

[30] For analyses of both the Czech text and the English translation, I excluded pronouns, prepositions, conjunctions, and numbers from the KW list. Difference between lower and upper case was also ignored. Minimal frequency was set at three, and percentage of types listed as KW was ten percent. The statistical method was log-likelihood, and the significance level was set at 0.001.

[31] Keywords are words with unexpectedly high relative frequency in a text in comparison with a reference corpus, and they act as signposts for interpretative analysis of a text. Thematic concentration identifies content words with abnormally high frequency in a target text and gives us an objective idea of thematic compactness; unlike KW analysis, TC analysis is not influenced by changing the reference corpus. DIN scores reflect prominence of a word: a DIN of −100 means that the word is present only in the reference corpus, 0 means equal presence, and +100 means presence only in the target text. The DIN scores here do not differ significantly between the two reference corpora used. Note also that both *lidskost*-related words in the Czech original and "human"-related words in the translation are evenly dispersed throughout the text.

[32] Different reader receptions of the same text are made in Fidler and Cvrček (2015) using keyword analysis; see their concluding observations for more details (Fidler & Cvrček, 2015, p. 219ff).

Table 7.7 KWords analysis of *Politika a svědomí* (SYN2015 as reference corpus)

KWs: *lidský* and *lidství*				
TCs: *světa* ('world') and *jen* ('only's')				
KW ranking				
Rank	Form	DIN	Text freq	Ref freq
14	*lidství* (noun)	99.42	7	331
74	*lidské* (adj)	92.16	12	7935
79	*lidskou* (adj)	91.6	3	2130
KW links				
lidství: *neosobní* 'impersonal' (1); *přirozený* 'natural' (1); *obětovat* 'sacrifice' (1); *svědomí* 'conscience' (1); *odpovědnosti* 'responsibility' (1); *západní* 'western' (1); *moci* 'power' (1); *nestojí* 'not worth' (1); *světa* 'world' (1); *svět* 'world' (1); *smysl* 'meaning' (1); *ukazuje* 'shows' (1); *naopak* 'on the contrary' (1); *totiž* 'that is' (1); *tedy* 'that is' (1)				
lidské: *přirozeného* 'natural' (1); *veskrze* 'through' (1); *předsudků* 'biases' (1); *přirozeny* 'natural' (1); *přírodu* 'nature' (1); *věda* 'science' (2); *moci* 'power' (1); *odpovědnost* 'responsibility' (2); *lidské* 'human' (2); *politiky* 'politics' (1); *světa* 'world' (2); *svět* 'world' (1); *smysl* 'meaning' (1); *obsah* 'content' (1); *sílu* 'power' (1); *lze* 'it is possible' (1); *tedy* 'that is' (2); *jen* 'only' (2)				
lidskou: *zkušenost* 'experience' (1); *osobně* 'personally' (1); *vědy* 'science' (1); *odstranit* 'to eliminate' (1); *dnešního* 'contemporary' (1); *světa* 'world' (1); *zemědělství* 'agriculture' (1)				

there is a qualitative difference between the KW links based on analysis via the two different reference corpora.[33] While KW links through the lens of Totalita yield 6 weak results (the concept of *lidskost* is related to 'objectivity, one's own, conscience, world, meaning, personal'), KW-link analysis through a contemporary lens yields most of these and more with some stronger connections (i.e., 'natural, nature, world, science, power'). Through the contemporary lens, we highlight *lidskost*'s connections also to "sacrifice, the West, conscience, biases, politics, possibility." The contemporary reading as summarized by KW links in comparison to the SYN2015 corpus is, needless to say, the way Havel would have wanted the essay to be read, and it moreover hints at Havel's elevation of *lidskost* to the level of a political phenomenon grounded in the personal (i.e., in a personal sense of responsibility for the world), a point to which we will return shortly.

Comparison of the Czech and English Versions of the Text

KWords analysis of the English translation in comparison to the corpus InterCorp-EN v8 yields a reading similar to the Czech text as filtered through the lens of SYN2015, but less complex in terms of KW links (Table 7.8).

[33] The *number* of KWs might also be related to the size of the reference corpus. With a higher number of KWs, there is also a higher probability of establishing a link between any two of them. Nonetheless, there is no denying the differences in the *type* of KW links.

Table 7.8 KWord analysis of "Politics and Conscience" (BNC as reference corpus)

KWs: "human," "humanity," "humans"				
TCs: "all," "world," "power," "human"				
KW ranking				
Rank	Form	DIN	Text freq	Ref freq
26	"humanity"	97.94	9	1199
44	"humans"	96.12	8	2021
71	"human"	91.27	33	19,255
KW links				
"humanity": totalitarianism (1); impersonal (1); transcends (1); conscience (1); slogan (1); confront (1); humans (1); personally (1); evil (1); natural (1); human (1); contemporary (1); power (2); world (2); responsibility (2); struggle (1); fundamental (1); means (1); sense (1); political (1); better (2); all (1); must (1)				
"humans": heavens (1); humanity (1); chimney (1); evil (1); manipulation (1); politics (2); natural (2); human (2); science (2); contemporary (1); truth (1); power (2); world (3); responsibility (1); technology (1); ways (1); sense (1); all (1)				
"human": Bělohradský (2); neighbors (1); totalitarian (1); rationalism (1); impersonal (3); objectivity (2); meaningful (1); conscience (1); humanity (1); abolish (2); horizon (1); deployed (1); illusion (1); humans (2); personally (1); beings (3); morality (3); fiction (1); socialism (1); politics (4); mystery (1); absolute (1); guided (1); natural (4); barrier (1); abstract (1); human (6); modern (4); science (1); truth (1); phenomenon (1); power (5); tradition (2); world (7); responsibility (5); weapons (1); experience (3); personal (3); lived (1); systems (2); nature (1); reason (3); sense (3); political (1); all (7); own (1); must (1)				

One difference between the KWords analysis of the original Czech text and its English translation lies in the analysis of thematic concentration: the English text has a more fully developed set of TCs, which includes the word "human," a concept that is a KW in the Czech text, but surprisingly not a TC.

The reason for this difference is clear, although the explanation is somewhat convoluted. I compared the two versions of the text by hand for contexts that involved "human" or *lid*-related words, and the result is a complex picture of cross-linguistic interplay. What ultimately gives "human" status as a TC in the English text, however, is that it is, as concordance analysis demonstrates, strongly correlated with the noun "being(s)." In general, where the translators opt for the phrase "human being(s)," Havel never uses the literal equivalent of either *lidská bytost* in the singular or *lidské bytosti* in the plural; instead, he more often than not focalizes his discourse by using the singular word for "a person" (*člověk*). Thus, in the 17 contexts where the English text has "humans," "human being," or "human beings," Havel's original text gives us *člověk* "a person" (12 times), *lidé* "people" (three times), and *blížní* "dear ones" (one time) with one context where there is no original equivalent for "humans" at all.

That Havel singularizes is not in doubt: the word *člověk* ("a person") is used 35 times in the essay (*lidé* or "people" is used 18 times). In the English text, "people" occurs 12 times, "person" five times, and "persons" three times. While none of these English words appears on the lists of KWs for the text, two forms of *člověk* receive KW status (in 96th and 123rd place) when the Czech text is compared with SYN2015 as the reference corpus.[34] There are also five instances where the English text has a plural form (e.g., "human beings") for an original singular *člověk* and four cases where singular *člověk* yields an English collective noun ("humanity" or "humankind"). There are also a number of cases where Havel uses *lidství* in a singularized and personal sense (as in *jeho konkrétní lidství*, which could be translated, literally but awkwardly, as "his concrete humanness") where the English text has the more general "humanity."

Another difference between the Czech and English KWords analyses that is starkly evident in the data sets is the sheer number of KW links for the English translation. The explanation for this is likely the same as for the difference in TCs: the prolific use of "human" (and related words) in the translation. This is especially true for thematic concentration, given that TCs in a text are not dependent on the reference corpus.

Through KWords analysis, then, we arrive at a somewhat ironic conclusion: the translated text seems to present a more "human" picture than the original Czech text. At the same time and as I have already shown, we have to take into account that the meaning of "human" (and related words) in English does differ significantly from the meaning of equivalent words in Czech, and the semantic and cultural connotations of the Czech words will prove largely inaccessible for readers of the text in translation.

The Lidskost *Orientation of Havel's Essay*

As analysis and comparison of the KWs and KW links in both versions of the essay make clear, Havel's concern in "Politics and Conscience" is with a modern world that is characterized, to its great detriment, by the "eschatology of the impersonal."[35] Havel defines the "eschatology of the impersonal" as the "rule of a bloated, anonymously bureaucratic power, not yet irresponsible but already operating outside all conscience, a power grounded in an omnipresent ideological fiction which can rationalize anything without ever having to come in contact with the truth (Havel, 1984, p. 260 and Havel, 1999, vol. 4, p. 431); this type of power "has achieved what is its most complete expression so far in the totalitarian systems" (Havel, 1984, p. 258 and Havel, 1999, vol. 4, p. 429). His goal in the essay is twofold: in the first place, to describe the modern sociopolitical framework that is characterized by the "impersonal" and thereby deprives individual human beings of political agency, and, in doing so, to attempt to restore agency and power to those individuals. In this respect, the thematic concentrations produced by KWords for the essay's English translation are right on target: "all, world, power, human."

What may be less clear at first glance, however, is that Havel grounds himself in the semantics of *lidskost* in order to craft his argument: he relies on the meaning of *lidskost* as we have seen it represented in the CNC, and then extends it, enlarging its

[34] When Totalita is used as the reference corpus, three forms of *člověk* receive KW status (in 89th, 109th, and 110th place).

[35] As Havel makes clear in the essay, he borrows this phrase from the Czech philosopher Václav Bělohradský (see Bělohradský1982 for a fuller account of his views).

scope and magnifying its potential import. In this sense, then, Havel follows in the footsteps of Comenius, promoting the pedagogue's intellectual and spiritual legacy. How exactly does he do this?

First and foremost, Havel assumes that readers recognize *lidskost* as a worthwhile value, a fact of human interpersonal experience. Then, as we saw above, he focalizes the essay largely through the eyes of an individual person who confronts, at times despairingly, modern-world challenges. These challenges are given "human" form in the central images that Havel evokes throughout the essay: the factory smokestack belching toxic smoke into our neighbors' (or our own) windows and the private bathroom that serves lamentably as a place of exile for each individual's conscience. How individuals react to modern-world challenges thus becomes a measure of complicity in the "eschatology of the impersonal." Do we object to the smokestack only when the smoke comes into our own house? Do we allow our personal conscience to guide our behavior in the public, and not merely private, sphere?

As we saw in the corpus analysis, *lidskost* is, however, a concept that spans domains of experience—it links personal, interpersonal, and sociocultural circles of home. Therein, for Havel, lies humanity's hope. Our personal and private "humanness" can serve as the basis for a restoration of "humanness" in the public sphere: the values that guide our behavior in our most intimate circles of home may be extrapolated outward. Implicit in Havel's thinking, then, is a deep faith in Comenius's idea of "education for how to be human." In regard to the Velvet Revolution, Krapfl summarizes the same point in different language when he writes that Czechoslovak citizens "experienced the revolution first and foremost as the genesis of a transcendent new sense of community," which in turn became a "signifier [that] served as the first principle in an expanding universe of signifiers by means of which citizens sought to express their collective ideals and map them onto social, political, and economic institutions" (Krapfl, 2013, p. 9).

We should recall here collocates for *lidskost* in the CNC: 'decency, empathy, faith, justice, love, morality, civility, responsibility, tolerance, humility, modesty, kindness, respect, considerateness,' and yes, even sometimes 'bravery.' These might be expected aspects of "being human" with family, friends, neighbors, professional colleagues, and perhaps even people we have only just met, but if they are extrapolated as norms to larger human circles of home, they gain the power to transform the world for the better.

In the course of the essay, Havel extends the concept of "humanness" to include a collocate that we do not find represented in the CNC, but that we do find linked as a keyword to "humanness" in both the Czech and English versions of the essay—namely, conscience (*svědomí*).[36] The crux of Havel's extension here is captured in the powerful rhetorical question that ends the essay in the form of a personal challenge to the reader:

> Netkví perspektiva lepší budoucnosti tohoto světa v jakémsi mezinárodním společenství otřesených, které nedbajíc hranic států, politických systémů a mocenských bloků, vně

[36] See Danaher (2015) (294ff) for a comparative analysis of "conscience" and *svědomí* in Havel's writings.

> vysoké hry tradiční politiky, neaspirujíc na funkce a sekretariáty, pokusí se učinit reálnou politickou sílu z fenoménu dnes technology moci tak vysmívaného, jakým je lidské svědomí?
> "Does not the perspective of a better future depend on something like an international community of the shaken which, ignoring state boundaries, political systems, and power blocs, standing outside the high game of traditional politics, aspiring to no titles and appointments, will seek to make a real political force out of a phenomenon so ridiculed by the technicians of power—the phenomenon of human conscience?"

One final move in Havel's argument is the extension of its applicable scope from the Eastern Bloc to the modern world as a whole. This address was, after all, written for a Western venue, and, as an accomplished playwright, Havel was always conscious of his audience. The "eschatology of the impersonal," he argues, is a generally modern problem, grotesquely exaggerated in the (post-)totalitarian countries of the East, but also evident, in different and perhaps more insidious ways, in the democratic West. In making this move, Havel extends the scope of *lidskost* as central human value beyond the boundaries of Czechoslovakia.

Conclusion: *Lidskost* as Revolutionary Principle

In exploring the semantics of *lidskost* both through corpus analysis and interpretation of a literary text, we are in a much better position to appreciate how the concept became (and still might become again) a revolutionary ideal. Indeed, this potential was in place well before 1989, as Havel's (1984) essay goes to show and as the legacy of Comenius through Masaryk and Patočka, among others, confirms. It is a concept with deep roots in the Czech cultural and intellectual tradition.

We should be clear that *lidskost* is not a moral principle in an abstract sense of the word and therein lies its true potential as a political force. The everydayness of "being human" as a lived-through experience in our personal circles of home is its conceptual ground. We see definite traces of that ground in corpus analysis of its usage.

Following in the footsteps of his intellectual predecessors, Havel urges that we extrapolate the standards inherent in personal *lidskost* to broader spheres of human activity: we should normatize *lidskost* at all levels of human engagement. He exploits the semantic potential of the concept, and it is precisely this potential that turns *lidskost* into a revolutionary value. It is not understood as an abstract political slogan, but rather as a conceptual space for personal empowerment at the sociopolitical level. By expanding the concept outward, individuals who understand *lidskost* in the context of their own lives become potentially powerful agents of political transformation. Moreover, if Havel is to be believed, this proves true not just for Czechoslovaks during the Velvet Revolution but also potentially for all of us living in the modern world.[37]

[37] I am grateful to Václav Cvrček and Masako Fidler for organizing and leading a corpus-training workshop at Brown University in April 2016 as well as for their detailed suggestions on a draft of this contribution. I am also grateful to Kieran Williams for reading and commenting on the same draft. Any errors that remain are my own.

References

Baker, P. (2007). *Using corpora in discourse analysis*. London: Continuum.

Bělohradský, V. (1982). *Krize eschatologie neosobnosti*. London: Rozmluvy.

Bolton, J. (2012). *Worlds of dissent: Charter 77, the plastic people of the universe, and Czech culture under communism*. Cambridge, UK: Harvard University Press.

Čapková, D. Bacík, F., Pařízek, V., & Skalková, J. (1991). Komenského dílna lidskosti a úsilí o humanizaci vzdělávání a výchovy. *Časopis pro pedagogické vědy, ročník XLI* 5-6, 659–667.

Cvrček, V., Čermáková, A., & Křen, M. (2016). Nová koncepce synchronních korpusů psané češtiny. *Slovo a slovesnost, 77*(2), 83–101.

Cvrček, V., & Vondřička, P. (2011a). *SyD - Korpusový průzkum variant*. Prague, Czech Republic: FF UK, from http://syd.korpus.cz

Cvrček, V., & Vondřička, P. (2011b). Výzkum variability v korpusech češtiny. In F. Čermák (Ed.), *Korpusová lingvistika (2. Výzkum a výstavba korpusů)* (pp. 184–195). Prague, Czech Republic: NLN.

Cvrček, V., & Vondřička, P. (2013). *KWords*. Prague, Czech Republic: FF UK, from http://kwords.korpus.cz

Danaher, D. (2010). An ethnolinguistic approach to key words in literature: Lidskost and duchovnost in the writings of Václav Havel. In *Ročenka textů zahraničních profesorů* (Vol. 4, pp. 27–54). Prague, Czech Republic: Charles University.

Danaher, D. (2015). *Reading Václav Havel*. Toronto, Canada: University of Toronto Press.

Fidler, M., & Cvrček, V. (2015). A data-driven analysis of reader viewpoints: Reconstructing the historical reader using keyword analysis. *Journal of Slavic Linguistics, 23*(2), 197–239.

Fronek, J. (2000). *Velký česko-anglický slovník*. Prague, Czech Republic: LEDA.

Havel, V. (1984). Politics and conscience. In *Open letters* (E. Kohák & R. Scruton Trans., pp. 249–271). New York: Knopf.

Havel, V. (1991). In P. Wilson (Ed.), *Open letters*. New York: Knopf.

Havel, V. (1999). *Spisy*. Prague, Czech Republic: Torst.

Krapfl, J. (2013). *Revolution with a human face: Politics, culture, and community in Czechoslovakia, 1989-1992*. Ithaca, NY: Cornell University Press.

Křen, M., Cvrček, V., Čapka, T., Čermáková, A., Hnátková, M., Chlumská, L., et al. (2015). *SYN2015: reprezentativní korpus psané češtiny*. Prague, Czech Republic: Ústav Českého národního korpusu FF UK, from http://www.korpus.cz

Křen, M., Cvrček, V., Čapka, T., Čermáková, A., Hnátková, M., Chlumská, L., et al. (2016). SYN2015: Representative corpus of contemporary written Czech. In *Proceedings of the tenth international conference on language resources and evaluation (LREC'16)* (pp. 2522–2528). Portorož, Slovenia: ELRA.

Rosenberg, T. (1996). *The haunted land: Facing Europe's ghosts after communism*. New York: Vintage.

Škrabal, M., & Vavřín, M. (2017). Databáze překladových ekvivalentů Treq. *Časopis pro moderní filologii, 99*(2), 245–260.

Vavřín, M., & Rosen, A. (2015). *Treq*. Prague, Czech Republic: FF UK, from http://treq.korpus.cz

Williams, K. (1997). *The Prague spring and its aftermath: Czechoslovak politics, 1968-1970*. Cambridge, England: Cambridge University Press.

Part III
Understanding Discourse

Chapter 8
Keeping and Bearing Arms in Czech

Kieran Williams

Abstract Determining the plain or primary meaning of words in legal language is crucial to compliance with and enforcement of laws, but also controversial if the methods used are subjective and unsystematic. Corpus linguistics is a potential remedy. This chapter uses corpus analysis to compare the usage of the Czech noun *zbraň* (weapon), verbs *držet* (keep) and *nosit* (bear), and adjectives *bezúhonný* (upstanding) and *spolehlivý* (reliable) in Czech gun law against their usage in wider discourse. The results suggest a marked misalignment between the two usages, with the words taking on connotations at law that would not be self-evident. Although the population of gun owners in the Czech Republic is small, the potential cost of misunderstanding the key terms of gun law has risen with the attempt in 2017 to create a constitutional right to keep and bear arms to assist the state in protecting national security.

Keywords Corpus-based approach · Czech · Legal language · Statutory interpretation · Political discourse · Gun control

Corpus Linguistics and Gun Law

One of the newest and still contentious applications of corpus linguistics is as a tool for making sense of statutes and constitutions. No matter how plain the authors of a law may have tried to make its language, there is often a vagueness or ambiguity about key words that require interpretation and construction (Solum, 2010). Lawyers and judges have searched in dictionaries, electronic databases, and on Google to ascertain a word's "plain" or "primary" meaning, but the methods they have used have been derided as subjective, unsystematic, and unreproducible (Phillips, Ortner, & Lee, 2016). Corpus linguistics, albeit with its own pitfalls and shortcomings,

K. Williams (✉)
Drake University, Des Moines, IA, USA
e-mail: kieran.williams@drake.edu

M. Fidler, V. Cvrček (eds.), *Taming the Corpus*, Quantitative Methods in the Humanities and Social Sciences, https://doi.org/10.1007/978-3-319-98017-1_8

provides a basis on which to make claims about a word's usage with a higher degree of confidence. This would be especially welcome in an area such as gun law, in which uncertainty about the meaning of a word or phrase could have huge implications for compliance and enforcement. It was in regard to guns that the US Supreme Court produced a problematic ruling based in part on a justice's searches in the Lexis/Nexis and Westlaw databases (to determine whether the phrase "carries a firearm" could reach to conveyance in a vehicle), while a justice of the Utah Supreme Court used corpus linguistics to determine the meaning of "discharge" with regard to firing a weapon (Mouritsen, 2010, 2017; Ortner, 2016).

These examples come from a legal system in which case law plays an enormous role, but we should resist the positivist myth that judges and counsel in European civil-law systems do not likewise wrestle with the meaning of words (Müller, 2000). Confusion could still arise if seemingly authoritative statutory definitions diverge from common usage. The possibility of confusion is all the greater when a statutory matter is elevated to a constitutional one, thereby attaining more publicity and political texture. One such occasion was the drive in 2017 to pass an amendment to article 3 of the Czech Republic's Constitutional Act 110/1998 on national security. (A constitutional act is a law passed by a three-fifths supermajority that is not inserted into the constitution but is treated as part of the broader "constitutional order" of the country.) The proposed addition would guarantee a new right in regard to certain enumerated purposes:

> Občané České republiky mají právo nabývat, držet a nosit zbraně a střelivo, k naplňování úkolů uvedených v odstavci 2.
> 'Citizens of the Czech Republic have the right to acquire, keep and bear arms and ammunition for the fulfilment of tasks referred to in clause 2.'

The second clause of paragraph 3 of Constitutional Act 110/1998 act states:

> Státní orgány, orgány územních samosprávných celků a právnické a fyzické osoby jsou povinny se podílet na zajišťování bezpečnosti České republiky.
> 'State organs, organs of regional self-governing units and legal and physical persons are obliged to participate in the safeguarding of the security of the Czech Republic.'

What "security" means is expansively defined in the opening paragraph of Constitutional Act 110/1998:

> [...] zajištění svrchovanosti a územní celistvosti České republiky, ochrana jejích demokratických základů a ochrana životů, zdraví a majetkových hodnot je základní povinností státu.
> '[...] the basic duty of the state is ensuring the sovereignty and territorial integrity of the Czech Republic, protection of its democratic foundations and protection of lives, health and property values.'

The amendment was not proposed in response to events in the Czech Republic, a country with few homicides by gun and a *rising* sense of general safety: a poll in December 2016 found that 81% of Czechs felt safe, up 5% from the year before and up 36% from 2002 (Pilnáček, 2017). Rather, it was a reaction to a change in the European Union's Firearms Directive, itself prompted by terrorist attacks in several countries reportedly involving semiautomatic Czech pistols (the CZ 85) and repurposed Cold-War firearms such as the *vzor* 58 (a Czechoslovak service rifle). In May 2017, the European Parliament prohibited civilian use of short semiautomatic firearms capable of firing more than 20 rounds without reloading, and long semiautomatics shooting more than ten rounds. Czech lobbying groups such as LEX—The Association to Protect the Rights of Gun Owners (*Sdružení na ochranu práv majitelů zbraní*) and the Czech-Moravian Hunters' Union (*Českomoravská myslivecká jednota*, ČMMJ) rallied members and sympathizers in Czech parties of left and right, and the amendment was co-sponsored by 35 members of the lower house, the Chamber of Deputies (Mařík, 2016; ver, 2017). The amendment was passed easily on June 28, 2017, with 139 of 168 deputies present voting in favor. It failed to pass the Senate in December 2017, but guns remained on the agenda, as the European Union's directive had to be incorporated into domestic law by September 13, 2018.

During the amendment's readings, skeptics challenged the amendment's validity, as it would not overrule the European Firearms Directive, and they questioned its necessity, as the Czech criminal code already allowed for the use of proportionate force by any person in self-defense and in extreme situations like a terrorist attack. A constitutional expert, Jan Kysela, noted that the amendment referred only to the acquisition, keeping, and bearing of arms, not to their actual use (Kotalík, 2017); in the absence of a "concrete proposal," said one legislator, it was unclear how gun owners would actually exercise their new right.[1]

This observation, which assumes a distinction between keeping/bearing a weapon and firing it, brings us to the perspective of corpus linguistics: are key terms in the amendment and gun laws to be understood differently from how they are used in general parlance? Applicants for a gun owner's permit have to pass a written test of their knowledge of the law, and thus become versed in its terminology, but permit holders numbered only 300,307 at the start of 2017, or 2.8% of the Czech population. Of those, 241,229 qualified for a group E permit, allowing them to carry a weapon to protect life, health, or property—the values enumerated in the constitutional act on security (*Tisk* 1021, 2017). The overall number of gun owners plateaued in 1998 after a 5-year surge following the end of Communist rule, and even with a slight recent upturn, the level in 2017 was well below the peak of 321,215 in 2001 (Šimek, 2017). So, how might the 97.2% of Czechs who have not gone through the tests to obtain a gun owner's permit read the language of the amendment, which was widely reprinted in the press?

For corpus analysis, I focus on the verbs *držet* and *nosit*, and the noun *zbraň*—generally equivalent to the "keep," "bear," and "arms" in the Second Amendment of

[1] Martin Plíšek, from the TOP 09 party, in the Chamber of Deputies, April 12, 2017, at http://www.psp.cz/eknih/2013ps/stenprot/056schuz/s056213.htm#r2. The amendment itself anticipated follow-up passage of a statute to limit the right and clarify conditions for its exercise.

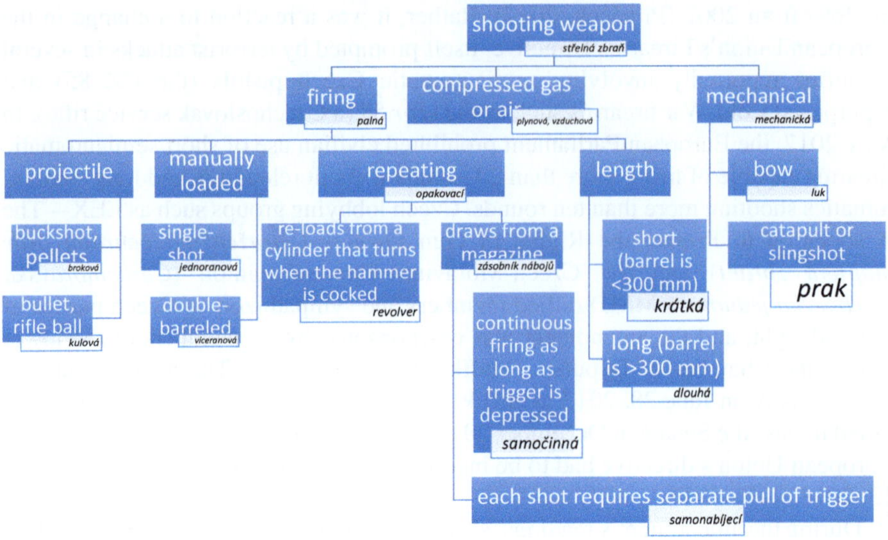

Fig. 8.1 Types of shooting weapon (*střelná zbraň*)

the US Constitution.[2] I also examine two adjectives from sections 22 and 23 of the 2002 firearms act regarding attributes that a person must evince in order to obtain a permit: being *bezúhonný* (upstanding) and *spolehlivý* (reliable). I use the SYN series of synchronic corpora of written Czech amassed as part of the Czech National Corpus project (Hnátková, Křen, Procházka, & Skoumalová, 2014), primarily version 5 (2017 release), which contains 3.8 billion non-punctuation tokens drawn from 14.8 million texts (Křen, Richterová, & Škrabal, 2017).

Zbraň

The starting point is the object that, under the proposed amendment, a person would have the right to wield in service of national security: *zbraň*. Not restricted to "gun" or "firearm," *zbraň* is "weapon" in the broadest sense. Since a Habsburg imperial patent in 1852, the many different kinds of *zbraň* have been sorted into a matrix of legal categories, with guidelines for possession and carrying (Sedláček, 2010). Acts passed in 1995 and 2002 understand a *střelná zbraň* to be any weapon that shoots a

[2] In the Czech National Corpus (SYN v.5), a common translation of the second clause of the Second Amendment, "the right of the people to keep and bear Arms, shall not be infringed," is "*právo lidu držet a nosit zbraně nesmí být proto omezováno*" (13 hits). A variant of this is "*právo lidu držet a nosit zbraně nesmí být porušeno*" (*Mladá fronta DNES*, April 18, 2007.) Another uses *mít* (to have) in place of *držet*: "*nebudiž dotčeno právo lidu mít a nosit zbraň*" (*Literární noviny*, 1/2013).

Table 8.1 Ten highest instances per million positions of *zbraň** in SYN v5 since 1989

Year	Frequency	i.p.m.
1993	4818	209.98
1992	4669	206.45
1991	1826	194.29
1994	5642	188.67
1995	6504	164.63
2003	22,546	151.91
1996	10,705	147.39
2001	19,875	141.15
1999	19,236	134.25
2002	18,435	132.23

projectile over a defined range through the instantaneous release of energy. This in turn can be broken down into types of energy, with variations per projectile and capacity. These are summarized in Fig. 8.1.

A *střelná zbraň* can also be categorized according to its social use rather than its design: whether it is for sport (*sportovní*), hunting (*lovecká*), the military (*vojenská*), or historical interest (*historická*, made before 31 December 1890).[3]

The lemma *zbraň* occurs 432,869 times in SYN v5, or 94.11 instances per million (i.p.m.).[4] There is no evidence of a rising salience of weapons in Czech discourse in recent years; the average i.p.m. over the 10 years from 2005 to 2015 is 79.46. There was a slight upturn in 2015, following a mass shooting in the town of Uherský Brod in February, but the i.p.m. was 85.35, still below the corpus average. In the decades since the end of Communist rule in Czechoslovakia in 1989, the years in which *zbraň* had the highest i.p.m. were in the first half of the 1990s, when the press was full of stories about weapons of all kinds, including nuclear, chemical, and biological (see Table 8.1).

If we filter the search for i.p.m. of the lemmas *zbraň* and *střelný* one place to the left, the corpus turns up 20,371 instances, with an i.p.m. of 4.43. Ranking by year since 1989, here too the phrase incurred its highest i.p.m. in the 1990s (see Table 8.2), and there was no evident spike in usage in the years before the push to amend the constitutional act in 2017.

We can now expand the range of collocation candidates with *zbraň* (setting a window span of −3 to +3 positions), focusing on the top 20 lemmas as ranked by logDice. I also provide the Mutual Information (MI) scores and T-scores (Table 8.3).[5]

[3] See also https://zbranekvalitne.cz/zbrojni-prukaz/nauka-o-zbranich for a helpful overview of the Czech terms for gun components.

[4] When the lemma for a noun or adjective has been used in a query, it will be indicated in the results table with an asterisk (*).

[5] With logDice, the theoretical maximum score is 14, if all occurrences in a corpus of word X co-occur with word Y, and vice-versa. Scores are normally below 10. See Rychlý (2008). MI scores are more sensitive to the size of the corpus and tend to give high scores to words that may occur infrequently (Baker, 2006).

Table 8.2 Ten highest instances per million positions of *střeln* zbraň** in SYN v5 since 1989

Year	Frequency	i.p.m.
1993	181	7.89
1994	186	6.22
1996	438	6.03
1999	820	5.72
2000	775	5.55
2003	824	5.55
2002	768	5.51
2008	1572	5.51
1995	215	5.44
2001	754	5.35

Table 8.3 Collocation candidates with *zbraň**

	Lemma	Translation	Frequency	logDice	MI	T-score
1.	střelný	shooting (adj.)	20,813	10.515	12.700	144.245
2.	jaderný	nuclear	22,084	10.093	9.996	148.461
3.	ničení	destruction	11,651	9.687	12.003	107.914
4.	hromadný	mass (adj.)	11,636	9.304	9.505	107.722
5.	složit	to lay down	10,575	9.207	9.518	102.695
6.	chemický	chemical	8175	8.893	9.379	90.280
7.	legálně	legally	6019	8.671	10.296	77.520
8.	držený	held, kept (adj.)	5556	8.669	12.015	74.521
9.	palný	firing (adj.)	5009	8.550	13.375	70.768
10.	střelivo	ammunition	5073	8.549	12.281	71.211
11.	použít	to use	8993	8.309	7.590	94.339
12.	biologický	biological	4878	8.304	9.475	69.745
13.	použití	use (noun)	5875	8.217	8.189	76.386
14.	ruka	hand	13,717	7.881	6.628	115.935
15.	držení	possession, ownership	3431	7.833	9.243	58.478
16.	lovecký	hunting (adj.)	3105	7.740	9.577	55.650
17.	munice	munitions	3010	7.692	9.500	54.788
18.	účinný	effective	3763	7.687	7.915	61.089
19.	služební	service (adj.)	3333	7.678	8.460	57.568
20.	ruční	hand (adj.), small (gun)	3065	7.624	8.736	55.233

These collocates can be grouped into three categories. The first concerns weapons that are not guns: nuclear, chemical, biological, mass, and destruction. The second comprises adjectives and nouns that could be associated with guns: shooting, hunting, firing, legally, service, hand, and ammunition. The third covers verbs associated with weaponry of all kinds: lay down, use, and keep. More will be said about verbs below, but right away we see one substantial difference between the corpus and the language of gun law: the prominence in the corpus of "use" (*použít*) and the low ranking—in 44th place—of one of the key verbs in statutes and the amendment to the constitutional law, "bear" (*nosit*), with a logDice of 6.807. *Držet*,

Table 8.4 Verbs among the collocations with *zbraň**

Rank	Verb (lemma)	Translation	Frequency	logDice	MI	T-score
5.	složit	lay down	10,575	9.207	9.518	102.695
11.	použít	use	8993	8.309	7.590	94.339
23.	skládat	lay down	2873	7.386	7.875	53.372
24.	odevzdat	surrender, give up	2585	7.351	8.317	50.683
26.	vytáhnout	pull (out)	3032	7.253	7.205	54.690
32.	namířit	point, aim	2022	7.133	9.098	44.885
44.	nosit	carry, bear, wear	2314	6.807	6.654	47.626
58.	ohrožovat	threaten	1591	6.510	6.926	39.559
59.	střílet	shoot	1686	6.499	6.652	40.653
64.	používat	use	2839	6.467	5.607	52.189
68.	vlastnit	own	1361	6.416	7.340	36.664
71.	obrátit	turn	1803	6.381	6.117	41.850
72.	přepadnout	attack	1305	6.371	7.373	35.907
80.	vystřelit	shoot, fire	1209	6.269	7.309	34.551
84.	vyrábět	produce, manufacture	1766	6.218	5.768	41.252
89.	zastřelit	shoot (someone)	1139	6.178	7.193	33.518
93.	vyhrožovat	threaten	1080	6.097	7.092	32.623
95.	mířit	point, aim	1427	6.016	5.711	37.054
98.	vyvíjet	develop	1151	6.014	6.344	33.509
100.	donutit	force	1019	5.970	6.761	31.627
105.	držet	keep, hold	2091	5.910	4.974	44.272
106.	najít	find	4422	5.896	4.553	63.666
112.	nalézt	find, discover	1321	5.842	5.447	35.513
119.	zabavit	seize, confiscate	837	5.798	7.211	28.736
129.	bojovat	fight	1609	5.663	4.814	38.687
136.	požadovat	demand, require, request	1056	5.584	5.281	31.660
144.	vyrobit	produce, manufacture	954	5.543	5.415	30.163
145.	sáhnout	reach, touch	832	5.530	5.813	28.331
146.	tasit	draw	615	5.528	10.671	24.784
147.	opatřit	provide, supply, furnish, obtain	683	5.514	6.997	25.930
150.	disponovat	have, possess	727	5.499	6.360	26.635

to keep or hold, appears even farther down, in 105th place, although adjectives and nouns derived from it are in the top 15 collocates. Table 8.4 ranks all the lemmatized verbs extracted from the top 150 collocation candidates.

This list abounds with verbs that describe the physical grasp and use (including firing) of a weapon; recall the prominence of a body part, the hand (*ruka*), as one of the most frequent collocates in Table 8.3. Several verbs relate to action by states or firms, such as the manufacture, storage, and elimination of weapons, including ones other than guns. The legal notion of a private person bearing arms, conveyed in law by the verb *nosit*, is present but only secondarily, especially in comparison to its seemingly more frequent partner, keeping, in the derived forms of the adjective *držený* and noun *držení* (the eighth and 15th top collocates in Table 8.3). As the next section will show, however, we have to distinguish the ways in which *držet* and its derivatives are used in the corpus.

Držet

The first comprehensive post-Communist firearms law, Act 288/1995, offered a definition of "keeping" weapons and ammunition: "*mít u sebe nebo je jinak přechovávat ve stavu vylučujícím jejich okamžité použití*" ('have on oneself or otherwise store them in a condition that excludes their immediate use'). As this gloss was parsimonious to a fault, Act 119/2002 expanded it into a two-part definition:

1. zbraň nebo střelivo uvnitř bytových nebo provozních prostor nebo uvnitř zřetelně ohraničených nemovitostí se souhlasem vlastníka nebo nájemce uvedených prostor nebo nemovitostí,
2. zbraň nenabitou náboji v zásobníku, nábojové schránce, nábojové komoře hlavně nebo nábojových komorách válce revolveru a uloženou v uzavřeném obalu za účelem jejího přemístění z místa na místo [...].
1. '[have] the weapon or ammunition inside places of housing or business or inside clearly demarcated immovable properties with the agreement of the owner or tenant of said places or properties,
2. [have] the weapon not loaded with a cartridge in a clip, fixed box magazine, the breech or the chambers of a revolver cylinder, and [have it] placed in a closed container for the purpose of transporting it from one place to another [...].'

As can be gleaned from the report accompanying the bill (*Tisk* 1071, 2001), the distinction between keeping and bearing arms turned on whether the weapon was loaded, so the expanded definition allowed for situations in which someone might be transporting an unloaded weapon outside the home or workplace and that did not qualify as "bearing" (*nošení*).

One confusion that this definition has caused is whether *držet* is a synonym for *vlastnit* (to own) or the phrase *nabývat do vlastnictví* (to acquire ownership), as they also appear in Act 119/2002 but are left undefined. From the text, it is clear that ownership is a separate aspect of permission to keep a weapon, and the two do not necessarily go together: section 12, paragraph 5 states, "*Příslušný útvar policie vydá povolení vlastnit nebo držet zbraň kategorie B, pokud má k tomu žadatel řádný důvod*" ('The appropriate police department shall give permission to own or keep a weapon in category B, so long as the applicant has a regular reason for doing so').[6]

[6] Category B is based on the taxonomy in the European Union's Firearms Directive and covers repeating or semiautomatic weapons.

Similarly, per paragraphs 6 and 7, police permission to bear weapons in category B is a separate consideration; the applicant has to request expressly that permission to own, keep, and bear be granted simultaneously.[7] The act consistently uses the formula "to keep or bear," not "keep and bear" arms.

When the legislature was voting on the amendment to the constitutional act in 2017, even visitors to a gun enthusiasts' online discussion forum were unsure of the different meanings and separability of the rights in question.[8]

> Jim11: Jaký je vlastně rozdíl mezi právem vlastnit a držet zbraň?
> 'What exactly is the difference between the right to own and keep a weapon?'
> Petzold (a moderator): Vlastnit můžeš třeba zbraně, z nějakého důvodu uložené v policejním skladu, ke kterým se nedostaneš. Držení a nošení je víš co, ne?
> 'You might own a weapon that for some reason is stored in a police storeroom, which you can't get at. You know what keeping and bearing are, don't you?'
> Mao: Právní výrazivo, někdy neodpovídá na 100% běžně užívané Č[sic]eštině .... např můžeš zbraň držet, a přitom nevlastnit, anebo naopak ....
> 'Legalese, sometimes it doesn't correspond 100% to commonly-used czech... e.g. you can keep a weapon while not owning it, or vice-versa.'
> Petzold: Nebo tak. Každopádně je pro nás výhodnější "držet a nosit" s příjemným bonusem "vlastnictví." 
> 'Something like that. In any event it is better for us to "keep and bear" with the pleasant bonus of "ownership.'

The uncertainty of "Jim11" and "Mao" is all the more understandable when we query the corpus for uses of *držet*. When we search for collocations in SYN v5, with a window span of −3 to +3, the logDice rankings turn up strong physical associations (especially of holding in the hand) or turns of phrase (holding a record, keeping pace, and sticking to a diet) (Table 8.5).

I then narrowed the search to generate a concordance for the lemmas *držet* and *zbraň*, again with a window span of −3 to +3. As this returned 2091 results, I randomly derived a subset of 250 instances for closer reading. It became clear that 234 (93.6%) of them fell into two groups:

- 136 (54.4%) described the physical brandishing of a weapon;
- 98 (39.2%) implied legal possession, sometimes as a synonym for ownership.

As *ruka* 'hand' had turned up as a strong collocation candidate with *zbraň* (see Table 8.3) and with *držet* on their own, I added a positive *ruka* filter (using a window span of −5 to +5), and found that 636 (30%) of the 2091 concordance results of *zbraň* and *držet* also included reference to a "hand." There is thus a strong associa-

---

[7] That this does arise and does cause confusion is attested to by the long thread, running intermittently from November 2004 to March 2016, on an online gun discussion board at http://www.strelectvi.cz/forum/povoleni-k-nabyti-drzeni-noseni-a-registrace-dle-ucelu-t360.html.

[8] http://www.strelectvi.cz/forum/post432712.html#p432712.

Table 8.5 Collocation candidates with the lemma *držet*

	Lemma	Translation	Frequency	logDice	MI	T-score
1.	palec	finger	28,235	10.204	11.215	167.962
2.	ruka	hand, arm	46,559	9.450	7.683	214.725
3.	krok	step	29,291	9.388	8.037	170.495
4.	pohromadě	together	10,323	8.799	10.330	101.523
5.	pevně	firmly	8945	8.484	9.025	94.396
6.	dieta	diet	7367	8.292	9.568	85.718
7.	rekord	record	10,004	8.259	7.487	99.462
8.	stále	still, increasingly, always	22,151	8.054	6.153	146.741
9.	dlouho	long, a long time	14,428	8.048	6.442	118.735
10.	příčka	place, rung	7242	7.769	6.950	84.411
11.	huba	mouth	4192	7.562	10.412	64.698
12.	akcie	shares, stock	6538	7.525	6.542	79.990
13.	míč	ball	6410	7.384	6.243	79.005
14.	uzda	rein, bridle	3670	7.370	10.227	60.530
15.	pozice	position	6424	7.260	5.970	78.871
16.	náskok	lead, head start	4463	7.143	6.471	66.052
17.	hladovka	hunger strike	3003	7.096	10.616	54.765
18.	nad	over, above	17,343	7.085	5.020	127.633
19.	nadále	still (continuing)	4628	7.077	6.176	67.089
20.	zub	tooth	3462	7.010	7.025	58.387

tion in the corpus of a weapon with being physically held, usually in view and ready for use. Other examples imply the same even without *ruka*:

1. Základ je *zbraň* dobře *držet*, což je umění. [...] Zvládnout střelbu nevyžaduje velkou sílu, musíte ale vyvinout správný odpor a *držet zbraň* stabilně.
   'The basic thing is to *hold* the *gun* well, which is a skill. [...]. To master shooting does not require great strength, but you have to develop the right resistance and *keep the weapon* stable.' (Source: *Zdravotnické noviny*, 6/2014)
2. Předseda Okresního mysliveckého spolku v Uherském Hradišti Karel Blahušek se sice o případu nedoslechl, za bezpečnost při honu ale podle něj odpovídá vždy každý myslivec sám. "Je to nezodpovědnost střelce, který *drží zbraň* a střílí, protože když střílí na zvěř, vždycky musí mířit tak, aby nezpůsobil žádnou škodu na majetku ani újmu na zdraví."
   'While the chairman of the district hunters' association in Uherské Hradište, Karel Blahušek, had not heard about the case, according to him every hunter is responsible himself for safety during a hunt. 'It is irresponsible of a hunter who *holds* a *gun* and shoots, because when he is shooting at game, he must always aim so that he causes no damage to property or injury to health.' (Source: *Deníky Moravia*, November 10, 2009)
3. Zápas se smrtelnou nemocí se ničím neliší od boje s nepřítelem, který *drží* nabitou *zbraň* a je připraven stisknout kohoutek.
   'A struggle with a fatal illness is no different from fighting with an enemy who *is holding* a loaded *gun* and is prepared to pull the trigger.' (Source: *Reflex*, 27/2010)

In some instances, *držet* is used in the more legal sense of "keeping," but keeping loaded and ready for use, contrary to the meaning at law.

4. "Velká vina leží i na rodičích, kteří ve svém domku *drželi* ostře nabité *zbraně* a děti k nim měly volný přístup," řekla u předběžného slyšení soudkyně.
   "'Great blame also lies with the parents, who *kept* heavily loaded *guns* in their home and the children had unfettered access to them,' said the judge at the preliminary hearing.'" (Source: *Blesk*, August 11, 1999)
5. Například Francouzi, jejichž úsek s československým sousedí, jsou zvyklí *držet zbraně* neustále v pohotovosti, připraveni je použít.
   'For example the French, whose sector borders on the Czechoslovak, are used to *keeping* their *guns* in constant readiness, prepared to use them.' (Source: *Respekt*, 6/1993)

Finally, the metaphor of holding a gun in one's hands (plural) can be used to connote possession, possibly owning, rather than literal brandishing:

6. Navíc se ale svěřil se svými obavami, kolik střelných *zbraní drží* Američané ve svých rukou.
   'Furthermore, he opened up about his fears as to how many *guns* Americans *have* in their hands.' (source: *Rytmus života*, 3/2015)

In sum, these corpus results help explain why even people keen on guns might have difficulty reconciling the everyday use of the verb *držet* with the specific meaning given it in gun law. The potential for trouble only grows when we couple it with "bearing."

Nosit

Act 288/1995 provided a succinct definition of bearing arms: "*mít u sebe nebo je jinak přechovávat ve stavu umožňujícím jejich okamžité použití*," 'to have on oneself or otherwise store [weapon and ammunition] in a state making possible their immediate use.' Act 119/2002, having expanded the definition of "to keep," reduced its gloss for "bear": "*mít zbraň nebo střelivo u sebe, s výjimkou případů uvedených v písmenu a)*" 'To have a weapon or ammunition on oneself, with the exception of the cases referred to in paragraph a) [on keeping arms].' The defense and security committee of the Chamber of Deputies had suggested making it more explicit that "bearing" involved a loaded weapon ready to be used, but this was not factored into the final text.[9] Only later in the act, in section 28, can it be gleaned that if the person has a group E permit (to protect life, health, and property) and the weapon falls into category B (repeating or semiautomatic arms), "bearing" means having on oneself no more than two guns, and that neither they nor the ammunition can be carried openly. Bearing arms under Czech law is thus a matter of mandatory concealment.

[9] *Usnesení výboru pro obranu a bezpečnost z 61. schůze dne 16. ledna 2002* [decision of the committee for defense and security from its 61st meeting on January 16, 2002], at http://www.psp.cz/doc/pdf/00/05/69/00056978.pdf.

Before comparing the usage of *nosit* in the Czech corpus, we should address the prepositional phrase *u sebe* that features in the definition in Acts 288/1995 and 119/2002. It had also been part of the definition of "keeping" in Act 288/1995 but was then replaced by a more descriptive reference to places of housing or business, which suggests that in that context *u sebe* had meant with oneself in a location and not necessarily on one's person. Neither act clarifies what *u sebe* means in the context of "bearing" a weapon, although in the context of an arms permit it appears to mean that the permit must be within reach to be produced for inspection when required. After querying the SYN v.5 corpus for a concordance of *nosit* and *zbraň* (window span of −3 to +3, results discussed below), I added a positive filter for *u sebe*, which produced 201 hits. Hand analysis of these extracts found that virtually all of them could be translated by the English phrase, "have on (oneself)" or "go about armed." This was borne out from passages translated from English-language novels, which I compared to the original texts. In some instances, *u sebe* serves to amplify where the English simply uses "carry," as if *nosit* alone would not suffice:

7. From Arthur Conan Doyle, *The Valley of Fear* (1915), 91:
   "There's one thing you should know. He always went about armed. His revolver was never out of his pocket."
   Translated: "Jednu věc byste měl vědět: stále *u sebe* nosil zbraň, nikdy nedal revolver z kapsy."
8. From Tami Hoag, *Ashes to Ashes* (1999), 80:
   "She suspected everyone of everything, rode a Harley Hog in good weather, and had been known to carry weapons."
   Translated: "Podezírala každého ze všeho, když bylo hezky, jezdila na harleyi a vědělo se o ní, že *u sebe* nosí zbraně."
9. From Margaret Millar, *The Iron Gates* (1945), 295:
   "'Do you carry a gun?' Andrew said."
   Translated: "'Nosíte *u sebe* zbraň?' zeptal se Andrew."

The main task for corpus analysis is to test the requirement of concealment in Act 119/2002: what is the likelihood that a Czech speaker unfamiliar with gun law would *not* expect bearing arms to entail their overt display? First, to get a feel for the usage of *nosit* in general, I queried the corpus for the top collocations (with a window span of −3 to +3); Table 8.6 ranks the top 20 candidates by logDice.

The immediate impression of this list is that *nosit* operates in the semantic field of clothing and accessories such as glasses and bags—mostly items in plain view, with potentially powerful social signifiers (fashion, team membership, and rank). In the Czech National Corpus's Treq database of translation equivalents, using InterCorp v9, *nosit* is rendered into English as "to wear" in around 65% of the examples, far more than "to carry," "to bear," or "to bring." In this company (*zbraň* is in 26th place, with a logDice score of 6.805), a weapon would not automatically be assumed to be something kept out of sight.

To tease out ways in which written Czech might convey whether a weapon is something carried openly, I generated a concordance for the lemmas *nosit* and *zbraň*, which returned 2310 results, and then added a positive filter for the adverb used in the law, *viditelně* (visibly, conspicuously), on a very broad window span (−7

Table 8.6 Collocation candidates for the lemma *nosit*

	Lemma	Translation	Frequency	logDice	MI	T-score
1.	brýle	glasses, spectacles	5007	8.925	9.979	70.690
2.	oblečení	clothes, clothing	4239	8.234	8.523	64.931
3.	uniforma	uniform	2518	7.976	9.147	50.091
4.	kalhoty	trousers	2389	7.869	8.954	48.779
5.	šaty	dress, clothes	2451	7.650	8.213	49.341
6.	šátek	scarf, kerchief	1640	7.579	9.712	40.449
7.	sukně	skirt	1666	7.557	9.422	40.757
8.	vlas	hair	2896	7.554	7.708	53.557
9.	dres	jersey, uniform	3090	7.495	7.520	55.285
10.	bota	shoe	2380	7.477	7.857	48.575
11.	kapsa	pocket	2042	7.405	7.995	45.011
12.	oblek	suit	1465	7.297	8.817	38.190
13.	domů	home	3703	7.279	7.021	60.384
14.	tričko	T-shirt	1495	7.234	8.439	38.554
15.	dárek	gift	2378	7.226	7.341	48.464
16.	kabelka	handbag, purse	1450	7.111	8.098	37.940
17.	klobouk	hat	1319	7.097	8.440	36.213
18.	hlava	head	6336	7.050	6.496	78.717
19.	džíny	jeans	1073	7.009	9.450	32.710
20.	kapitánský	captain's (adj.)	997	6.992	10.552	31.554

to +7) to see how often it arose. This turned up 26 results, four of which did not relate to a Czech setting; all but one of the rest imparted that Czech law forbids open carry of guns. So, while it could be said that the usage of *viditelně* in the corpus was in line with the law, it accounts for only 1% of all collocations of *nosit* and *zbraň* (and six of the hits were essentially the same story reprinted in multiple newspapers). I then ran a positive filter for *ruka*, because of how high it ranked in collocations with *zbraň* and *držet* and because it would be a direct physical indicator of open carry. This query (on a window span of −5 to +5) produced only nine results. Filtering for the adverb *veřejně* (publicly) likewise turned up only ten hits, of which nine referred to non-Czech settings. Filtering for adjectives such as the lemmatized adjectives *zakrytý* (covered) and *ukrytý* (hidden, concealed) produced only one result, from an American setting.

I concluded by generating a random sample of 250 results from the *nosit-zbraň* concordance to see if hand analysis could turn up other indicators of open or concealed carry. Only 17 (6.8%) contained enough additional information, in 12 cases to signal concealment, although not always in a Czech setting. In these cases, it has to emerge through some sort of discovery that someone has a gun on them:

10. O ochranu požádal též královéhradecký státní zástupce Miroslav Antl, který zároveň přiznal, že u sebe z obavy o svou bezpečnost neustále *nosí* střelnou *zbraň*. 'Protection was also requested by the Hradec Králové state attorney Miroslav Antl, who at the same time admitted that he always *carries* a *gun* out of fear for his safety.' (From: *Právo*, November 2, 2000)

11. "Když jsem se dověděl, že jsou kolegové, kteří prý *zbraně nosí* do objektů parlamentu, přešel po mně mráz," přidává se poslanec Jiří Štětina (VV).
'"When I learned that there are colleagues who reportedly *bring weapons* onto the premises of the parliament, a chill went down my spine," joins in Deputy Jiří Štětina (VV).' (From: *Lidové noviny*, June 8, 2012)
12. Na dotaz přítomných přiznala, že u sebe *nosí zbraň*, protože to považuje za vhodné.
'At the request of those present, she admitted that she *was carrying* a *weapon*, because she considered it advisable.' (From: *Deníky Bohemia*, November 2, 2007)

In almost all instances in the sample, the verb *nosit* was used in a very general way that would not impress on the reader or listener that the weapon could not be seen. We can thus tentatively conclude that common usage of *nosit* does not prime the public to equate bearing arms with the concealed carry required by law. In one online discussion thread, when one visitor asked whether it was legal for guards in shops to openly carry their weapons, another—a forum moderator!—replied by citing the definition of "keeping" in Act 119/2002, in the mistaken belief that it meant that a person could openly carry a weapon with the consent of the shop's owner.[10] As a reminder that even professionals can get it wrong, the corpus contains a cautionary tale about the bodyguards for the owner of a soccer team:

13. Na stadionu se oba muži objevili se samonabíjecí puškou a samonabíjecí brokovnicí v ruce. Podle policie *zbraně* sice *drželi* legálně, podle zákona je ale nemohou *nosit* viditelně. Při sportovním utkání k tomu navíc potřebují souhlas policie, který neměli. Dopustili se tak přestupku.
'Both men showed up in the stadium with a semi-automatic rifle and semi-automatic shotgun in hand. According to the police they did *possess* the *weapons* legally but according to the law they must not *carry* them openly. Moreover, for a sporting event they would need the approval of the police, which they did not have. They thus committed an offense.' (From: *Deníky Bohemia*, January 2, 2006)

Bezúhonný and Spolehlivý

The reference in that story to an offense (*přestupek*) leads us to the requirement in section 18 of Act 119/2002 that in order to obtain a gun permit, applicants must satisfy a list of conditions such as minimum age, residence, demonstration of medical fitness, and a clean (recent) criminal record. They thus have to assure the police that they are *bezúhonný* and *spolehlivý*. According to Treq, *bezúhonný* is most commonly translated into English as "respectable, blameless, upstanding, and of good

[10] See the exchange between "Marthy" and "MarK" on June 8, 2007, at http://www.strelectvi.cz/forum/muze-ochranka-viditelne-neskryte-nosit-zbran-t3503.html. "MarK" was soon set straight by another contributor, "Steiner," but many other posts in the thread suggest widespread uncertainty about what constitutes keeping and bearing at law. The thread continued into June 2014, with 164 posts.

repute or integrity," while *spolehlivý* is "reliable, sound, dependable, and credible." In the context of Czech gun law, an applicant is judged not to be *bezúhonný* if they have been convicted of one of the serious felonies enumerated in section 22 and a set time has not yet elapsed since the custodial sentence was completed, for example, 10 years since the end of a prison term of more than 2 years. An applicant is judged not to be *spolehlivý* if they have been given a suspended sentence and are still on probation, or are "demonstrably" consuming alcohol to excess or taking addictive substances, or pose a "serious danger" for having been convicted within the previous 3 years of an offense relating to arms, armaments, public order, national defense, property, civic peace, or poaching.

The detail in these sections minimizes the risk of abuse of police discretion when deciding whether to issue a permit, while ensuring that potentially dangerous applicants can be weeded out. (Mental as well as physical health checks are covered in section 20.) The corpus can be used, however, to check whether the law's usage of these two adjectives is rooted in ordinary speech or employs them as a specialized nomenclature. I queried the SYN v5 corpus for the top collocation candidates for both adjectives and their noun forms (lemmatized), using a widened window span (−5 to +5) to catch more of the context in which they appear.[11] The results are presented in Tables.8.7, 8.8, 8.9, and 8.10, ranked by logDice.

Table 8.7 Top collocation candidates for *bezúhonn**

	Lemma	Translation	Frequency	logDice	MI	T-score
1.	morálně	morally	153	8.072	13.233	12.368
2.	trestně	criminally	176	8.031	13.098	13.265
3.	mravně	morally, ethically	58	7.677	13.660	7.615
4.	občansky	civically	38	7.460	14.386	6.164
5.	způsobilý	eligible, competent, fit	131	7.319	12.300	11.443
6.	pohlížet	to view, regard, see, treat	55	6.130	11.129	7.413
7.	bezúhonný		24	6.129	11.772	4.898
8.	bezúhonnost	integrity, good repute, probity	24	6.088	11.691	4.897
9.	trestaný	punished (adj.)	38	6.004	11.141	6.162
10.	plnoletý	of age, adult	23	5.856	11.315	4.794
11.	svéprávný	legally competent, *sui juris*	18	5.674	11.278	4.241
12.	přihlédnout	to take into account	26	5.422	10.545	5.096
13.	polehčující	attenuating, mitigating (adj.)	15	5.405	11.004	3.871
14.	úkon	act, operation	84	5.303	10.067	9.157
15.	spolehlivý	reliable, sound, dependable, credible	102	5.179	9.912	10.089
16.	projevený	shown, demonstrated (adj.)	9	5.076	11.204	2.999
17.	odborně	technically, expertly, professionally	33	4.892	9.776	5.738
18.	spořádaný	orderly	13	4.830	10.152	3.602
19.	přísedící	observer, examiner	10	4.816	10.412	3.160
20.	rejstřík	register, registry	55	4.763	9.533	7.406

[11] I also ran the collocations on a window span of −3 to +3, with negligible differences in the word rankings and scores.

Table 8.8 Collocation candidates for *bezúhonnost**

	Lemma	Translation	Frequency	logDice	MI	T-score
1.	způsobilost	eligibility, competence, capacity	372	8.654	13.532	19.286
2.	přihlédnout	to take into account, allow for	189	8.261	13.326	13.746
3.	doznání	confession	84	7.761	13.234	9.164
4.	spolehlivost	reliability	216	7.593	12.411	14.694
5.	polehčující	mitigating, attenuating (adj.)	69	7.567	13.125	8.306
6.	prokazování	proof, demonstration of (something)	42	7.146	13.072	6.480
7.	bezdlužnost	not being in arrears, indebted	29	7.010	13.935	5.385
8.	bezúhonnost		45	6.955	12.518	6.707
9.	morální	moral	325	6.897	11.559	18.022
10.	čestnost	honesty, integrity	30	6.838	13.095	5.477
11.	výpis	statement, record, extract	152	6.805	11.574	12.325
12.	mravní	moral, ethical	108	6.776	11.631	10.389
13.	rejstřík	register, registry	185	6.506	11.203	13.596
14.	plnoletost	being of age, legal majority	24	6.266	12.084	4.898
15.	doložení	support, evidence, attestation	21	6.189	12.184	4.582
16.	prokazovat	to show, demonstrate, prove	91	6.139	10.920	9.534
17.	dosavadní	current, existing, to date	807	6.137	10.722	28.391
18.	trestní	criminal, penal	658	6.137	10.727	25.636
19.	osvědčení	certificate	80	6.114	10.923	8.940
20.	trestněprávní	penal, relating to criminal justice	20	6.094	12.051	4.471

Table 8.9 Collocation candidates for *spolehliv**

	Lemma	Translation	Frequency	logDice	MI	T-score
1.	plátce	payer	665	7.672	10.770	25.773
2.	politicky	politically	725	7.393	9.460	26.888
3.	partner	partner	2968	7.310	8.226	54.297
4.	pracovitý	hardworking, industrious	500	7.183	9.992	22.339
5.	spojenec	ally	557	6.752	8.483	23.535
6.	metoda	method	1241	6.730	7.796	35.069
7.	spolehlivý		494	6.545	8.241	22.153
8.	antikoncepce	contraception	281	6.442	9.600	16.741
9.	robustní	robust, sturdy	283	6.435	9.513	16.800
10.	dodávka	supply, delivery	793	6.348	7.502	28.005
11.	důvěryhodný	trustworthy	288	6.324	8.939	16.936
12.	dodavatel	supplier, contractor	713	6.306	7.504	26.555
13.	indikátor	indicator	244	6.303	9.790	15.603
14.	vysoce	highly	472	6.290	7.818	21.629
15.	výkonný	efficient, effective, executive, managing	687	6.245	7.439	26.060
16.	záruka	guarantee	467	6.197	7.668	21.504
17.	stoprocentně	one-hundred-percent (adverb)	347	6.184	8.046	18.557
18.	stabilní	stable	435	6.163	7.685	20.755
19.	rychlý	quick	1755	6.156	7.016	41.569
20.	pomocník	assistant, helper	321	6.154	8.124	17.852

Table 8.10 Collocation candidates for *spolehlivost**

	Lemma	Translation	Frequency	logDice	MI	T-score
1.	životnost	(service) life, lifetime, durability	853	8.259	11.044	29.192
2.	úvěrový	credit (adj.)	677	7.927	10.713	26.004
3.	přesnost	precision	587	7.927	10.829	24.215
4.	bezúhonnost	respectability	216	7.593	12.411	14.694
5.	provozní	operational, operating	1021	7.395	9.829	31.918
6.	robustnost	robustness	170	7.390	13.315	13.037
7.	dodávka	supply, delivery	1125	7.131	9.503	33.495
8.	spolehlivost		259	7.111	10.303	16.081
9.	jednoduchost	simplicity	227	7.096	10.489	15.056
10.	funkčnost	functionality, functioning	225	7.064	10.432	14.989
11.	bezpečnost	safety, security	1601	7.034	9.342	39.951
12.	flexibilita	flexibility	161	6.899	10.802	12.681
13.	odolnost	resilience	276	6.796	9.673	16.593
14.	trvanlivost	durability, shelf life	142	6.697	10.555	11.908
15.	hospodárnost	economy, efficiency	110	6.649	11.626	10.485
16.	upřímnost	honesty, sincerity, candor	128	6.551	10.418	11.305
17.	pracovitost	diligence, industry	118	6.551	10.714	10.856
18.	komfort	comfort, amenity	273	6.548	9.299	16.496
19.	věrnost	loyalty	158	6.525	9.857	12.556
20.	kvalita	quality	2000	6.517	8.773	44.619

Bezúhonný is not a frequently used term—it appears in the corpus 5619 times, an i.p.m. of 1.22, but it does have associations that tally with its usage in gun law to communicate the lack of a criminal record. Its noun form appears 5951 times in the corpus, and its collocations bear a similar connection to the legal, especially criminal, process (although neither it nor *spolehlivost* are concepts used in the criminal code).

More problematic is *spolehlivý*, a word that occurs more often in everyday speech and 86,656 times in the SYN v5 corpus (18.84 i.p.m.). Its noun form *spolehlivost* occurs 30,706 times, with an i.p.m. of 6.68. The collocations emanate primarily from the semantic field of commerce, not crime and punishment.

This is the discourse of modern business, in which a person is valued and evaluated for being diligent, dedicated, and efficient, whether as one's equal partner or in a hierarchy of superior and subordinate. There are secondary associations with product reliability, and to a still lesser degree with politics. In the context of gun law, it would be a good fit with section 29 of Act 119/2002, which sets out the obligation of a gun-permit holder to keep records in order, prevent misuse of the permit, and store properly any weapon or ammunition. It is a less apposite heading for section 23, which seems to be an extension, albeit less grave, of the preceding section's requirement of *bezúhonnost*.

Conclusion

Corpus analysis leaves us with the impression of a misalignment between the language of general written (especially journalistic) Czech and that of gun law. The verbs in the corpus would suggest that to "keep" a weapon is to hold or own it, and to "bear" it is to carry it like a garment or accessory. Critical legal distinctions, such as whether the gun is loaded or concealed, do not automatically come with the verbs but need to be extracted through immersion in gun law and its community—and even there, as online discussion boards show, confusion can persist. Criteria for holding a gun permit are summarized by moral modifiers that are apt but recondite (*bezúhonný*) or familiar but mismatched (*spolehlivý*).

Such matters would be problematic for only the small set of citizens who hold permits or might consider applying for one, were it not for the attempted constitutionalization of the right to keep and bear arms in response to the European Firearms Directive. The publicity surrounding the amendment raised public awareness but also the stakes for understanding what the key terms mean. Confusion over the purpose of the constitutional act was compounded by confusion about the kind of situation it envisioned, and what arms-bearing citizens would be permitted or expected to do beyond the criminal code's allowance of defensive force in extremis so long as it is proportionate to the nature of the attack.

Rather than clarify the terms of engagement, the amendment's sponsors hoped that the need to shoot would never arise if a potential attacker, unable to ascertain whether his targets could fight back (because of the legally mandated concealment of weapons), abandoned his plan. The sponsors' bill report (*Tisk* 1021) could validate this hypothetical scenario with citations to just two law review articles published in the 1990s in the USA, from which the (very tenuous) conclusion "*might* be drawn that *at least to some extent* the deterrence of a potential attacker *might* share in the drop in the number of such cases" (emphases added).[12] Accordingly, the main contribution of keeping and bearing arms to national security would lie in their not being wielded and fired, but sitting unloaded in a safe or tucked unseen into a shoulder holster. Even if this were true, many Czechs could be forgiven if that was not what first came to their minds on reading the words of the amendment.

References

Baker, P. (2006). *Using corpora in discourse analysis*. London: Bloomsbury.
Hnátková, M., Křen, M., Procházka, P., & Skoumalová, H. (2014). The SYN-series corpora of written Czech. In *Proceedings of the ninth international conference on language resources and evaluation (LREC'14)* (pp. 160–164). Reykjavík, Iceland: ELRA.

[12] One of the authors of those articles, Judge Richard Posner of the US Court of Appeals for the Seventh Circuit, was also the author of an opinion who tried to use a Google search to arrive at the plain meaning of the verb "to harbor." For a critique of that method, see Kilgarriff (2007).

Kilgarriff, A. (2007). Googleology is bad science. *Computational Linguistics, 33*, 147–151.
Kotalík, Jakub. (2017). Ústavní právo držet zbraň? Nejsme USA v 18. století, kroutí hlavou právník [A constitutional right to keep arms? We are not the USA of the eighteenth century, a lawyer shakes his head]. *iDnes.cz*. http://zpravy.idnes.cz/uprava-ustavy-ustavni-zakon-drzeni-zbrani-pravnik-jan-kysela-p6j-/domaci.aspx?c=A170103_141800_domaci_jkk. Accessed 22 Sept 2017.
Křen, Michal, Richterová, Olga, & Škrabal, Michal. (2017). Corpus SYN version 5. http://wiki.korpus.cz/doku.php/en:cnk:syn:verze5. Accessed 7 Oct 2017.
Mařík, Martin. (2016). Myslivci: mocná lobby [Hunters: A powerful lobby]. *Dotyk*. http://www.dotyk.cz/publicistika/myslivci-mocna-lobby-20161013.html. Accessed 22 September 2017.
Mouritsen, S. C. (2010). The dictionary is not a fortress: Definitional fallacies and a Corpus-based approach to plain meaning. *Brigham Young University Law Review, 35*, 1915–1980.
Mouritsen, S. C. (2017). Corpus linguistics in legal interpretation: An evolving interpretative framework. *International Journal of Language and Law, 6*, 67–89.
Müller, F. (2000). Observations on the role of precedent in modern continental European law from the perspective of structuring legal theory. *Stellenbosch Law Review, 11*, 426–436.
Ortner, D. (2016). The merciful corpus: The rule of lenity, ambiguity and corpus linguistics. *Boston University Public Interest Law Journal, 25*, 101–142.
Phillips, J. C., Ortner, D. M., & Lee, T. R. (2016). Corpus linguistics & original public meaning: A new tool to make originalism more empirical. *Yale Law Journal Forum, 126*, 21–32.
Pilnáček, M. (2017). *Hodnocení bezpečnostní situace v ČR a Evropě - Prosinec 2016* [*Evaluation of the security situation in the Czech Republic and in Europe – December 2016*]. Prague, Czech Republic: Centrum pro výzkum veřejného mínění, Sociologický ústav AV ČR.
Rychlý, P. (2008). A lexicographer-friendly association score. In P. Sojka & A. Horák (Eds.), *Proceedings of recent advances in Slavonic natural language processing* (pp. 6–9). Brno, Czech Republic: Masaryk University.
Sedláček, Petr. (2010. *Právní úprava držení a nošení zbraní v letech 1945–1989*. Diplomová práce [*The legal regulation of keeping and bearing arms in 1945–1989*. Thesis], Právnická fakulta Masarykovy univerzity, Brno.
Šimek, Jiří. (2017). Počet držitelů zbrojních průkazů a zbraní v roce 2016 [The number of holders of gun permits and weapons in 2016]. https://gunlex.cz/clanky/hlavni-clanky/75-dulezite/2641-pocet-drzitelu-zbrojnich-prukazu-a-zbrani-v-roce-2016. Accessed 26 May 2017.
Solum, L. B. (2010). The interpretation-construction distinction. *Constitutional Commentary, 27*, 95–118.
ver. (2017). Majitelé zbraní: České zákony o zbraních patří k nejlepším na světě. Ústava je má ochránit [Gun owners: Czech laws on weapons are among the best in the world. The constitution should protect them]. Česká televize 24. http://www.ceskatelevize.cz/ct24/domaci/2027510-majitele-zbrani-ceske-zakony-o-zbranich-patri-k-nejlepsim-na-svete-ustava-je-ma. Accessed 26 May 2017.

Bills and Sponsor Reports

Tisk 1021. (2017). Novela ústav. z. o bezpečnosti České republiky [Amendment to the constitutional act on the security of the Czech Republic]. http://www.psp.cz/sqw/text/tiskt.sqw?O=7&CT=1021&CT1=0. Accessed 7 October 2017.
Tisk 1071. (2001). Vládní návrh zákona o zbraních – EU [Government draft of an act on weapons – EU]. http://www.psp.cz/sqw/text/tiskt.sqw?o=3&ct=1071&ct1=0. Accessed 7 Oct 2017.

Promulgated Acts

Act 119/2002. Zákon o střelných zbraních a střelivu [Law on weapons and ammunition]. In *Sbírka zákonů* [*Collection of laws*] (Vol. 52, pp. 3038–3070.

Act 288/1995. Zákon o střelných zbraních a střelivu [Law on weapons and ammunition]. In *Sbírka zákonů* [*Collection of laws*] (Vol. 75, pp. 3922–3942).

Constitutional Act 110/1998. Ústavní zákon ze dne 22. dubna 1998 o bezpečnosti České republiky [Constitutional act of 22 April 1998 on the security of the Czech Republic]. In *Sbírka zákonů* [*Collection of laws*] (Vol. 39, pp. 5386–5387).

Chapter 9
Image of Politicians and Gender in Czech Daily Newspapers

Adrian Jan Zasina

Abstract The issue of the representation of women in politics has received increasing global attention in recent years. This article discusses the representation of female politicians in the Czech daily press, contrasted to that of male politicians. It uses corpus methods to investigate the extent to which the image of women in politics in Czech media is stereotypical. The study is based on adjectival collocations of two lexemes: *politik* 'male politician' and *politička* 'female politician.' The research uses a subset of the SYN corpus, which contains texts published in six different editions of Czech daily newspapers from 1991 to 2014. Two case studies were carried out: one focuses on the positive and negative connotations of premodifiers collocating with the target lexemes to reveal the similarities and dissimilarities between male and female politicians; the other investigates the top 20 collocates for both lexemes with attention to tokens that capture the nature of prevailing discourse. This study brings new insight into this area in contrast to similar studies that highlight gender differences: the behavior of the adjectival collocates of the two target lexemes reveals a more complex picture of gender image. It shows similarities rather than differences between men and women in politics and projects a "non-stereotypical" image of female politicians. These attribute properties are more subtle than outright stereotypes. What is more, in some spheres women are represented as having potential, although they are also represented as already holding power.

Keywords Women in politics · Gender studies · Corpus linguistics · Corpus-based approach · Language and gender · Discourse analysis · Sociolinguistics

---

A. J. Zasina (✉)
Univerzita Karlova, Prague, Czech Republic
e-mail: adrian.zasina@ff.cuni.cz

M. Fidler, V. Cvrček (eds.), *Taming the Corpus*, Quantitative Methods in the Humanities and Social Sciences, https://doi.org/10.1007/978-3-319-98017-1_9

Introduction

Gender in politics has taken center stage in several disciplines during the last 50–60 years. The political significance of gender originates in the 1970s (Lovenduski, 1992, p. 603) and has been expanded to other areas of scholarship. Besides political scientists (e.g., Lovenduski, 1992; Mackay, 2004; Lim, 2009) and sociologists (e.g., Čermáková, 1995; Havelková, 1999; Kunovich, 2003), linguists now analyze gender and politics as well (e.g., Valdrová, 1997; Shaw, 2000; Lakoff, 2003).

The aim of the present chapter is to examine how journalistic texts reflect the situation of female politicians relative to male ones after 1989 in the Czech Republic. In particular, it focuses on the collocational patterns of adjectives that premodify two lemmas in selected Czech daily newspapers from 1991 to 2014: *politik* 'male politician' and *politička* 'female politician.'

At the same time, the paper explores the possible presence of stereotypical gender representation in these texts. By gender "stereotypes," I mean the identification of two desirable identities: "hegemonic masculinity" and "preferred femininity" (Valdrová, 2006, pp. 8–10). Many psychological studies state "that a typical woman is seen as warm, gentle, kind, and passive, whereas a typical man is viewed as tough, aggressive, and assertive" (Huddy & Terkildsen, 1993, p. 121). Men and women are associated, respectively, with activity and passivity; the stereotypical woman is weak, dependent, modest, and sensitive, while the stereotypical man powerful, self-confident, brave, rational, etc.[1]

A similarly stereotypical representation of men and women has been noticed by linguists as well. Previous studies (e.g., Pearce, 2008; Caldas-Coulthard & Moon, 2010) report that women are not stereotypically represented as being in a powerful position. Czech data however presents a different view: female politicians, just as male politicians, are represented as having strong personalities but, in some spheres, are represented as having "potential," with the negative meaning expressed in a more indirect, subtle way.

First, I describe the theoretical framework used in this study, outlining a few examples of studies on discourse and gender. After briefly presenting the overview of the representation of women in politics, I explain the methodology and the data, and justify the selection of the subcorpus and the examined lexemes. Next, I zoom in on the analysis of adjectival collocations. Finally, I conclude and discuss the results.

Corpus-Assisted Discourse Studies and Gender

This chapter applies an approach to discourse laid out in *Corpus-assisted discourse studies* (CADS). CADS is a "form of discourse analysis that uses corpus linguistics methods and tends to take a critical approach to the analysis" (Baker & Ellece, 2011,

---

[1] Hausen (1976, p. 368) presents a more detailed comparison of typically grouped male and female characteristics.

pp. 24–25). In other words, it offers us a new perspective on exploring topics focusing on social and political issues. Researchers use specialized software to identify frequencies of particular linguistic phenomena and/or word collocations in large sets of language data as possible symptoms of a specific discourse and ideological stance. CADS combines close reading with statistical analysis that allows the analyst to establish a detailed image of what is typical for a specific type of discourse (Partington & Marchi, 2015, p. 217), shedding new insights into how discourses function. The following are the three most widely used statistical techniques in CADS (ibid., p. 217): frequency distribution of words and clusters (also called n-grams or lexical bundles (cf. Chlumská, this volume); keyword analysis (cf. Fidler and Cvrček, this volume), and the use of concordances that display the context before and after a node word (McEnery & Hardie, 2012, pp. 35–37). Moreover, corpus linguistics is a suitable method to explore discourse when corpora contain large amounts of texts representing natural language (Baker, 2006, p. 13). A researcher's biases can be minimized by conducting quantitative research using large corpus data.

The vast majority of corpus-based research on gender examines representations of men and women in English-language discourse. One of the first studies is by Pearce (2008) who examines collocations of the lexemes *man* and *woman* in the British National Corpus. Pearce divides collocates into grammatical categories. Then, he analyzes their collocational behavior and interprets the cultural significance they represent. He concludes that collocations of the lexemes *man* and *woman* are often of a stereotypical nature (e.g., *lead*, *conquer*, and *wise man* vs. *weep*, *cry*, and *hysterical woman*). Macalister (2011) explores gender representation in texts for children in the *School Journal*. The main objective was to capture changes in gender roles in the twentieth-century writing by sampling at 30-year intervals. The study shows that female characters have become more visible and are represented as being more independent of male characters over time. Taylor (2013) is one of the few scholars who focuses on the similarities between the genders, rather than the differences. Her case study provides analysis of the lexemes *boy* and *girl* in the British press in 1993, 2005, and 2010; she concludes that dissimilarities outweigh similarities, however. Stubbs (1996, pp. 81–100) examines two short messages from Baden-Powell, the ideological leader and founder of the Scout Movement, to the scouts and the girl guides.[2] He uses collocations, words, and grammar structures to demonstrate that these messages contain a male-chauvinistic character.

A recent influential gender corpus analysis has been carried out by Baker. He examines collocations of single men and women, namely *bachelor* and *spinster* (Baker, 2006, pp. 95–120, 2010a, pp. 129–130). This study clearly demonstrates that *bachelor* has a positive connotation while *spinster* traditionally has a negative connotation. Baker (2014, pp. 157–195) also focuses on the collocations of lexeme *man* in dating adverts. His research is based on three corpora consisting of personal adverts in Indian English, Singaporean English, and Australian English. The results show how the lexeme emphasizes different qualities in these three different countries:

[2] The Girl Scouts were introduced later.

Indians underline social status and education, Australians concentrate more on personality, and Singaporeans on ethnicity. Shaw (2000) provides a slightly different type of corpus-based gender discourse analysis. She examines gender in political debates in the British parliament and shows that men interrupt speeches more often than women.

Gender in language is also discussed by Czech linguists (Čmejrková, 1995; Valdrová, 1997) predominantly using qualitative methods; these studies explore the preferential use of generic nouns to refer to men and women, rather than using both the masculine and feminine forms. Čmejrková (2003) focuses on the relationship between grammatical gender and references to women with a focus on noun asymmetries and lexical gaps. Valdrová (2006) examines referential devices for men and women in society and the image of gender in advertisements and media language. Other scholars study women's magazines to explore gender differences reflected in their representation of the relationship between men and women. Hoffmannová (2004) concludes that magazines are full of stereotypical gender roles. Šonková (2011) was perhaps the first to use quantitative methods to investigate gender differences in the spoken language, using the Prague Corpus of Spoken Czech (Čermák, Adamovičová, & Pešička, 2001). Her study shows that women tend to use a greater number of expressions connected with emotions than their male counterparts. The present chapter specifically focuses on the Czech media's images of female and male politicians.

The Representation of Women in Politics

In this section, I present some motivations for examining the media image of women in politics with a focus on Czech data.

The existing literature on gender and politics focuses mostly on *differences*: Lovenduski, e.g., states that more visibility and power are ascribed to men than to women in public discourse and particularly in political discourse (2001, p. 744). The recent global increase in women's participation, however, suggests a need to revisit a view that focuses on differences. The data from the Inter-Parliamentary Union (2015) shows a rising trajectory of the representation of women internationally in the single and lower houses of parliament from 1995 through 2015: the representation of women shows an overall upward tendency, from 1995 (11.3%) to 2015 (22.1%).

According to this report, the highest increase is observed in the Americas with 13.7 percentage points (26.4% in 2015), and the lowest in Asia (5.3 percentage points; 18.5%) and in Nordic countries (5.1 percentage points; 41.5%). The underlying factors for these numbers, however, may vary widely. A fast increase in the representation of women in the Americas is mostly caused by new or revised quota policies (Inter-Parliamentary Union, 2015, pp. 4–5). While the slower growth in

Nordic countries is due to the consistently higher number of women already integrated into politics, the similarly slow increase in Asia is most likely caused by the unfavorable status of women in the public sphere (ibid., pp. 5, 9–10). A slower but nonetheless increasing tendency in the Arab nations might be caused by the democratization processes in the region and movements for women's political rights (16.1% in 2015; ibid., pp. 7–8).

Increased of women participation in politics may also be a result of gender quotas. Some countries apply political party quotas or legalized quotas and/or a combination of the two. Others reserve seats for female politicians. In 2015, the largest share of women's political representation was found in Rwanda (63.8%), which reserves seats for women, and in Bolivia (53.1%), which applies political party quotas (Inter-Parliamentary Union, 2015, p. 13). But, the existence of gender quotas is not the only cause for increased female participation in politics. Andorra, Cuba, and Seychelles already had high percentages of female politicians (50%, 48.9%, and 43.6%, respectively) without introducing gender quotas. The raw numbers of women in politics therefore evidently do not give a complete story of where women stand in politics in a state and/or regions.

In view of the complexity involved accounting for the participation of women in politics, this chapter explores how the Czech media views the topic. In contrast to other European countries, the share of women in parliament for the Czech Republic in 2015 is not high (19%, cf. Finland (42.5%) and Spain (41.1%); Inter-Parliamentary Union, 2015, pp. 16–19). Against the backdrop of these numbers, the findings in this study are meaningful in two aspects: it not only presents an in-depth view of women in politics but also serves as a case study to demonstrate the difficulties in using numbers of women alone to assess where they stand in politics.

In the following sections, I will present the data, methodology, and adequacy of the subcorpus and the examined lexemes (section 'Data and Method'), followed by my analysis (section 'Analysis'), which is divided into two case studies. These studies (sections 'Evaluative Adjectives Collocating with *Politik* and *Politička*' and 'Top 20 Collocates with *Politik* and *Politička*') discuss the analysis of collocations from two different angles and their interpretations. Finally, I will summarize my observations in 'Conclusions.'

Data and Method

The present section is divided into three subsections. The first presents the language corpus used in the case studies and its contents; the next describes the method used in this study. The last subsection explains the choice of the corpus and the lexemes; this part also comments on the occurrences of the lexemes in daily newspapers from 1991 to 2014.

Data

My research was conducted on the material of the SYN corpus version 4 (Hnátková, Křen, Procházka, & Skoumalová, 2014; Křen et al., 2016) which consists of all synchronic written corpora in the SYN series (SYN2000, SYN2005, SYN2006PUB, SYN2009PUB, SYN2010, SYN2013PUB, and SYN2015) and additionally contains an as-yet unpublished journalistic component that exceeds 200 million words predominantly from the years 2010–2014 in yearly volumes.

For the purpose of my study, I worked with a subcorpus that contains the six most popular daily newspapers in the Czech Republic, i.e., *Mladá Fronta Dnes* (MF Dnes), *Lidové noviny* (LN), *Deník Moravia* (DM), *Deník Bohemia* (DB), *Právo*, and *Hospodářské noviny* (HN). All the articles in this subcorpus were published in the years 1991–2014.[3] The table below presents the total number of tokens from each newspaper (Table 9.1).

MF Dnes, LN, Právo, and HN are the national news publications with the most subscribers. DM and DB are regional presses. As seen in Table 9.2, the dailies represent diverse political orientations

Table 9.1 Subcorpus structure[a]

Daily	MF Dnes	LN	DM	DB	Právo	HN	Total
Total	825,379,860	268,637,818	474,248,541	842,330,128	355,693,962	220,734,144	2,987,024,453

[a]Not all the tokens are selected from 1991: MF Dnes (1992–2014). DM and DB (2004–2014), and Právo and HN (1995–2014). More detailed information is available upon request

Table 9.2 Descriptions of daily presses in subcorpus

Daily	Website	Political orientation	Description
MF Dnes	http://www.mfdnes.cz/	Center-right, liberal	One of the most subscribed daily newspapers[a] in the Czech Republic. Founded in 1990, *MF Dnes* has one of the biggest editorial offices in the country
LN	http://www.lidovky.cz/	Center-right, liberal conservatism	One of the most read newspapers. Similar circulation as MF Dnes. LN states that its history dates back to the nineteenth century
HN	http://ihned.cz/	Center-right, liberal conservatism	First appeared in 1990. Focus on economy politics
Právo	http://www.pravo.cz/	Center-left, social democrat	Founded in the early 1990s. A left-wing newspaper with focus on social issues
DB and DM	http://www.denik.cz/	Regional focus does not allow a single nationwide orientation	Regional newspapers from a single publisher (Vltava Labe Media). They consist of 71 regional newspapers in Bohemia, Moravia, and Silesia. World and regional news

[a]Cf. https://domaci.ihned.cz/c1-64423550-nejctenejsim-denikem-zustal-blesk-roste-zajem-o-casopisy-novinam-ctenari-ubyvaji

[3] Newspapers beginning from the year 1989 were not included because data collection of journalistic texts for the CNC did not start until 1991.

Method

The main goal of my study is to examine the relative image of female politicians in Czech daily newspapers, based on collocations involving the lexemes *politik* 'male politician' and *politička* 'female politician.'[4] The lemmas *politik* and *politička* were analyzed only in the singular forms because the masculine plural form of *politik* (i.e., *politici*) can refer to both male and female politicians.

The corpus interface KonText (Machálek & Křen, 2013) was used to extract collocation candidates. In the subcorpus of journalistic texts, I looked for collocation candidates by lemma rather than by word form. The minimum collocate frequency in the corpus and the minimum collocate frequency in the span were set to five hits. Collocates were identified within a span of four words on the left side, as this study focuses on attributive adjectives, which predominantly precede a noun (Cvrček, 2010, pp. 303–304). The LogDice measure was used to rank the adjectival collocates. Upon collecting the first 350 collocation candidates[5] for each lexeme, I sorted them manually and identified 184 adjectives for *politik* and 154 for *politička* for my analysis.[6]

The categories of adjectives used in this study result from a synthesis of the studies by Caldas-Coulthard and Moon (2010) and Zasina (2016). Caldas-Coulthard and Moon (2010, p. 111) divide adjectives into three main categories: functionalization, identification, and appraisement, with each group breaking down into further subcategories. Functionalization distinguishes subcategories: occupation, role, and function. Identification contains four subgroups: classification (age, gender, provenance, ethnicity, sexuality, class, wealth, religion, politics, etc.), relational (kinship, work relationship, personal relationship, etc.), physical (size, coloring, appearance, clothing, attractiveness, etc.), and personal (emotional state, behavioral traits, intellect, morality, etc.). Finally, appraisement has general evaluatives and affectives as subcategories. Zasina's categorization is partially based on Caldas-Coulthard and Moon's study, but the number of categories is reduced to ten with the following labels: age, strength/supernatural power, appearance/attractiveness, character/psychological state/adjectives evoking positive/negative emotions, maternity, nationality/ethnicity, action, material status, sexual orientation, and others.

This study, as seen in Table 9.3, uses seven categories—a somewhat reduced version of Zasina (2016), roughly speaking—omitting the categories of strength and supernatural power, maternity, action, material status, and sexual orientation, which I consider redundant, and adding two categories: one adopted from Caldas-Coulthard and Moon, which concerns provenance, and the other new category referring to political orientation. Zasina's category of evoking positive and negative emotions

[4] These words are the best targets of my research because they provide the most generic reference, compared to more specific terms such as *poslanec/poslankyně* 'MP,' *starosta/starostka* 'mayor,' *primátor/primátorka* 'mayor of a city'; these lexemes are also less frequent than *politik/politička* and more often used to refer to specific individuals. As my goal is to have a maximally general image of politicians in the press, I did not include these lexemes in my analysis.

[5] The given results of collocation candidates contained other parts of speech as well.

[6] The lowest LogDice index for *politička* is 1.26 and for *politik* is 3.30.

Table 9.3 Semantic categories of adjectives collocating with the lexemes *politik* and *politička*

Semantic category	Example
Age specification	*padesátiletý politik* '50-year-old politician,' *třiapadesátiletá politička* '53-year-old female politician'
Appearance and attractiveness	*mladý politik* 'young politician,' *blonďatá/pohledná/elegantní politička* 'blond and beautiful/pretty/ elegant female politician'
Character, social, and emotional states	Character traits (including the level of intelligence): *důvěryhodný/zkušený/ambiciózní politik* 'trustworthy/experienced/ ambitious politician,' *charismatická/zásadová/pracovitá politička* 'charismatic/principled/ hardworking female politician,' *inteligentní/profesionální poltik/ politička* 'Intelligent/professional male/female politician,' positive emotional states: *populární* 'popular,' *vlivný* 'influential,' negative emotional states: *kontroverzní* 'controversial,' *špatný* 'bad,' adjectives characterized by positive or negative prosody: *popravená politička* 'executed female politician'
Nationality and ethnicity	*slovenský/černošský politik* 'Slovak/black politician,' *pákistánská/ palestinská politička* 'Pakistani/Palestinian female politician'
Political orientation	*konservativní* 'conservative,' *demokratický* 'democratic,' *liberální* 'liberal'
Provenance	*lokální* 'local,' *regionální* 'regional,' *bavorský* 'Bavarian'
Others	*typický* 'typical,' *bývalý* 'ex-,' *normální* 'normal, typical'

was relabeled as "character, social, and emotional states" to avoid possible confusion, because it does not consist of only evaluative adjectives. This category is the most heterogeneous and consists of adjectives having a potential to evoke either positive or negative emotion; such association can be direct (e.g., *populární politik* 'popular politician' evoking positive emotional state) or indirect (e.g., *zavražděná politička* 'murdered female politician' evoking negative emotional state).

Indirect association is closely connected with semantic prosody (Sinclair, 2004) which is not implicit, but realized in specific contexts; *popravený* 'executed' is not an evaluative adjective, but it evokes negative emotion in discourse. The words in this category are for the most part evaluative adjectives and adjectives arousing (or having the potential to arouse) positive and negative emotions.

I categorized these adjectives to the best of my knowledge by looking at their functions by individual context. Table 9.3 above presents semantic categories with some examples.

Adjectives concerning age, appearance/attractiveness, nationality/ethnicity, political orientation, provenance, and not categorized adjectives were separated from the data since they do not help characterize the image of gender. All the other adjectives were subject to further analysis.

Adequacy of the Subcorpus and the Examined Lexemes

This section attempts to justify the selection of the subcorpus and the lexemes. It summarizes the representation of the lexemes *politik* and *politička* from 1991 to 2014 in the subcorpus presented in section 'Data.' It is a sufficiently large set to analyze prevailing tendencies in the use of references to female and male politicians over a 24-year period.

Figures 9.1 and 9.2 show relative frequencies (instances per million[7]) of lemmas *politik* 'male politician' and *politička* 'female politician' in the singular over time.

The figures clearly show different trajectories. While the initial high frequency of references to male politicians gradually declines, the frequency of references to female politicians shows a continuous increase. Not only do the trends develop in opposite directions (Spearman's correlation coefficient $r = -0.59$), but their frequency bounds also differ; in 2014, there are 33.03 ipm for male and 3.59 ipm for female.

The data is consistent with the observation by Šprincová and Adamusová who note a growing number of women in politics in the Czech Republic (Šprincová & Adamusová, 2014, p. 23; www.padesatprocent.cz). The representation of women in the Czech Lower House from 1996 until 2017 grew by 7% and representation in the upper house grew by 8.7% (until 2016), with continual upward tendencies.[8] The increased references to female politicians are most probably connected with the increased appearance (and therefore visibility) of women in politics, resulting in more frequent dissemination of information about them in the daily press. To the

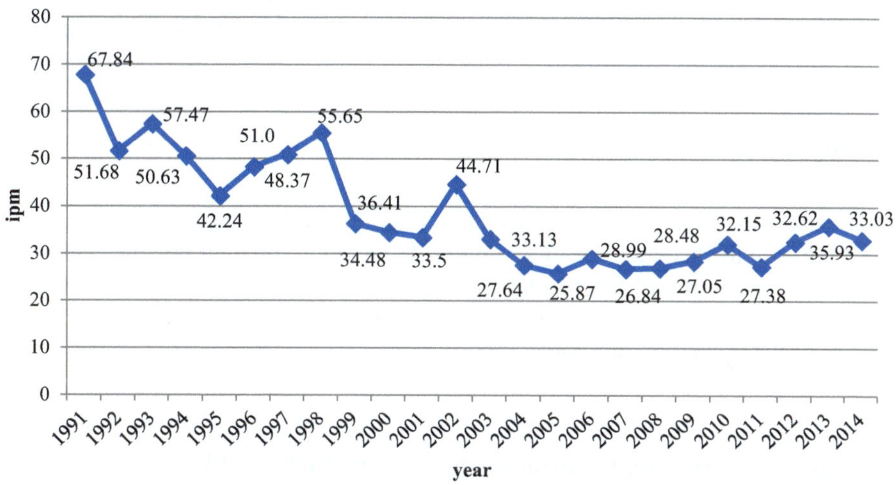

Fig. 9.1 Instances per million of the lexeme *politik* in daily newspapers, 1991–2014

[7] This decision is based on the fact that the number of texts varies from year to year.

[8] This paper does not present data from the early 1990s because the Czech Republic was a part of Czechoslovakia till the end of 1992 and its statistics include Slovakia as well (cf. www.volby.cz).

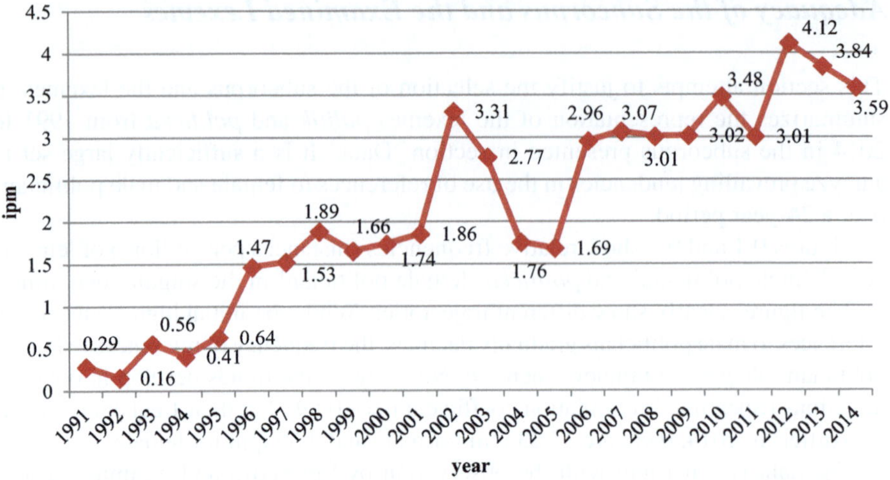

Fig. 9.2 Instances per million of the lexeme *politička* in daily newspapers, 1991–2014

extent that the results from this section are in accord with the actual trends in increased female participation in Czech politics, it is reasonable to assume that the selection of the subcorpus and the two lexemes constitute adequate material to explore the image of female politicians.[9]

The following section will present two kinds of collocation analysis and will answer our research question about the image of female politicians in Czech journalistic texts and how it differs from or resembles the image of male politicians.

Analysis

The current analysis consists of two parts. First, I look at evaluative adjectives collocating with the lexemes *politik* and *politička* and focus on their positive and negative meanings to reveal the similarities and differences between male and female politicians. Second, I discuss the top 20 collocates for both lexemes and capture the nature of the prevailing discourse.

Evaluative Adjectives Collocating with Politik *and* Politička

In this study, the most appropriate set for analysis is the semantic category "character, social, and emotional states" because it describes positive and negative character traits as well as emotions. Some of the selected adjectives are evaluative and enable

[9] The Czech media covers female politicians not only at home but also abroad. This study therefore reflects the image of female politicians in general.

us to rate the degrees of good and bad qualities. I first manually checked the context of collocation candidates to verify that the collocations are premodifying adjectives.[10] In the end, I obtained 129 types of adjectival collocates co-occurring with *politik* and 72 with *politička*. I divided the adjectives into two groups: "positive" and "negative." Positive adjectives are those adjectives that either evoke positive emotions in the reader or describe positive human characteristics. In contrast, negative adjectives are those adjectives that either evoke negative emotions in the reader or describe negative human characteristics. Table 9.4 below shows all of the adjectival collocates (lemmas).

Table 9.5 shows that positive and negative attributes are almost equally shared by male and female politicians. The "positive collocates" for *politik* account for 63.57% of the types and the negative 36.43%. Similarly, the positive collocates for *politička* comprise 69.44% and negative 30.56%. The results do not sufficiently substantiate Lakoff's statement that a powerful woman is perceived in media as ambivalent, that she is "variously sexualized, objectified, or ridiculed," and that she is also reduced "to her traditional role of *object*, one who is seen rather than one who sees acts" (Lakoff, 2003, pp. 172–176).

The shared adjectival collocates differ by gender. Table 9.6 presents the percentages of positive and negative collocates that modify both *politik* and *politička*. Both lexemes share 44 positive and 12 negative adjectives: the shared positive adjectives constitute 34.11% of all the adjectival collocates for *politik* (and almost 54% of all positive collocates for *politik*) and 61.11% for *politička* (88% of positive); the shared negative adjectives constitute 9.30% for *politik* (25.53% of all negative collocates for *politik*) and 16.67% for *politička* (54.55% out of the negative ones). It is important to point out that the apparent difference between the total percentages of shared positive and negative adjectives out of all collocations (43.41 for *politik* and 77.78 for *politička*) does not lead to an observation that Czech newspapers draw a straightforward distinction between the genders.

However, a better picture of the portrayal of genders in politics is obtained by comparing positive and negative context based on the number of tokens (Table 9.7). The positive meaning for both lexemes, *politik* and *politička,* is comparable, although the positive meaning for female politicians is slightly higher (18.28% vs. 17.59% for male politicians). In the case of negative meaning, at 3.02%, female politicians have almost twice as high a percentage of negative adjectives than male politicians with 1.64%. It confirms the statement in other corpus studies (Baker, 2006; Romaine, 2000 *in* Pearce, 2008) that words with negative meanings tend to appear more frequently with female rather than male counterparts. At the same

[10] Since Czech lemmatization (cf. Jelínek, 2008; Jelínek & Petkevič, 2011) labels adjectives with the prefix *ne-* as a surface manifestation of a positive form (e.g., adjective *nepopulární* 'unpopular' is lemmatized as *populární* 'popular'), I manually checked all the instances of each lemma and grouped the forms with *ne-* as a separate lemma. There were also examples of indirect negation, such as *ne příliš populární politik* 'not a very popular politician,' *Nemyslím, že je tak vynikající politik* 'I do not think he is such a outstanding politician'; these instances were rare and negligible.

time, however, the results above show that both female and male politicians in Czech daily newspapers are for the most part praised.

Moreover, female politicians are not represented with stereotypically "feminine" attributes, as will be shown in the following section. These findings are unexpected in contrast to the observations in other studies on English. Earlier research (Caldas-

Table 9.4 Positive and negative collocations of lexemes *politik* and *politička*

	Politik	Politička
Positive	aktivní 'active,' ambiciózní 'ambitious,' chari[sz] matický[a] 'charismatic,' chytrý 'clever,' ctižádostivý 'ambitious,' čelný 'leading,' čestný 'honorable,' čitelný 'legible,' dynamický 'dynamic,' důvěryhodný 'trustworthy,' energický 'energetic,' (nejlépe) hodnocený[b] '(the best) rated,' ideální 'ideal,' inteligentní 'intelligent,' kariérní 'career,' kompetentní 'competent,' konkrétní 'concrete, specific,' korektní 'upright,' mediální 'media,' mocný 'powerful,' moderní 'modern,' moudrý 'wise,' nadějný 'promising,' nekontroverzní 'uncontroversial,' nezkorumpovaný 'uncorrupted,' nezávislý 'independent,' oblíbený 'favorite,' obratný 'skillful,' odpovědný 'responsible,' odvážný 'courageous,' ostřílený 'seasoned,' osvícený 'enlightened,' perspektivní 'perspective,' poctivý 'honest,' populární 'popular,' pracovitý 'hardworking,' pragmatický 'pragmatic,' profesionální 'professional,' prominentní 'prominent,' protřelý 'savvy,' prozíravý 'farsighted,' přední 'leading,' (vysoce) postavený[c] '(high-)ranking,' racionální 'rational,' razantní 'vigorous,' realistický 'realistic,' reformní 'reform,' respektovaný 'respected,' rozhodný 'resolute,' rozumný 'reasonable,' rozvážný 'prudent,' rázný 'spirited,' schopný 'capable,' sebevědomý 'confident,' seriózní 'serious,' skutečný 'real,' slušný 'decent,' soudný 'judicious,' správný 'right,' sympatický 'likable,' šikovný 'nifty,' špičkový 'top,' talentovaný 'talented,' tvrdý 'tough,' umírněný 'moderate,' uvolněný 'relaxed,' uvážlivý 'prudent,' uznávaný 'moderate,' úspěšný 'successful,' vlivný 'influential,' vrcholný 'supreme,' vrcholový 'top,' vynikající 'outstanding,' výrazný 'significant,' významný 'significant,' význačný 'prominent,' vzdělaný 'educated,' zdatný 'proficient,' zkušený 'experienced,' známý 'famous,' zodpovědný 'responsible,' zásadový 'principled'	aktivní 'active,' ambiciózní 'ambitious,' cílevědomý 'ambitious, go-getter,' čelný 'leading,' dynamický 'dynamic,' důvěryhodný 'trustworthy,' energický 'energetic,' chari[sz] matický 'charismatic,' chytrý 'clever,' inteligentní 'intelligent,' mocný 'powerful,' nadějný 'promising,' nekompromisní 'uncompromising,' neústupný 'unyielding,' oblíbený 'favorite,' obratný 'skillful,' odvážný 'courageous,' ostřílený 'seasoned,' populární 'popular,' pracovitý 'hardworking,' pragmatický 'pragmatic,' profesionální 'professional,' prominentní 'prominentní,' proslulý 'renowned,' přední 'leading,' (vysoce) postavený '(high-) ranking,' razantní 'vigorous,' realistický 'realistic,' respektovaný 'respected,' rázný 'spirited,' schopný 'capable,' sebevědomý 'confident,' seriózní 'serious,' slušný 'decent,' sympatický 'likable,' šarmantní 'charming,' tvrdý 'tough,' umírněný 'moderate,' uznávaný 'recognized,' úspěšný 'successful,' vlivný 'influential,' vrcholný 'supreme,' vrcholový 'top,' vytrvalý 'resilient,' výrazný 'significant,' významný 'significant,' vzdělaný educated, zkušený 'experienced,' známý 'famous,' zásadový 'principled'

(continued)

Table 9.4 (continued)

	Politik	Politička
Negative	arogantní 'arrogant,' bezvýznamný 'insignificant,' (nejhůře) hodnocený '(the worst) rated,' kontroverzní 'controversial,' neaktivní 'inactive,' nechari[sz]matický 'non-charismatic,' nečestný 'dishonest,' nečitelný 'unclear,' nedůvěryhodný 'untrustworthy,' neinteligentní 'unintelligent,' nekompetentní 'incompetent,' nekorektní 'uprigh,' nemediální 'non-media,' nemoderní 'unprogressive,' nemoudrý 'unwise,' neoblíbený 'unpopular,' neobratný 'clumsy,' neodpovědný 'irresponsible,' nepoctivý 'dishonest,' nepopulární 'unpopular,' neprofesionální 'unprofessional,' neprozíravý 'improvident,' nerazantní 'unvigorous,' nerealistický 'unrealistic,' nerozhodný 'indecisive,' nerozvážný 'thoughtless,' neschopný 'unable,' neseriózní 'unserious,' nesoudný 'injudicious,' nesympatický 'unlovable,' neuvolněný 'not relaxed,' neuvážlivý 'imprudent,' neúspěšný 'unsuccessful,' nevzdělaný 'uneducated,' nevýrazný 'unclear,' nevýznamný 'insignificant,' nezkušený 'inexperienced,' neznámý 'unknown,' nezodpovědný 'irresponsible,' obviněný 'accused,' špatný 'bad,' vysloužilý 'retired,' zavražděný 'murdered,' zesnulý 'deceased,' zhrzený 'despised,' zkorumpovaný 'corrupt,' závislý 'dependent'	kontroverzní 'controversial,' křehký 'fragile,' naivní 'naive,' napadený 'attacked,' nedůvěryhodný 'untrustworthy,' neobratný 'clumsy,' nepohodlný 'inconvenient,' nepopulární 'unpopular,' neschopný 'unable,' nesympatický 'unlovable,' neúspěšný 'unsuccessful,' nevýrazný 'unclear,' nezkušený 'inexperienced,' neznámý 'unknown,' odsouzený 'condemned,' popravený 'executed,' postřelený 'been shot,' unesený 'kidnaped,' vězněný 'imprisoned,' zabitý 'killed,' zavražděný 'murdered,' zesnulý 'deceased'

[a]This adjective appears in two different spellings: *(ne)charizmatický* and *(ne)charismatický* (hereinafter *(ne)chari[sz]matický*). Both were counted as a single lemma.

[b]The adjective *hodnocený* is not evaluative per se. However, it acquires evaluating meaning when combined with an adverb that is either positive (*nejlépe* 'the best,' *nejvýše* 'the best,' *dobře* 'the best,' *nejpozitivněji* 'the most positively,' *přiměřeně* 'reasonably') or negative (*nejnegativněji* 'the most negative,' *nejhůře* 'the worst,' *nejpříkřeji* 'the most harshly'). For the purpose of this analysis, I took into account the combination adverb + *hodnocený*

[c]This adjective appears only in a phrase with adverb *vysoce* 'high,' otherwise as a word in isolation reports a different meaning—, standing'

Table 9.5 Percentage of positive/negative adjectives collocating with *politik* and *politička*

Lexeme	All	% all	Positive	% positive	Negative	% negative
Politik	129	100	82	63.57	47	36.43
Politička	72	100	50	69.44	22	30.56

Table 9.6 Adjectival collocates shared by both *politik* and *politička*

Lexeme	Total	%	Positive adjectives	% shared out of positive	Negative adjectives	% of shared out of negative	% shared out of all
Politik	129	100	44	53.66	12	25.53	43.41
Politička	72	100		88.00		54.55	77.78

Table 9.7 Percentage of positive and negative contexts for studied lexemes based on tokens

Lexeme	Positive tokens	% positive	Negative tokens	% negative	Total tokens
Politik	17,012	17.59	1583	1.64	96,691
Politička	1511	18.28	250	3.02	8268

Coulthard & Moon, 2010) based on British newspaper articles argues that men are described in terms of their power, function, and social status in society, while women are portrayed as far from being in powerful positions and are more likely to be described in terms of their appearance and sexuality. Also, Pearce (2008) concludes that collocates of *men* and *women* point to gender stereotypes. His study shows that men in the British National Corpus are associated with competitiveness, adventurousness, independence, rationality, and aggression and are shown as strong, rugged, and muscular characters, while women are characterized with gentility, cooperativeness, passivity, emotions, sympathy, and physical weakness.

Positive Adjectives

Table 9.8 demonstrates that anticipated stereotypes for female politicians are not predominant. It presents positive collocates that modify only male politicians, only female politicians, and politicians of both genders. There is a big overlap between both genders.

Table 9.8 shows a large group of similar adjectives for both *politik* and *politička*. The group suggests that the image of women is far from stereotypical. Female politicians as well as male politicians receive attributes that are associated with determination (active, energetic), power (powerful, tough), decisiveness (leading), self-confidence (ambitious, confident), intelligence (clever, intelligent), and popularity (favorite, popular, significant). Women in politics are clearly viewed as powerful figures. Tables 9.9 and 9.10 explore in more detail the adjectives that modify female or male politicians and also both genders. The adjectives are categorized further into semantic subgroups.

Table 9.9 zooms in on the positive adjectives that collocate with both *politik* and *politička* from Table 9.8. The adjectives are further divided into semantic subcategories. Many of the attributes can be seen as reporting stereotypically "masculine" traits: leading, powerful, top, and influential (Pearce, 2008, p. 8). It is noteworthy that such traits are shared by both genders.

The data above confirms that both genders are generally associated with "strong" personalities. The subcategories indicate many traits that are stereotypically attributed to men. Apparently, such straightforward stereotypes are not applied to men and women in politics in the Czech media. More subtle differences, however, can be found in those collocates that are used exclusively for one or the other gender.

Table 9.8 Distribution of positive attributes for male and female politicians

Category	Positive collocates
Adjectives that modify only male politicians	*ctižádostivý* 'ambitious,' *čestný* 'honorable,' *čitelný* 'legible,' (*nejlépe*) *hodnocený* '(the best) rated,' *ideální* 'ideal,' *kariérní* 'career,' *kompetentní* 'competent,' *konkrétní* 'concrete, specific,' *korektní* 'upright,' *mediální* 'media,' *moderní* 'modern,' *moudrý* 'wise,' *nekontroverzní* 'uncontroversial,' *nezkorumpovaný* 'uncorrupted,' *nezávislý* 'independent,' *odpovědný* 'responsible,' *osvícený* 'enlightened,' *perspektivní* 'perspective,' *poctivý* 'honest,' *protřelý* 'savvy,' *prozíravý* 'farsighted,' *racionální* 'rational,' *reformní* 'reform,' *rozhodný* 'resolute,' *rozumný* 'reasonable,' *rozvážný* 'prudent,' *skutečný* 'real,' *soudný* 'judicious, reasonable,' *správný* 'right,' *šikovný* 'nifty,' *špičkový* 'top,' *talentovaný* 'talented,' *uvolněný* 'relaxed,' *uvážlivý* 'prudent,' *vynikající* 'outstanding,' *význačný* 'prominent,' *zdatný* 'proficient,' *zodpovědný* 'responsible'
Adjectives that modify only female politicians	*cílevědomý* 'ambitious, go-getter,' *nekompromisní* 'uncompromising,' *neústupný* 'unyielding,' *proslulý* 'renowned,' *šarmantní* 'charming,' *vytrvalý* 'resilient'
Adjectives that modify politicians of both genders	*aktivní* 'active,' *ambiciózní* 'ambitious,' *charismatický* 'charismatic,' *chytrý* 'clever,' *čelný* 'leading,' *dynamický* 'dynamic,' *důvěryhodný* 'trustworthy,' *energický* 'energetic,' *inteligentní* 'intelligent,' *mocný* 'powerful,' *nadějný* 'promising,' *oblíbený* 'favorite,' *obratný* 'skillful,' *odvážný* 'courageous,' *ostřílený* 'seasoned,' *populární* 'popular,' *pracovitý* 'hardworking,' *pragmatický* 'pragmatic,' *profesionální* 'professional,' *prominentní* 'prominent,' *přední* 'leading,' (*vysoce*) *postavený* '(high-)ranking,' *razantní* 'vigorous,' *realistický* 'realistic,' *respektovaný* 'respected,' *rázný* 'spirited,' *schopný* 'capable,' *sebevědomý* 'confident,' *seriózní* 'serious,' *slušný* 'decent,' *sympatický* 'likable,' *tvrdý* 'tough,' *umírněný* 'moderate,' *uznávaný* 'moderate,' *úspěšný* 'successful,' *vlivný* 'influential,' *vrcholný* 'supreme,' *vrcholový* 'top,' *výrazný* 'significant,' *významný* 'significant,' *vzdělaný* 'educated,' *zkušený* 'experienced,' *známý* 'famous,' *zásadový* 'principled'

Now, let us look at the positive adjectival collocates that appear either with *politik* or with *politička* from Table 9.8. Their semantic subcategories are presented in Table 9.10.

The semantic subgroups in Table 9.10 look different from those modifying both *politik* and *politička* in Table 9.9. The former does not contain adjectives that belong to subgroups reporting determination, high energy level, and quick action, nor power and dominance; furthermore, this table includes five subgroups not seen in Table 9.9: integrity, decision-making abilities, vision for the future, perfection and persistence, and hard-headedness. While most subgroups of adjectives modify *politik*, fewer subgroups modify *politička*. A *politik* is likely to be portrayed as someone who makes decisions, has visions for the future, has integrity and high status, and experience and intelligence. It is notable that *politička* differs from *politik* in that the

Table 9.9 Positive adjectival collocates modifying both *politik* and *politička*

Semantic subgroups	Positive collocates
Self-confidence and ambition	*ambiciózní* 'ambitious,' *sebevědomý* 'confident'
Determination, high energy level, and quick action	*aktivní* 'active,' *dynamický* 'dynamic,' *energický* 'energetic,' *razantní* 'vigorous,' *rázný* 'spirited'
High social status	*čelný* 'leading,' *(vysoce) postavený* '(high-)ranking,' *prominentní* 'prominent,' *přední* 'leading,' *vrcholný* 'supreme,' *vrcholový* 'top'
Experience, intelligence, and deal-making abilities	*chytrý* 'clever,' *inteligentní* 'intelligent,' *obratný* 'skillful,' *ostřílený* 'seasoned,' *pracovitý* 'hardworking,' *profesionální* 'professional,' *úspěšný* 'successful,' *vzdělaný* 'educated,' *zkušený* 'experienced'
Popularity and recognition	*oblíbený* 'favorite,' *populární* 'popular,' *respektovaný* 'respected,' *uznávaný* 'moderate,' *významný* 'significant,' *známý* 'famous'
Likable/trustworthy personality	*chari[sz]matický* 'charismatic,' *důvěryhodný* 'trustworthy,' *slušný* 'decent,' *sympatický* 'likable'
Power and dominance	*mocný* 'powerful,' *odvážný* 'courageous,' *tvrdý* 'tough,' *vlivný* 'influential'
Others	*nadějný* 'promising,' *pragmatický* 'pragmatic,' *realistický* 'realistic,' *schopný* 'capable,' *seriózní* 'serious,' *umírněný* 'moderate,' *výrazný* 'significant,' *zásadový* 'principled'

former, unlike the latter, collocates with adjectives reporting persistence and hard-headedness, and likableness. Furthermore, there are some subtle but important differences between the portrayal of *politik* and *politička* as manifested by other adjectival collocates in the subcategories of adjectives that do not modify female politicians[11] such as: high status, experience, intelligence and deal-making abilities, integrity, and decision-making abilities. These subcategories suggest that *politik* is described as a leader with a powerful position in politics and as someone who is more suitable for political positions (c.f. *špičkový* 'top,' *kompetentní* 'competent,' *čestný* 'honorable,' *perspektivní* 'perspective'). Other examples are adjectives representing the subgroup of perfection. The adjectives *ideální* 'ideal,' *skutečný* 'real,' or *správný* 'right' are collocates only for male politicians; this suggests that the prototype of the perfect politician is associated with maleness.

The positive attributes for male and female politicians for the most part are similar. However, the adjectives *nekompromisní* 'uncompromising,' *neústupný* 'unyielding,' and *vytrvalý* 'resilient' which modify only female politicians seem to refer to the difficulties women face in their political career (Kunovich, 2003, p. 286). Moreover, the adjective *šarmantní* 'charming' shows that female politicians are expected to be accepted by others in politics.

[11] The adjectival collocates for *politička* from the corpus with a LogDice index <1.26 were excluded from the research material beacause they were not prominent.

Table 9.10 Positive adjectival collocates modifying only *politik* or *politička*

Semantic subgroups	Positive adjectival collocates co-occurring only with	
	Politik	*Politička*
Ambition	*ctižádostivý* 'ambitious'	*cílevědomý* 'ambitious, go-getter'
High status	*špičkový* 'top,' *vynikající* 'outstanding'	
Experience, intelligence, and deal-making abilities	*kompetentní* 'competent,' *moudrý* 'wise,' *osvícený* 'enlightened,' *protřelý* 'savvy,' *prozíravý* 'provident' *rozumný* 'reasonable,' *šikovný* 'nifty,' *talentovaný* 'talented'	
Popularity, reputation, and recognition	*(nejlépe) hodnocený* '(the best) rated,' *význačný* 'prominent'	*proslulý* 'renowned'
Likableness		*šarmantní* 'charming'
Integrity	*čestný* 'honorable,' *korektní* 'upright,' *nezkorumpovaný* 'uncorrupted,' *odpovědný* 'responsible,' *poctivý* 'honest,' *racionální* 'rational,' *rozvážný* 'rational,' *zodpovědný* 'responsible,' *uvážlivý* 'prudent'	
Decision-making abilities	*rozhodný* 'resolute,' *nezávislý* 'independent,' *soudný* 'judicious, reasonable'	
Vision for the future	*moderní* 'modern,' *perspektivní* 'perspective,' *reformní* 'reform'	
Persistence and hard-headedness		*nekompromisní* 'uncompromising,' *neústupný* 'unyielding,' *vytrvalý* 'resilient'
Perfection	*ideální* 'ideal,' *skutečný* 'real' or *správný*	
Others	*čitelný* 'legible,' *kariérní* 'career,' *konkrétní* 'concrete, specific,' *mediální* 'media,' *nekontroverzní* 'uncontroversial,' *uvolněný* 'relaxed,' *zdatný* 'proficient'	

Negative Adjectives

Compared to the group of positive adjectival collocates, the group of negative adjectival collocates for *politik* and *politička* is smaller, but it shows even more differences between the genders. Collocates co-occurring only with female politicians suggest implicit prejudice. My data can thus be contrasted with the gender differences observed by other scholars, but we have to bear in mind that the lexemes *politik* and *politička* are being compared with other gender-associated words: *woman/man*, *girl/boy*, and *spinster/bachelor*. Romaine's study on collocations with the lexemes *man/woman* and *boy/girl* (Romaine, 2000 *in* Pearce, 2008) shows that words with negative meaning tend to appear more frequently with *woman/girl* than *man/boy*. Baker (2006, pp. 95–120) draws a similar conclusion analyzing the

Table 9.11 Distribution of negative attributes for male and female politicians

Category	Negative collocates
Adjectives that modify only male politicians	*arogantní* 'arrogant,' *bezvýznamný* 'insignificant,' (*nejhůře*) *hodnocený* '(the worst) rated,' *neaktivní* 'inactive,' *nechari*[*sz*]*matický* 'non-charismatic,' *nečestný* 'dishonest,' *nečitelný* 'unclear,' *neinteligentní* 'unintelligent,' *nekompetentní* 'incompetent,' *nekorektní* 'unseemly,' *nemediální* 'non-media,' *nemoderní* 'unprogressive,' *nemoudrý* 'unwise,' *neoblíbený* 'unpopular,' *neodpovědný* 'irresponsible,' *nepoctivý* 'dishonest,' *neprofesionální* 'unprofessional,' *neprozíravý* 'improvident,' *nerazantní* 'unvigorous,' *nerealistický* 'unrealistic,' *nerozhodný* 'indecisive,' *nerozvážný* 'thoughtless,' *neseriózní* 'unserious,' *nesoudný* 'injudicious,' *neuvolněný* 'not relaxed,' *neuvážlivý* 'imprudent,' *nevzdělaný* 'uneducated,' *nevýznamný* 'insignificant,' *nezodpovědný* 'irresponsible,' *obviněný* 'accused,' *špatný* 'bad,' *vysloužilý* 'retired,' *zhrzený* 'despised,' *zkorumpovaný* 'corrupt,' *závislý* 'dependent'
Adjectives that modify only female politicians	*křehký* 'fragile,' *naivní* 'naive,' *napadený* 'attacked,' *nepohodlný* 'inconvenient,' *odsouzený* 'condemned,' *popravený* 'executed,' *postřelený* 'been shot,' *unesený* 'kidnaped,' *vězněný* 'imprisoned,' *zabitý* 'killed'
Adjectives that modify politicians of both genders	*kontroverzní* 'controversial,' *nedůvěryhodný* 'untrustworthy,' *neobratný* 'clumsy,' *nepopulární* 'unpopular,' *neschopný* 'unable,' *nesympatický* 'unlovable,' *neúspěšný* 'unsuccessful,' *nevýrazný* 'unclear,' *nezkušený* 'inexperienced,' *neznámý* 'unknown,' *zavražděný* 'murdered,' *zesnulý* 'deceased'

Table 9.12 Negative adjectival collocates modifying both *politik* and *politička*

Semantic subgroups	Negative collocates
Unpopularity	*nepopulární* 'unpopular,' *neznámý* 'unknown'
Lack of likability and trust	*nedůvěryhodný* 'untrustworthy,' *nesympatický* 'unlovable'
Incompetence and lack of experience	*neobratný* 'clumsy,' *neschopný* 'unable,' *neúspěšný* 'unsuccessful,' *nezkušený* 'inexperienced'
Facts about death or crime	*zavražděný* 'murdered,' *zesnulý* 'deceased'
Others	*kontroverzní* 'controversial,' *nevýrazný* 'unclear'

lexemes *bachelor* and *spinster*, positing that the mainstream discourse of *spinster* has more outright negative associations. Instead, the current data is more consistent with the observations in Macalister (2011) and Zasina (2016). Macalister demonstrates that negative collocations with *girl/s* in child-centered texts do not occur more frequently than with *boy/s*. Also, a study based on Czech journalistic texts (Zasina, 2016) shows that positive and negative adjectives occur with both the lexemes *muž* 'man' and *žena* 'woman,' and the only distinction was seen in the co-occurrence of attributes in specific genres. The current chapter, however, shows a more complex nature of gender differences (Tables 9.11, 9.12, and 9.13). Table 9.11 shows that only twelve adjectives modify both *politik* or *politička*.

The subcategories of negative collocates shared by both genders in Table 9.12 can be contrasted with their positive counterparts in Table 9.9. Lack of popularity, trust, and experience seem to be damaging traits in politics both for men and women.

Table 9.13 Negative adjectival collocations modifying only *politik* or *politička*

Semantic subgroups	Negative adjectival collocates co-occurring only with	
	Politik	*Politička*
Lack of determination and stagnation	*neaktivní* 'inactive,' *nerazantní* 'lacking vigor'	
Lack of professionalism and intelligence	*neinteligentní* 'unintelligent,' *nemoudrý* 'unwise,' *nekompetentní* 'incompetent,' *neodpovědný* 'irresponsible,' *neprofesionální* 'unprofessional,' *nerozvážný* 'thoughtless,' *nevzdělaný* 'uneducated,' *nezodpovědný* 'irresponsible'	
Unpopularity	*bezvýznamný* 'insignificant,' *(nejhůře) hodnocený* '(the worst) rated,' *neoblíbený* 'unpopular,' *nevýznamný* 'insignificant'	
Bad character traits	*arogantní* 'arrogant,' *nechari[sz]matický* 'non-charismatic,' *špatný* 'bad'	
Unfair dealing	*nečestný* 'dishonest,' *nekorektní* 'unseemly,' *nepoctivý* 'dishonest,' *neseriózní* 'unserious,' *neuvážlivý* 'imprudent,' *zkorumpovaný* 'corrupt'	
Lack of decision-making abilities	*nerozhodný* 'indecisive,' *nesoudný* 'injudicious,' *závislý* 'dependent'	
Description of death or crime	*obviněný* 'accused'	*napadený* 'attacked,' *odsouzený* 'condemned,' *popravený*[a] 'executed,' *postřelený* '(been) shot,' *unesený* 'kidnapped,' *vězněný* 'imprisoned,' *zabitý* 'killed'
Sensitivity		*křehký* 'fragile'
naiveté		*naivní* 'naive'
Being inconvenient		*nepohodlný* 'inconvenient'
Others	*nemediální* 'non-media,' *nemoderní* 'unprogressive,' *neprozíravý* 'improvident,' *nerealistický* 'unrealistic,' *neuvolněný* 'not relaxed,' *nečitelný* 'unclear,' *vysloužilý* 'retired,' *zhrzený* 'despised'	

[a]This adjective is entirely related to Milada Horáková (cf. section "Top 20 Collocates with *Politik* and *Politička*")

The semantic subgroups in Table 9.12 can be contrasted with those in Table 9.13, which present negative adjectives used for either *politik* or *politička*

Table 9.13 does not contain adjectives that belong to subgroups reporting a lack of likability and trust, nor incompetence or lack of experience; furthermore, the table includes subgroups not seen in Table 9.12: lack of determination and stagnation, lack of professionalism or intelligence, bad character traits, unfair dealing, lack of decision-making abilities, sensitivity, naiveté, and being inconvenient. *Politik* and *politička* share only one semantic subcategory: description of death or crime. However, there are differences even here. Female politicians are presented as victims (*napadený* 'attacked,' *popravený* 'executed,' *postřelený* 'been shot,' *unesený* 'kidnaped,' *vězněný* 'imprisoned'). Such tendencies partially and indirectly resonate with the observation by Beauvoir (1949/2012) that women were always stereotypically seen as weak, and as dependent and subordinate to men.[12]

It is also worth noting that only *politik* is negatively represented in terms of determination and activity, professionalism and intelligence, character traits, fair dealing, or incompetence in making decisions. For the most part, these adjectival collocates are the negation of the attributes seen in Table 9.8, e.g., *neinteligentní* 'unintelligent,' *nemoudrý* 'unwise,' *neoblíbený* 'unpopular,' *nevýznamný* 'insignificant,' *nečestný* 'dishonest,' *nekorektní* 'unseemly,' *nerozhodný* 'indecisive.' The larger number and types of collocates even suggest that the image of male politicians might be more negative than that of female politicians, who are not described with such bad traits as *arogantní* 'arrogant,' *nechari[sz]matický* 'non-charismatic,' *špatný* 'bad.' Moreover, attributes concerning unfair dealing (*nečestný* 'dishonest,' *nekorektní* 'unseemly,' *nepoctivý* 'dishonest,' *neseriózní* 'unserious,' *neuvážlivý* 'imprudent,' *zkorumpovaný* 'corrupt') do not appear with female politicians. What is more, adjectives such as *nečestný*, *nepoctivý*, and *zkorumpovaný* indicate that *politik* is often connected with corruption. There is no such evidence for associating female politicians with corruption. This observation is consistent with Coate's statement that women are often seen as fair-minded, attending to the general good, while men tend to pursue their goals at any cost (Coates, 1986, pp. 151–152).[13]

Table 9.13 also indicates that different measuring sticks are used for male and female politicians. Male politicians are criticized for their lack of determination and activity, their lack of professionalism and intelligence, bad character traits, unfair dealing, and lack of decision-making abilities; female politicians are criticized for naiveté and fragility. For instance, adjectives such as *křehký* 'fragile' and *naivní* 'naive' represent women as oversensitive and gullible. These collocates are commensurate with the image of women as unstable or pet-like in the BLOB corpus, consisting of English texts from around 1930 (Baker, 2010b), and with observations in contemporary English by Caldas-Coulthard and Moon (2010, p. 117) that women tend to appear with negative attributes such as *naive*, *hysterical*, or *distressed*. The implicit image of female politicians as naive can additionally be compared to *racionální* 'rational,' *rozvážný* 'rational,' *uvážlivý* 'prudent,' positive adjectives that appear only with male politicians. These adjectives as well as the negative adjec-

[12] Pearce (2008, p. 19) draws a similar conclusion: "[p]hysical weakness and subordination are evident in the extent to which women are represented as the victims of violence (in object verbs such as *rape* and *assault*)."

[13] When it comes to the adjective *nepohodlný* 'inconvenient,' three of four cases relate to Milada Horáková, a Czechoslovak politician executed under fabricated charges in 1950. She was sentenced to death as an "inconvenient" person for the communist government at the time (Thompson, 2014, p. 54–64). One occurrence of *nepohodlný* concerned the contemporary politician Zuzana Moravčíková. The adjective *nepohodlný* in my study does not reflect a general image of women in politics but only appears in the press as a strong collocate with very specific female politicians.

tives specific to female politicians thus suggest an implicit assumption that they *should* be prudent and rational thinkers (but they are often not).

Positive and Negative Adjectives: Summary

Analyzing positive and negative premodifying adjectives for *politik* and *politička* leads to the question of whether male and female politicians are represented differently. As seen above, there are similarities between men and women in politics, mainly in terms of positive collocations. Even positive adjectives modifying only female or male politicians are similar in terms of focus of praise, but it is still possible to observe some subtle differences. Furthermore, some overt differences in the type of negative adjectival collocates are found. They suggest implicit references to stereotypical views of women as weak, subordinate, oversensitive, or gullible. Negative collocates for male politicians are for the most part the mirror image of their positive counterparts: bad character traits, unfair dealing, lack of popularity, lack of professionalism, etc. This section thus presents a more complex picture of gender, unlike some previous studies (Pearce, 2008, p. 21; Taylor, 2013, p. 108) that note gender differences within semantic categories.

In the subsections above, I compared the list of positive and negative adjectives collocating with male and female politicians, with a particular emphasis on comparison with respect to adjective type. The two sets for both lexemes were consistent with the different number of types. The following section, in contrast, compares the same number of top-frequency collocates for *politik* and *politička* to further verify the differences found in this section.

Top 20 Collocates with Politik and Politička

In the preceding section, I examined the adjectival collocates of *politik* and *politička*. I compared two sets of adjectives (co-occurring with 'male' and 'female' politician), focusing on the *type* of collocates for each lexeme. In this section, I take a look at the same data from a different perspective. I focus only on the top 20 collocates for both lexemes. The collocates were ranked with respect to absolute frequency. In contrast to the previous section predominantly focused on collocates as types, this section attempts to capture the nature of the prevailing discourse based on *tokens*. This approach helps to answer the question of whether gender in politics is connected with evaluative meaning, either positive or negative.

I chose 20 adjectival collocates from Table 9.4 with the highest frequencies for both *politik* and *politička* in the singular form in my subcorpus (96,691 and 8268 times, respectively).[14] Table 9.14 contains information about the collocates, includ-

[14] Errors were manually removed. Negated forms were considered as separate lemma (cf. footnote 10) and the two adjectives *chari[sz]matický* were counted together as one lemma.

Table 9.14 Most frequent collocations with study lexemes

No	Politik				Politička			
	Collocate	Instances	%[a]	Group	Collocate	Instances	%	Group
1.	**populární** 'popular'	1731	1.79	Positive	**populární** 'popular'	268	3.24	Positive
2.	**oblíbený** 'favorite'	1385	1.43	Positive	**oblíbený** 'favorite'	163	1.97	Positive
3.	**významný** 'significant'	1286	1.33	Positive	**úspěšný** 'successful'	145	1.75	Positive
4.	**zkušený** 'experienced'	1021	1.06	Positive	**zkušený** 'experienced'	127	1.54	Positive
5.	**vlivný** 'influential'	846	0.87	Positive	**známý** 'famous'	110	1.33	Positive
6.	**známý** 'famous'	778	0.80	Positive	**významný** 'significant'	56	0.68	Positive
7.	**kontroverzní** 'controversial'	678	0.70	Negative	**kontroverzní** 'controversial'	47	0.57	Negative
8.	**úspěšný** 'successful'	614	0.64	Positive	**výrazný** 'significant'	41	0.50	Positive
9.	**(vysoce) postavený** '(high-)ranking'	552	0.57	Positive	**vlivný** 'influential'	40	0.48	Positive
10.	**schopný** 'capable'	500	0.52	Positive	**schopný** 'capable'	35	0.42	Positive
11.	**přední** 'leading'	499	0.52	Positive	chari[sz]matický 'charismatic'	33	0.40	Positive
12.	vrcholný 'top'	483	0.50	Positive	nadějný 'promising'	33	0.40	Positive
13.	**profesionální** 'professional'	388	0.40	Positive	mocný 'powerful'	32	0.39	Positive
14.	důvěryhodný 'trustworthy'	305	0.32	Positive	zavražděný 'murdered'	32	0.39	Negative
15.	aktivní 'active'	293	0.30	Positive	**(vysoce) postavený** 'high-ranking'	31	0.37	Positive
16.	umírněný 'moderate'	267	0.28	Positive	vězněný 'imprisoned'	31	0.37	Negative
17.	**výrazný** 'significant'	230	0.24	Positive	**přední** 'leading'	29	0.35	Positive
18.	**ambiciózní** 'ambitious'	229	0.24	Positive	**ambiciózní** 'ambitious'	25	0.30	Positive
19.	odpovědný 'responsible'	228	0.24	Positive	**profesionální** 'professional'	24	0.29	Positive
20.	slušný 'decent'	216	0.22	Positive	popravený 'executed'	22	0.27	Negative
	total	12,529	12.96		**total**	1,324	16.01	
	politik total	96,691	100		**politička total**	8,268	100	

[a]The percentage of single collocates relative to the overall frequency of *politik* and *politička*, respectively

ing their absolute frequencies, and the proportion of single collocates out of the overall frequency of *politik* and *politička*, respectively. Each adjective is labeled as presenting a positive or negative meaning. Collocations shared by both lexemes are shown in boldface; negative meaning is highlighted with a gray shadow.

Just as in the preceding section, the data in Table 9.14 shows more similarities between male and female politicians than differences. Out of 20 total adjectives, 14 are shared by two examined lexemes. There are six collocates that even received the same ranking for both *politik* and *politička*, such as *populární* 'popular,' *oblíbený* 'favorite,' *zkušený* 'experienced,' *kontroverzní* 'controversial,' *schopný* 'capable,' and *ambiciózní* 'ambitious.' The top 11 adjectival collocates for *politik* and the Top ten adjectival collocates for *politička* are shared by both analyzed lexemes. However, gender differences start to appear below these levels, as I discuss later in this section.[15]

It is notable that the first two collocates (*populární* and *oblíbený*) concern popularity and recognition in society. Regardless of gender, acceptance by the public seems to be one of the most important criteria for politicians. The adjectives shared by both genders can be classified into the semantic subcategories mentioned above: adjectives reporting popularity (*populární* 'popular,' *oblíbený* 'favorite,' *významný* 'significant,' *známý* 'famous'), intelligence and experience (*zkušený* 'experienced,' *úspěšný* 'successful,' *profesionální* 'professional'), powerfulness (*vlivný* 'influential'), high status (*vysoce postavený* 'high-ranking,' *přední* 'leading'), and ambitiousness (*ambiciózní* 'ambitious'). These adjectives report traits that are crucial for a political career but tell us very little about gender stereotypes.

Among the adjectival collocates shared by both genders is the negative adjective *kontroverzní* 'controversial' which was not assigned to any subcategory in section 'Negative Adjectives.' (cf. Table 9.12). *Kontroverzní* was ranked the same for both lexemes and has a comparable collocability (0.7% for male politicians and 0.57% for female politicians). This collocate indicates that both men and women in politics are often portrayed as having opponents and/or being confrontational. The word also suggests scandal or unforeseen actions contrary to people's expectations and to the ideology of the opposition parties. While *kontroverzní* is the only negative collocate that appears among the collocates for *politik,* three more negative collocates appear among the collocates for *politička.*

The negative adjectives that collocate only with female politicians are *zavražděný* 'murdered,' *vězněný* 'imprisoned,' and *popravený* 'executed.' These words relate to crime. They evoke negative emotions and have negative meaning as well but, as premodifiers of *politička,* present inconvenient or fatal situations that a female politician faces, rather than her criminal qualities. As I highlighted in Table 9.13, the adjective 'executed' appears only as a modifier for Milada Horáková, who faced political persecution in the late 1940s. The adjective 'imprisoned' relates to the Ukrainian politician Yulia Tymoshenko[16] in 29 cases out of 31. The remaining two instances of this adjective are used in reference to the Serbian politician Biljana Plavšić and the Colombian-French politician Íngrid Betancourt Pulecio. The last adjective 'murdered' is mostly connected with the Pakistani politician Benazir Bhutto (19 out of 32 times). This adjective also modifies Milada Horáková, the

[15] As the general frequency of *politička* is rather lower than that of *politik,* I used the relative ratios of each collocate between the genders and considered only those adjectival collocates over 0.27%. The discussion that follows is also about the adjectival collocates shared by both *politik* and *politička.*

[16] Czech spelling: Julija Tymošenková.

Russian politician Galina Starovoytova, the Swedish politician Anna Lindh, and the Polish-Jewish Marxist theorist Rosa Luxemburg. These examples show that female politicians are often depicted positively, but also as victims of unfair persecution. In other words, they are depicted as heroines (positively) who were killed or imprisoned (negative) by their political foes. These collocations appeared high up on the frequency list, as these topics stirred public opinion. Male politicians, in contrast, also generally appear as an object of crime (e.g., *murdered politician*), but these collocations are not as strong as with female politicians. The results are commensurate with Pearce's conclusion that "there is a tendency for women in the corpus to be represented as objects of sociological enquiry and discussion, which involves their marginalization and oppression being written and talked about" (2008, p. 11).

As to positive adjectives for male politicians, the top 20 collocates include *aktivní* 'active,' *vrcholný* 'top,' *důvěryhodný* 'trustworthy,' *umírněný* 'moderate,' *slušný* 'decent,' and *odpovědný* 'responsible.' For female politicians, in contrast, we obtained words such as *chari[sz]matický* 'charismatic,' *nadějný* 'promising,' and *mocný* 'powerful.' Here too, it is possible to discern some subtle differences. Men in politics are represented as active, top-notch, trustworthy, decent, and responsible (i.e., qualified to perform their duties), while women are represented as having potential: they are depicted as 'promising' and 'charismatic' (i.e., they may not be competent, but might yet become better or somehow influence people), and powerful (i.e., they may not be capable but hold power).

This section focused on the ranking of adjectival collocates for *politik* and *politička*: politicians, both male and female are viewed as popular, famous, and as having leadership qualities and ambition, but in some spheres women are represented as having potential (the possibility of improving their competence), although they are also represented as holding power. The observations in this section are commensurate with Havelková, who finds that the Czech media sees men and women as equally politically competent, but that there is some kind of *expectation of traditional feminine behavior* that limits women from achieving higher positions in politics (1999, pp. 147–148).

However, the present study brings new insights into women's position in Czech politics. Firstly, in contrast to Havelková who states that the political participations of women "are in general negative" (ibid., p. 161), in my study both male and female politicians are presented positively. Secondly, unlike Havelková's opinion that women lack self-confidence and are not interested in political power (ibid., p. 162), the positive collocates in my data refer to women's self-confidence and interest in political power. Thirdly, the negative collocates show subtle positioning of some female politicians as innocent victims; this was not mentioned in Havelková's study. There were also no indicators of immaturity attributed to male politicians, which Havelková (ibid., p. 162) discusses. This study based on language corpora therefore adds to previous studies in qualitative sociology.

Conclusions

The present study focused on the Czech newspaper discourse about female politicians compared and contrasted to male ones. The analysis of adjectival collocations with the lexemes *politik* and *politička* has shown that both male and female politicians are presented largely in a positive light. They both share a relatively large amount of associated adjectives. Women in politics are described as strong, powerful, and popular. An analysis of the positive collocations has shown that both male and female politicians have attributes pertaining to self-confidence, appreciation in society, determination, wisdom, and ability to negotiate or dominate. As for negative collocates, both male and female politicians were associated with a lack of popularity, a lack of sympathy and trust, incompetence and a lack of experience, and crime, but there were also noticeable differences between the two genders; some adjectives attributed to female politicians implicitly refer to weakness, submissiveness, oversensitivity, or naivety. In contrast to the existing literature, which emphasizes the differences between men and women and pursues clearly visible gender stereotypes, the present study found important similarities in the representation of both male and female politicians, and properties of attributes that are more subtle than outright stereotypes.

In my study, I also examined the top 20 collocates for *politik* and *politička* with the highest frequency. For the most part, the adjectives were positive, and 70% of them were shared between male and female politicians. This method further confirmed that women in politics are not so differently represented from men, are viewed as having strong personalities, and are able to make their careers in politics. Moreover, 30% of adjectives for each lexeme even placed the same rank on the list. This also indicates that male and female politicians have more in common than previously discussed. However, there were subtle differences as well. These reveal that women in politics are represented as having "potential" despite sharing these same traits with men. Female politicians are portrayed more often than men as victims of unfair persecution, and these negative connotations are rather indirect. The results of this study provide a more complex view than previous studies.

Journalistic texts after 1989 project a rather "non-stereotypical" image of female politicians in the Czech Republic. The present study has discovered a more subtle and complex picture of gender image in comparison with previous studies emphasizing the differences (Caldas-Coulthard & Moon, 2010; Pearce, 2008). It reveals not only positive and negative connotations of both male and female politicians and finds the similarities between them but also underlines that gender representation is expressed in a more subtle way and is not dichotomous in nature.

Gender issues in politics have so far only been analyzed in the Czech Republic from a sociological point of view (Havelková, 1999; Ferber & Raabe, 2003; Kunovich, 2003). The present study is the first attempt at corpus linguistic analysis of gender in politics. Expanded future research, through a study of both tabloid press and broadsheet newspapers (cf. Caldas-Coulthard & Moon, 2010), is expected to produce further findings.

Acknowledgments My thanks go to Zuzana Komrsková for her supportive comments and to Zbyněk Drugda for fielding my questions about politics and for his helpful comments. I would also like to show my gratitude to Masako Ueda Fidler and Václav Cvrček for the extraordinary support and expert advice that greatly improved the manuscript.

References

Baker, Paul. (2006). *Using corpora in discourse analysis*. New York: Continuum.

Baker, P. (2010a). *Sociolinguistics and corpus linguistics*. Edinburgh, Scotland: Edinburgh University Press.

Baker, P. (2010b). Will Ms ever be as frequent as Mr? A corpus-based comparison of gendered terms across four diachronic corpora of British English. *Gender and Language, 4*(1), 125–149.

Baker, P. (2014). *Using corpora to analyze gender*. London: Bloomsbury.

Baker, P., & Ellece, S. (2011). *Key terms in discourse analysis*. In London. New York: Continuum.

Beauvoir, S. d. (1949/2012). *The second sex*. New York: Vintage.

Caldas-Coulthard, C. R., & Moon, R. (2010). 'Curvy, hunky, kinky': Using corpora as tools for critical analysis. *Discourse & Society, 21*(2), 99–133.

Chlumská, Lucie. (this volume).

Coates, J. (1986). *Women, men and language: A sociolinguistic account of gender differences in language*. Harlow, UK: Longman.

Cvrček, V. (2010). *Mluvnice současné češtiny* [*Grammar of Contemporary Czech*]. Praha, Slovakia: Karolinum.

Čermák, F., Adamovičová, A., & Pešička, J. (2001). *PMK (Pražský mluvený korpus): přepisy nahrávek pražské mluvy z 90. let 20. století* [*Prague spoken corpus: Recordings transcriptions of the Prague speech from the 1990s*]. Praha, Slovakia: Ústav Českého národního korpusu FF UK http://www.korpus.cz

Čermáková, M. (1995). Women and family–the Czech version of development and chances for improvement. *Contribution in Sociology, 112*, 75–85.

Čmejrková, S. (1995). Žena v jazyce [Woman in language]. *Slovo a Slovestnost, 56*, 43–57.

Čmejrková, S. (2003). Communicating gender in Czech. In M. Hellinger & H. Bußmann (Eds.), *Gender across languages: The linguistic representation of women and men* (pp. 27–58). Amsterdam: John Benjamins Publishing Company.

Ferber, M. A., & Raabe, P. H. (2003). Women in the Czech Republic: Feminism, Czech style. *International Journal of Politics, Culture, and Society, 16*(3), 407–430.

Fidler, Masako, & Cvrček, Václav. (this volume).

Hausen, K. (1976). Die Polarisierung der "Geschlechtscharaktere" – Eine Spiegelung der Dissoziation von Erwerbs- und Familienleben [Polarization of the "sexual characters" – a reflection of the dissociation of working and family life]. In W. Conze (Ed.), *Sozialgeschichte der Familie in der Neuzeit Europas* (pp. 363–393). Stuttgart, Germany: Klett.

Havelková, H. (1999). The political representation of women in mass media discourse in the Czech Republic 1990–1998. *Czech Sociological Review, VII*(2), 145–165.

Hnátková, M., Křen, M., Procházka, P., & Skoumalová, H. (2014). The SYN-series corpora of written Czech. In *Proceedings of the Ninth International Conference on Language Resources and Evaluation (LREC'14)* (pp. 160–164).

Hoffmannová, J. (2004). Ženy a muži v časopisech pro ženy: Role, perspektivy, výrazové stereotypy [Woman and man in women's magazines: Role, perspectives, expressional stereotypes]. *Stylistyka, XIII*, 27–34.

Huddy, L., & Terkildsen, N. (1993). Gender stereotypes and the perception of male and female candidates. *American Journal of Political Science, 37*(1), 119–147.

Inter-Parliamentary Union. (2015). Women in parliament: 20 years in review. http://www.ipu.org/pdf/publications/WIP20Y-en.pdf. Accessed 18 March 2017.

Jelínek, T. (2008). Nové značkování v Českém národním korpusu [New tagging in the Czech National Corpus]. *Naše řeč*, (1), 13–20.

Jelínek, T., & Petkevič, V. (2011). Systém jazykového značkování současné psané češtiny [Language tagging system of contemporary written Czech]. In V. Petkevič & A. Rosen (Eds.), *Korpusová lingvistika Praha 2011, sv. 3: Gramatika a značkování korpusů* (pp. 154–170). Praha, Slovakia: Nakladatelství Lidové noviny.

Křen, M., Cvrček, V., Čapka, T., Čermáková, A., Hnátková, M., Chlumská, L., et al. (2016). *Korpus SYN, verze 4 [SYN Corpus, realise 4]*. Praha, Slovakia: Ústav Českého národního korpusu FF UK http://www.korpus.cz

Kunovich, S. (2003). The representation of Polish and Czech women in national politics: Predicting electoral list position. *Comparative Politics, 2003*, 273–291.

Lakoff, R. (2003). Language, gender, and politics: Putting 'women' and 'power' in the same sentence. In J. Holmes & M. Meyerhoff (Eds.), *The handbook of language and gender* (pp. 161–178). Oxford, UK: Blackwell Publishing.

Lim, E. T. (2009). Gendered metaphors of women in power: The case of Hillary Clinton as Madonna, unruly woman, bitch and witch. In K. Ahrens (Ed.), *Politics, gender and conceptual metaphors* (pp. 254–269). Basingstoke, UK: Palgrave Macmillan.

Lovenduski, J. (1992). Gender and politics. In M. Hawkesworth & M. Kogan (Eds.), *Encyclopedia of government and politics* (pp. 603–615). London: Routledge.

Lovenduski, J. (2001). Women and politics: Minority representation or critical mass? *Parliamentary Affairs, 54*(4), 743–758.

Macalister, J. (2011). Flower-girl and bugler-boy no more: Changing gender representation in writing for children. *Corpora, 6*(1), 25–44.

Machálek, T., & Křen, M. (2013). Query interface for diverse corpus types. In K. Gajdošová & A. Žáková (Eds.), *Natural language processing, corpus linguistics, e-learning* (pp. 166–173). Lüdenscheid, Germany: RAM Verlag.

Mackay, F. (2004). Gender and political representation in the UK: The state of the 'discipline'. *The British Journal of Politics and International Relations, 6*(1), 99–120.

McEnery, T., & Hardie, A. (2012). *Corpus linguistics: Method, theory and practice*. Cambridge: Cambridge University Press.

Partington, A., & Marchi, A. (2015). Using corpora in discourse analysis. In D. Biber & R. Reppen (Eds.), *The Cambridge handbook of English corpus linguistics* (pp. 216–234). Cambridge, UK: Cambridge University Press.

Pearce, M. (2008). Investigating the collocational behaviour of man and woman in the BNC using sketch engine. *Corpora, 3*(1), 1–29.

Romaine, S. (2000). *Language in society: An introduction to sociolinguistics*. Oxford, UK: Oxford University Press.

Shaw, S. (2000). Language, gender and floor apportionment in political debates. *Discourse & Society, 11*(3), 401–418.

Sinclair, J. (2004). *Trust the text: Language, corpus and discourse*. London: Routledge.

Stubbs, M. (1996). *Text and corpus analysis: Computer-assisted studies of language and culture*. Oxford, UK: Blackwell.

Šonková, J. (2011). Genderové rozdíly v mluvené češtině [Gender differences in spoken language]. In F. Čermák (Ed.), *Korpusová lingvistika. Praha 2011–2 Výzkum a výstavba korpusů* (pp. 150–165). Praha, Slovakia: Nakladatelství Lidové Noviny.

Šprincová, Veronika, & Adamusová, Marcela. (2014). Politická angažovanost žen v české republice. Přehledová studie (1993–2013) [Political engagement of women in the Czech Republic. Survey Study (1993–2013)]. http://aa.ecn.cz/img_upload/666f72756d35302d666931303 0313139/politicka-angazovanost-zen-v-ceske-republice_forum_1.pdf. Accessed 8 March 2017.

Taylor, C. (2013). Searching for similarity using corpus-assisted discourse studies. *Corpora, 8*(1), 81–113.

Thompson, E. (2014). Milada Horáková–The Tragic Destiny of a Czechoslovak Proto-Feminist. *Hungarian Review, 06*, 54–64.

Valdrová, J. (1997). K české genderové lingistice [Czech gender linguistics]. *Naše řeč, 80*(2), 87–91.

Valdrová, J. (2006). *Gender a společnost* [*Gender and society*]. Ústí nad Labem, Czech Republic: Univerzita J.E. Purkyně.

Zasina, Adrian Jan. (2016, November). *Adjective collocations with the lexemes muž 'man' and žena 'woman' in Czech journalistic texts*. Paper presented at the Young Linguists' Meeting in Poznań 2016. Poznań, Poland.

Chapter 10
Going Beyond "Aboutness": A Quantitative Analysis of *Sputnik Czech Republic*

Masako Fidler and Václav Cvrček

Abstract This paper is an attempt to unpack the "alternativeness" of *Sputnik Czech Republic*, an online news-opinion portal that targets the Czech-speaking audience. The overarching principle used in the analysis is prominence, a concept used in the corpus linguistic method of keyword analysis. The use of Multi-level Discourse Prominence Analysis (MLDPA), which combines quantitative data and concepts from critical discourse analysis and cognitive linguistics, expands the applicability of prominence beyond the lexicon to multiple levels of language and informs of the overarching rhetoric and ideology in a text. The centerpiece of MLDPA is "keymorph analysis," which applies the cognitive linguistic notion of morphemes as meaning-bearing units (Janda 1993; Janda and Clancy, The case book for Czech. Slavica, Bloomington, IN, 2006) to the existing corpus linguistic method of keyword analysis. MLDPA helps identify and objectivize the ideological content of news in media that creates the impression of objective and well-balanced news.

Keywords Multi-level discourse prominence analysis · Keywords · Keymorphs · Corpus-based discourse analysis · Alternative news

Introduction

Corpus linguistic methods have made substantial advances in the analysis of discourse. One such method is keyword analysis, which extracts words that are prominent relative to a point of reference. This paper extends the existing keyword analysis by also taking into consideration the cognitive linguistic notion of morphemes as

M. Fidler
Department of Slavic Studies, Brown University, Providence, RI, USA
e-mail: masako_fidler@brown.edu

V. Cvrček (✉)
Institute of the Czech National Corpus, Charles University, Prague 1, Czech Republic
e-mail: vaclav.cvrcek@ff.cuni.cz

M. Fidler, V. Cvrček (eds.), *Taming the Corpus*, Quantitative Methods in the Humanities and Social Sciences, https://doi.org/10.1007/978-3-319-98017-1_10

meaning-bearing units (Janda, 1993), especially the cognitive case semantics described in Janda and Clancy (2006). It shows how quantitative data reveal prominence at different linguistic levels, i.e., not only the most striking topics of a text, but also what critical discourse analysts call "discourse position" (Jäger & Maier, 2016, pp. 124–125)—the implicit ideology that permeates a text. The study therefore is grounded in notions of corpus linguistics, critical discourse analysis, and cognitive linguistics.

Texts in this study are selected from an "alternative" news portal: *Sputnik Česká republika* (https://cz.sputniknews.com/). *Sputnik* was established in November 2014 by the Russian state media group *Rossia segodnia*, which replaced the previous *RIA Novosti* (Heritage, 2013). *Sputnik Česká Republika* is one of more than 30 foreign-language portals of *Sputnik* for the international audience. Its "About us" page states: "Sputnik. Telling the untold."[1] In other words, *Sputnik* represents itself as an alternative news portal. *Sputnik*, however, is viewed as a venue that promotes a pro-Kremlin ideology. It is said to be engaged in disinformation activities (Smoleňová, 2015) and to provide "false stories" (MacFarquhar, 2016). Groll (2014) states that *Sputnik* is the "BuzzFeed" of the Kremlin's propaganda.

Discourse analysis substantiates and further facilitates our understanding of *Sputnik's* discourse mechanism. We present our initial observations (section "Initial Observations: Ideological Partiality"), then our methodology (section "Methodology"), the language material used in this paper (section "Language Data"), followed by five subsections on data and discussion ("KWs (Key Inflected Word Forms)," "Key Lemmas (KLs)," "Collocates and Key Lemmas Links (KL Links): Contextual Reading of Words," "Keymorph Analysis: A Glimpse into Discourse Position," "Density Of Prominent KLs in Sentences"), and Conclusions.

Initial Observations: Ideological Partiality

Linguistic patterns that promote a pro-Kremlin ideology are directly observable in lexical items, citations, reporting style, and the representation of statements made by Russian leaders. They motivate our initial formulation of a hypothesis about *Sputnik*'s discourse.

Some lexical items suggest a certain bias towards a specific view. One characteristic lexical item in SPU is *domobranec* 'home defender', used to refer to anti-Ukrainian forces whom western media refer to as Ukrainian separatists. Furthermore, the "republics" led by the Ukrainian separatists, although not internationally acknowledged, are often represented in abbreviations in *Sputnik*: *DLR* (*Doněcká Lidová Republika* 'Donetsk People's Republic') and *LLR* (*Luhanská Lidová Republika* 'Luhansk People's Republic'). These expressions resemble those of other internationally recognized states such as *ČLR* (*Čínská Lidová Republika* 'People's Republic of China') and *ČR* (*Česká Republika* 'Czech Republic').

Citation practices also suggest the nature of the *Sputnik* discourse. *Sputnik* draws from multiple sources, thereby adhering to a descriptive journalistic style (Smoleňová, 2015). In fact, the use of citations can be quantitatively examined by

[1] https://sputniknews.com/docs/about/index.html, accessed September 22, 2018.

Table 10.1 Frequencies of the preposition *podle* 'according to' in Sputnik vs. SYN2015

Podle 'according to'	Sputnik	SYN2015 (newspapers and magazines)
Frequency of *podle*	1155	59,532
Total size (*N*)	395,110	39,744,419
Relative frequency (ipm[a])	2923	1498

[a]Instances per million

studying the preposition *podle* 'according to'. Table 10.1 shows that the preposition *podle* 'according to' is used nearly twice as often in the corpus of Sputnik texts than in the periodicals in SYN2015.

Such markedly frequent use of this preposition can be interpreted as an overzealous effort to represent the portal as one that cites information from diverse sources, and to create an impression of providing a well-balanced view.[2] Sputnik seems[3] to cite even *Le Iene*, a comedy-satirical television show that provides "infotainment," a mixture of "journalistic inquiry with entertainment" (https://www.iene.mediaset.it/, accessed September 29, 2018) (example 1).

1. Zahraniční dobrovolníci bojující na straně domobranců[4] v Donbasu prozradili, že přijeli pomoci místním obyvatelům, kteří se ocitli uprostřed skutečného „masakru", píše Sputnik **s odkazem na reportáž italského programu Le Lene** [sic]. (https://cz.sputniknews.com/svet/20150331188150/)[5]
   'International volunteers fighting on the home-defenders' side in Donbas revealed that they came to help the local residents who found themselves in the midst of a real "massacre," writes Sputnik, **with a link to the story of [from] the Italian channel Le Iene**.' Examples (2–3) nonetheless suggest the selection of sources that promote Russia.

2. Zatímco USA připravovaly NATO vzdorovat[6] tomu, co považují za ruskou agresi, a chválily se za izolaci Ruska, Moskva přestavěla asijskou ekonomiku, prohloubila vztahy s Čínou, Indií, Jižní Koreou a Japonskem, píše v The Nation **americký politolog Scherle Schwenninger**. (https://cz.sputniknews.com/politika/20150613548757/)
   'While the USA was preparing NATO to defy what it considers to be Russian aggression and praising itself for isolating Russia, Moscow rebuilt the Asian economy and deepened relations with China, India, South Korea and Japan, **the American political scientist Scherle Schwenninger** writes in The Nation.'

3. **Vojtěch Filip**[7]: Ruská hrozba pro Evropu neexistuje. (https://cz.sputniknews.com/svet/20150314101536/)
   '**Vojtěch Filip**: the Russian threat for Europe does not exist.'

[2] The use of *podle* parallels the use of "neutral structuring verbs" (Caldas-Coulthard, 1994) that "introduce a saying without evaluating it explicitly" (Machin and Mayer, 2012, p. 59).

[3] The show is cited incorrectly as "Le Lene" instead of the actual "Le Iene."

[4] Emphasis in bold style by the authors.

[5] All the examples from SPUCz used in this article were last checked and were present on the web on June 22, 2018.

[6] The phrasing *připravovat* + the infinitive is not natural but not totally erroneous in Czech.

[7] Filip is the current chairman of the Czech Communist Party.

Table 10.2 References to state representatives

	Total frequency	Number of articles where the names appear	First and last names + title	First and last names + title (% of articles)
Putin	869	291	265	91.1%
Obama	130	70	36	51.4%

The use of prestigious titles and full names also indicates a bias. Note the differences in the use of first name/last name and title between Putin and Obama relative to the number of articles (Table 10.2):

This initial probe is consistent with previous scholars' conclusions that *Sputnik* renders ideological partiality behind the appearance of journalistic professionalism. The following sections attempt to verify and further uncover the way in which the portal represents the world by means of quantifiable data. The findings essentially show a methodology to unpack the content of "alternativeness."

Methodology

Keyword Analysis

This study assumes that any text can be characterized in terms of its prominent linguistic units. A prominent word (or a keyword, henceforth KW) can be identified by the corpus linguistic method of keyword analysis (KWA). KWA assumes that each text prefers one type of word to others.[8] A word is "keyed"[9] if two conditions are met: if there is a significant difference[10] between the relative frequencies of the word (raw frequency divided by the size of the text) in the target and reference corpora; and if the relative frequency of a unit in the target corpus is reasonably higher than

[8] "[a] word form which recurs within the text in question will be more likely to be key in it." (Scott & Tribble, 2006).

[9] Extraction of KWs is the first statistical step ("keywords are pointers, that is all" (Scott, 2010)). KWs are often further analyzed with other methods of corpus linguistics (e.g., collocation profiles and "semantic prosody" (Stewart, 2010)).

[10] Several statistical tests are used for comparison of relative frequencies, such as log-likelihood, chi^2, or Fisher exact tests (cf. Bertels & Speelman, 2013) to determine the statistical significance of the difference. However, the statistical significance expressed by p-value is a necessary but not sufficient condition of prominence. Given that these tests are typically asymptotically true, p-values (esp. when computed on large data sets) do not inform us of whether the difference between the frequencies carries any descriptive value (cf. Wilson, 2013). As a result, tests are often accompanied by the effect size estimation, such as the Difference Index (DIN), a ratio (multiplied by 100) of the difference between relative frequencies of an item in the target text, and the reference corpus and the mean of those relative frequencies (cf. Fidler & Cvrček, 2015).

its relative frequency in the reference corpus. KWs are connected with the topic and style of the text or discourse (Scott, 2010, p. 43).[11]

Scholars use KWA to study literary texts (e.g., Culpeper, 2002; Scott & Tribble, 2006; Walker, 2010) as well as media (e.g., Baker, 2005 on LGBT discourse; Baker & McEnery, 2005 on immigration; and Tabbert, 2015 on crime). While these studies use KWs as a starting point to analyze the content of texts, others use it to understand reader reception of texts. By using two reference corpora that reflect patterns of language use from two different times, Fidler and Cvrček (2015) show that KWs are likely to be ranked differently by present-day readers than by readers in the past[12] because of different degrees of exposure to socialist discourse. In this approach, KWs do not serve as indicators of "aboutness" or style, but more as a source of information about what might be striking (or surprising) for different readers.

Beyond KWA: Keymorph Analysis and Multi-level Discourse Prominence Analysis

KWA is largely carried out on texts written in English, a language with little inflection, where the difference between a given word form and lemma is minimal. In English, the principles of keyness have been applied to multi-word expressions or clusters (e.g., Fisher-Starcke, 2009; Mahlberg, 2007) or key semantic domains (based on semantic tagging, cf. Baker, 2009). Attempts were made to expand keyness to grammatical categories (cf. Culpeper & Demmen, 2015), but the scarcity of inflection in English seems to lead to the language-specific conclusion that grammatical information (parts of speech) contributes little to existing KWA (Culpeper, 2009, pp. 54–55). This view is not applicable to every language (Cvrček & Fidler, forthcoming). Keymorph analysis (KMA), as proposed by Fidler and Cvrček (2017), shows that prominent morphosyntactic features (keymorphs) can characterize more schematic components of discourse—the representation of events and participants in discourse, especially the degrees of agency expressed in texts. The study demonstrates that morphemes provide information that is fundamental to discourse *structure*, rather than discourse content.

This paper studies prominence on multiple levels: keyed word forms, keyed lemmas (and their context), keyed morphemes, and the properties of sentences marked by a high density of keyed lemmas. The motivations for adopting such a multilayered quantitative approach to texts are found in the literature. Hopper and Thompson (1980) find correlations between the discourse properties of foregrounding–backgrounding and

[11]The term KWs therefore differs from query terms in search engines or cultural keywords (Williams, 1976). The identification of KWs has a clear quantitative basis; "…it is less subject to the vagaries of subjective judgments of cultural importance … [and] it does not rely on researchers selecting items that might be important… but can reveal items that researchers did not know to be important in the first place." (Culpeper & Demmen, 2015, p. 90)

[12]More discussion on the influence of a reference corpus on the results of KWA can be found in Scott, 2013.

grammatical components on multiple levels. Quantitative studies by Biber (1993, 2006) show how lexical and morphosyntactic data facilitate the identification of linguistic registers in English. The interaction between grammar and discourse has been a point of discussion especially in Slavic linguistics: for example, variation in case and context in Russian (Ueda, 1992), deixis selection and thematic hierarchization (Kresin, 1998), and verbal aspect and discourse organization (Altshuler, 2010 on Russian; Chvany, 1990; Desclés & Guentschéva, 1990 on Bulgarian; Fielder, 1990; Sonnenhauser, 2008). This holistic approach to text, which we will call Multi-level Discourse Prominence Analysis (MLDPA), can help us understand what constitutes alternativeness in the news provided by *Sputnik Czech Republic*.

Language Data

This study uses texts from *Sputnik Czech Republic* as the target corpus (henceforth SPUCz). SPUCz contains texts published from March to June 2015 at https://cz.sputniknews.com/ and consists of all the texts containing the following seed words (stems) related to the Czech Republic, Russia, and Ukraine:

- Word stems related to the Czech Republic: *česk-* 'Czech, Czech Republic (noun, adjective)', *čr* (abbreviation of the Czech Republic), *prah-* 'Prague', *hrad-* 'Castle' (reference to the Czech equivalent of the White House), *zeman-* [president] 'Zeman'.
- Word stems related to Ukraine (and the Minsk agreements): *ukrajin-* 'Ukraine' (noun, adjective), *kyjev-* 'Kiev' (noun, adjective), *porošenk-* '[president] Poroshenko'; *bělorusk-* 'Belarus' (noun, adjective)', *minsk-* 'Minsk' (noun, adjective), *lukašenk-* '[president] Lukashenko'.
- Word stems related to Russia: *rusk-* 'Russia' (noun, adjective), *moskv-* 'Moscow', *putin-* [president] 'Putin'.

SPUCz is expected to show how *Sputnik* projects images of Russia and Ukraine during the Ukrainian crisis (Russia's annexation of Crimea, the Malaysian Air crash, and the Minsk Agreements) and their relations to the Czech Republic.[13] The reference corpus used for the analysis is SYN2015 (Křen et al. 2016), which reflects the general language usage pattern of contemporary written Czech (for the summary of the corpora used see Table 10.3).[14]

The following sections examine several aspects of SPUCz. First, we look at what keyed words and lemmas tell us about SPUCz.[15] Second, we zoom in on selected key lemmas (KLs; the texts were lemmatized and morphologically tagged by

[13] While the target corpus may be biased towards the presence of words formed from these stems, it allows us to focus on the image of these countries specifically (especially Russia and Ukraine).

[14] Both corpora are available upon request at www.korpus.cz.

[15] The significance level used in this study was set to 0.001 and the minimum effect size was set to DIN = 75.

Table 10.3 Description and size of target corpus and reference corpus

Name	Description	Size
Target corpus: *SPUCz*	A compilation of texts containing seed words published between March and June, 2015 in *Sputnik Česká Republika* (https://cz.sputniknews.com/)	395,110 tokens 336,653 words (excl. punctuation)
Reference corpus: *SYN2015*	A balanced, representative corpus of written Czech texts published mainly in 2010–2014	121,666,414 tokens 100,838,568 words (excl. punctuation)

MorphoDiTa (Straková, Straka, & Hajič, 2014)) and their immediate context by studying collocates and key lemma links. Our analysis includes two unusual KLs as samples of discourse-semantic "spin" in SPUCz. Third, we use morphosyntactic features of selected lemmas to explore the rhetoric and ideology implicit in SPUCz. Finally, we examine those sentences where KLs cluster to identify what they have in common. The entire analysis is associated with prominence: prominence of word forms, lemmas, morphosyntactic properties, and density of keyness.[16] This study study thus probes what is likely to be striking (and therefore to have an impact) in contrast to the language patterns to which Czech readers are routinely exposed.

KWs (Key Inflected Word Forms)

Word forms are obviously much more numerous than lemmas (which represent entire paradigms[17]). A highly ranked word form (KW) indicates prominence simultaneously in the lexical and the syntactic role. The most highly ranked KWs (DIN = 100) are informative[18] (Table 10.4):

The fem nom sg case of the adjective 'anti-Russian' highlights *Sputnik*'s emphasis on the anti-Russian rhetoric, campaign, and hysteria (all fem nouns) in particular. *Domobrancům* suggests contentious dispute over arms supply by Russia *to* the separatists and fighting *against* the separatists (dative case).

The representation of the Ukrainian separatists as home-defenders and the concern about anti-Russian actions and entities are all the more evident among KWs with a DIN above 99.5 and below 100 (in bold style) (Table 10.5).

Other KWs add more information about the content of anti-Russian actions (in italics): allegations of unfair behavior by the West and Ukraine against Russia ("moratorium"); "undelivered [gas]" and "undelivered [Mistrals]" (helicopter carri-

[16] This procedure involves the level of prominence (DIN), the number of prominent units, and the number of all content words in a sentence. It investigates sentence types that are likely to attract reader attention by measuring the density of KLs.

[17] For example, the lemma *hrad* 'castle' can appear in multiple word forms in Standard Czech: *hrad* (nom/acc sg), *hradu* (gen/dat sg), *hradě* (loc sg), *hradem* (instr sg), *hrady* (nom/acc/voc/instr pl), *hradů* (gen pl), *hradům* (dat pl), and *hradech* (loc pl).

[18] Here, we only discuss common nouns, as they are most likely to be associated with the representation of entities, individuals, and events.

Table 10.4 Keywords (DIN = 100)

Keyword (Non-Proper Nouns)	DIN
protiruská 'anti-Russian' (fem nom sg[a])	100.000
domobrancům 'to home-defenders' (dat pl)	100.000

[a]Theoretically, this could also be a neut pl nom or acc form, but all the instances here are in the fem nominative sg

Table 10.5 Keywords (99.5 < DIN < 100)

KWs	DIN
domobranců 'of home-defenders' (gen pl)	99.941
třístranná 'tri-lateral' (fem nom sg)	99.891
vrtulníkových 'of helicopter' (gen, loc pl)	99.891
domobranci 'home-defenders' (nom pl)	99.873
neonacismus 'neonacism' (nom acc sg)	99.869
default 'of default' (gen sg)	99.855
batalionů 'of batallions' (gen pl)	99.837
MZV 'Ministry of Foreign Affairs, abbreviation'	99.828
rusofobie 'Russophobia' (nom, gen sg)	99.813
valutových 'of foreign currency' (gen, loc pl)	99.813
přisunují '(they) move' (Non-past 3pl)	99.782
domobrance 'home-defender' (acc pl)	99.755
masmédiích 'mass media' (loc pl)	99.746
protiruských 'anti-Russian' (gen pl)	99.743
nedodaný 'not delivered [gas]' (masc acc sg)	99.720
moratoriu 'moratorium' (loc sg)	99.710
spolubesedník 'interlocutor, conversation partner' (nom sg)	99.710
mj 'besides'	99.704
čelení 'tackling' (gen acc loc sg)	99.673
odváděcí 'distracting' (nom sg)	99.673
protiruskými 'anti-Russian' (instr pl)	99.673
protiruským 'anti-Russian' (dat pl, instr sg)	99.673
dvoustranném 'bi-lateral' (masc loc sg)	99.637
rozmísťují '(they) deploy' (NP 3pl)	99.608
nedodané 'not delivered [Mistrals]' (masg inanim acc pl, fem acc pl)	99.608
ratifikovalo '(it) ratified' (Past neut sg)	99.608
masmédia 'mass media' (nom acc pl)	99.557
znepokojeno 'concerned' (pass part neu sg short)	99.534
protiruské 'anti-Russian' (fem nom acc pl; fem gen dat sg; neut nom sg; masc inanim acc pl)	99.523

ers which France did not deliver to Russia), which suggest Russia's unfair treatment at the hands of European states.

These KWs reveal salient words in their most prominent syntactic functions. The interpretation of KWs is not complete, however, without contextual information. Moreover, KWs may not necessarily rank prominent ideas (represented by lemma) highly, since the prominence of the lemma may be diluted when inflected forms are measured separately. We therefore need to look at prominent lemmas (KLs).

Key Lemmas (KLs)

The top 246 KLs (with a DIN value of at least 99.5) illustrate some of the most salient ideas in SPUCz[19] (Table 10.6).

Clearly, the information provided by KWs and KLs can overlap. Some of the KLs, like KWs, concern anti-Russian sentiments ('anti-Russian', 'Russophobia', and representation of the Ukrainian separatists as 'home-defenders'). KLs, however, point to other topics: to highly developed technology ('highly technological') and settlements of the Ukrainian crisis ('coordinated [agreement]'). KLs also suggest more detailed aspects of the Ukrainian crisis, as in "heroization" (of Ukrainian nationalists).

The KLs are clearly associated with prominent topics raised in SPUCz. The anticipated topics of anti-Russian actions, negotiations about Ukraine, and Ukrainian aggression could be obtained through qualitative analysis of texts. More importantly, KLs themselves do not directly show how the lemmas are used, as they are only pointers to what the text is about. This is especially the case with parts of

Table 10.6 KLs with DINs of at least 99.5[a] (excluding proper nouns and adjectives directly derived from proper nouns)

KLs	DIN
vysocetechnologický 'highly-technological'	100
eurointegrace 'Euro-integration'	100
ukrajinizace 'Ukrainization'	100
departament 'department'	99.984
průstřelný (as the negated form neprůstřelný 'bullet-proof')	99.9455
čekaný (as the negated form nečekaný 'unexpected')	99.9405
domobranec 'home-defender'	99.8895
rusofobie 'Russophobia'	99.8217
úřada (=úřad 'office')[a]	99.7821
zkoordinovaný 'coordinated'	99.7386
čelení 'facing'	99.6733
protiruský 'anti-Russian'	99.6554
antiteroristický 'anti-terrorist'	99.5918
odváděcí 'distracting'	99.5336
heroizace 'heroization'	99.5336

[a]Atypical KLs (*departament*), lemmatization errors (*úřada*), and parts of proper nouns (AT, *Antiteroristická Operace*) are not discussed here.

[19] Proper nouns and adjectives directly derived from them are not discussed here.

speech that do not stand on their own (modifiers). Moreover, the KLs themselves do not reflect discourse-semantic "spin"—a process of altering the connotation and/or the meaning of a word by embedding it in a less expected context. The following section will explore the interaction between selected KLs and context.

Collocates and Key Lemmas Links (KL Links): Contextual Reading of Words

In this section, we first look at modifiers: the two adjectives 'Russian, Ukrainian', and two groups of adverbs that must be understood in context. Then, we study two nouns ('separatist, genocide') as an illustration of the discourse-semantic spin in SPUCz. The adjectives *ruský* and *ukrajinský* were selected because of their objective values (high DINs) and their high relevance in the news (Ukrainian crisis); they were selected also because they themselves do not contain inherent evaluative meaning (in contrast to 'anti-Russian' or 'Russophobia'). The two groups of adverbs affirm or question actions and statements. The two nouns (*separatista* and *genocida*) were selected because they could potentially occur in texts about different regions and historical periods.

The analysis in this section is based on collocation[20] and KL-links. Collocation suggests the use of KLs in a phraseological and syntactic unit. KL-links deepen our understanding of key lemma use by showing connections among the prominent lemmas in discourse; the reader is expected to draw prominent thematic connections between KLs that appear in close proximity. Although these KLs are specific to the time of their publication and are mostly tied to the Ukrainian crisis, the results might be also informative of the general nature of SPUCz texts.

KL-Collocates and KL-Links of Ethnic-National Adjectives: **ruský** *'Russian' and* **ukrajinský** *'Ukrainian'*

Ethnic-national adjectives can modify specific sets of nouns to produce an image of a country and its people. Collocates are especially crucial for adjectives since their modified nouns can indicate what entities, qualities, and individuals are particularly

[20] Cf. "collocations create connotations" (Stubbs, 2005, p. 14). The contextual properties of keywords are thus examined by their links (Scott & Tribble, 2006) to other keywords (i.e., co-occurrence of KWs within a textual span).

Table 10.7 Collocates of *ukrajinský* 'Ukrainian' and *ruský* 'Russian'

	***ukrajinský* Collocates**	**FQ ≥ 14**	**LogDice ≥ 8.06**	***ruský* Collocates**	**FQ ≥ 23**	**LogDice ≥8.26**
1.	**voják 'soldier'**	54	9.94	prezident 'president'	162	10.54
2.	strana 'party, side'	55	9.73	Putin	112	10.15
3.	úřad 'office'	43	9.68	prohlásit 'to proclaim'	103	9.96
4.	**armáda 'army'**	43	9.65	Vladimir	82	9.94
5.	prezident 'president'	64	9.64	plyn 'gas'	76	9.79
6.	**silový 'of force'**	36	9.59	zahraniční 'foreign'	69	9.64
7.	krize 'crisis'	36	9.53	strana 'party, side'	69	9.53
8.	**konflikt 'conflict'**	41	9.52	věc 'affair, thing'	56	9.42
9.	Porošenko	38	9.44	ministr 'minister'	62	9.38
10.	vláda 'government'	38	9.37	federace 'federation'	48	9.31
11.	**složka '(army) division'**	28	9.27	ministerstvo 'ministry'	47	9.16
12.	příslušník 'member'	29	9.25	**vojenský 'of military'**	55	9.1
13.	**ozbrojený 'armed'**	30	9.21	Dmitrij	38	8.97
14.	**síla 'force'**	32	9.09	Sergej	37	8.86
15.	oznámit 'to announce'	26	8.7	diplomacie 'diplomacy'	35	8.84
16.	Petr	19	8.66	šéf 'head'	36	8.84
17.	premier 'prime minister''	19	8.54	který 'who/which (rel pron)'	70	8.76
18.	Petro	17	8.52	hranice 'border'	34	8.74
19.	ekonomika 'economy'	16	8.33	dodávka 'supply'	33	8.65
20.	hranice 'border'	16	8.31	společnost 'society'	34	8.65
21.	Arsenij	14	8.28	být 'to be'	168	8.63
22.	vnitřní 'internal'	14	8.26	vztah 'relationship'	34	8.61
23.	být 'to be'	121	8.26	oznámit 'to announce'	35	8.58
24.	ministr 'minister'	19	8.2	se 'reflx pron acc'	100	8.46
25.	který 'who, which'	39	8.2	Lavrov	29	8.44
26.	rada 'council'	16	8.18	mluvčí 'spokesman'	26	8.4
27.	se 'reflx pron acc'	74	8.18	tiskový 'of press'	26	8.35
28.	ministerstvo 'ministry'	15	8.13	delegace 'delegation'	24	8.33
29.	společnost 'society'	15	8.07	státní 'of state'	25	8.27
30.	stát 'state'	20	8.06	Vladimír	23	8.26
31.				economika 'economy'	24	8.26

associated with specific ethnic-national groups. Compare the collocates of *ukrajinský* 'Ukrainian' and *ruský* 'Russian' in Table 10.7.[21]

'Ukrainian' and 'Russian' tend to pattern with different semantic units. 'Ukrainian' has more collocates (lemmas, in bold style)[22] connected with military forces and political instability ('army', 'of force', 'crisis', 'conflict', '[army] divi-

[21] The collocates were searched within a span of three words on either side of the KWIC and were ranked first by LogDice and secondly by frequency.

[22] Collocates here are lemmas that are not necessarily keyed.

sion', 'armed', 'force') than 'Russian.' 'Russian' collocates with lemmas (in gray shading) report official negotiations and announcements ('diplomacy', 'relationship', 'spokesman', 'of press', 'delegation').[23]

The KL-links for these adjectives indicate different thematic connections (Table 10.8). A KL-link is established if two KLs appear in one sentence (regardless of their distance).

The KL-links for *ruský* show economic connections: 'sanction(s)' (against Russia) and 'gas' (each shaded in gray). In comparison, armed participants and conflict are prominent parts of the text connected with *ukrajinský* (KLs in bold style). Both the list of the KL links and the list of collocates consistently include 'armed' and 'conflict' for 'Ukrainian.'

Table 10.8 KL-links for *ruský* of Russia' and *ukrajinský* 'of Ukraine'

ukrajinský KL-links	Count ≥ 65	ruský KL-links	Count ≥ 110
Ukrajina 'Ukraine'	258	prezident 'president'	408
ukrajinský 'of Ukraine'	206	Rusko 'Russia'	370
prezident 'president'	206	ruský 'of Russia'	318
prohlásit 'to proclaim'	137	prohlásit 'to proclaim'	270
ruský 'of Russia'	129	Ukrajina 'Ukraine'	256
Porošenko	127	Putin	243
voják 'soldier'	124	ministr 'minister'	225
Rusko 'Russia'	118	**vojenský 'of military'**	193
Donbas	115	zahraniční 'foreign'	184
oznámit 'to announce'	114	Vladimir	176
konflikt 'conflict'	97	USA	175
Kyjev 'Kiev'	96	americký 'of America'	165
dohoda 'agreement'	94	oznámit 'to announce'	152
armáda 'army'	87	plyn 'gas'	143
americký 'of America'	78	Moskva	136
vojenský 'of military'	71	ukrajinský 'of Ukraine'	129
zbraň 'weapon'	69	Sergej	124
ozbrojený 'armed'	67	evropský 'European'	119
evropský 'European'	66	Evropa 'Europe'	115
USA	65	sankce 'sanction'	110

[23] The appearance of KWs referring to presidents among the collocations is expected, as the major seed words include names of presidents (e.g., Putin and Poroshenko).

KL Links for Adverbs

Just as adjectives modify entities and individuals, adverbs modify actions and states. Some adverbs can function as "amplifiers" of statements or denote an epistemic stance towards a statement (Biber et al., 1999, pp. 554–557). In our case, the former indicate commitment to the truthfulness of statements (e.g., 'definitely,' 'absolutely'), while the latter indicate distance from it (e.g., allegedly, seemingly). There were six keyed adverbs in SPUCz[24]: amplifiers or adverbs of commitment (*sporně*, occurring as *nesporně* 'undoubtedly' and *kategoricky* 'categorically') and "stance" adverbs expressing the speaker's evaluation that an event–action–situation is questionable (*zákonně* 'legally,' 4/5 instances as *nezákonně* 'illegally,' and *jednostranně* 'unilaterally') (Table 10.9).

The selected amplifiers attract more KLs related to Russia (gray shading) than to Ukraine (bold style). The texts express commitment to truthfulness.

4. A klíčovým okamžikem jsou tu **nesporně** prvky politického urovnání" řekl Putin. (https://cz.sputniknews.com/svet/201506195754751/)
   'And here **undoubtedly** the components of a political settlement constitute [lit. are] the key moment,' Putin said.'

In contrast, Ukraine is linked to stance adverbs expressing questionable behavior. Situations involving Ukraine are thus likely to be represented as somewhat suspect. KLs related to Ukraine have more links than those related to Russia. There are no links related to Russia for the adverb *nezákonně*.

5. Ve vedení Doněcké lidové republiky tvrdí, že kyjevští letečtí dispečeři **nezákonně** předali kontrolu letu malajsijského boeingu, který havaroval u Doněcku, svým dněpropetrovským kolegům oznámil portál Vesti.ru. (https://cz.sputniknews.com/svet/20150506361967/)
   'Someone in the leadership of the Donetsk People's Republic claims that the Kiev air dispatchers **illegally** transferred flight control of the Malaysian Boeing which crashed near Donetsk to their colleagues in Dnepropetrovsk, Vesti.ru announced.'

KL-links to amplifiers and stance adverbs suggest Russia and Ukraine are represented differently. Ukraine's actions are questioned, while Russia's actions are associated with determination and a commitment to the truth. These links, as they are keyed, are expected to stand out and be noticed by readers.

Contextual information can also show discourse-semantic spin, which alters the connotation and/or meaning of a word by placing it into a (slightly) different context. The following section will serve as an illustration.

[24] We excluded the remaining adverbs: *zahraničně* as part of the descriptive phrases *zahraničně-politický/-ekonomický/-obchodní* 'internationally-politically /-economically /-commercially,' and the adverb *odkladně* (used in *neodkladně* 'urgently').

Table 10.9 Amplifiers and stance adverbs (KL-links)[a]

Amplifiers				Stance adverbs (adverbs of questionable behavior)			
sporně (as *nesporně* 'undoubtedly'	count	*kategoricky* 'categorically'	count	*zákonně* (as *nezákonně* 'illegally' except one instance)	count	*jednostranně* 'unilaterally'	count
Napomáhat 'assist'	2	Genocida 'genocide'	1	**kyjevský 'of Kiev'**	1	**Kyjev 'Kiev'**	4
rozšiřování 'expansion'	2	západ 'west'	1	Boeing	1	doněcký 'of Donetsk'	4
summit	2	pohraniční 'of border'	1	zdůraznit 'to emphasize'	1	luhanský 'of Luhansk'	3
Rusko 'Russia'	2	kontrolovaný 'controlled'	1	premier 'prime minister'	1	**ukrajinský 'of Ukraine'**	3
Putin	2	letadlo 'airplane'	1	území 'territory'	1	urovnání 'settlement'	3
zasedání 'session'	2	Nizozemí 'the Netherlands'	1	oznámit 'to announce'	1	Dialog	2
stíhačka 'fighter jet'	2	komplex 'complex'	1	válka 'war'	1	DLR (Donetsk People's Republic)	2
Jaceňuk 'Yatsenyuk'	1	Rusko 'Russia'	1	Nulandová 'Nuland'	1	evropský 'of Europe'	2
plenární 'plenary'	1	Moskva 'Moscow'	1	malajsijský 'of Malaysia'	1	**Ukrajina 'Ukraine'**	2
Porošenko 'Poroshenko'	1	separatista 'separatist'	1	havarovat 'to have an accident'	1	minský 'of Minsk'	2
výzbroj 'armaments'	1	Donbas	1	Doněck	1	území 'territory'	2
rozmístění 'deployment'	1	domobranec 'home-defender'	1	dněpropetrovský 'of Dnepropetrovsk'	1	hodlat 'to intend'	1
mezinárodní 'international'	1	MH (flight no. of Malaysian Air)	1	doněcký 'of Donetsk'	1	Ihor	1
Moskva 'Moscow'	1	sestřelit 'to shoot down'	1	Vest	1	napomáhat 'to assist'	1
ekonomický 'economic'	1	konflikt 'conflict'	1	dispečer 'dispacher'	1	Rusko	1

[a]Collocates are not presented for these adverbs because there were too few of them.

Discourse-Semantic Spin

This section looks at two highly ranked KLs: *separatista* 'separatist' and *genocida* 'genocide.' They are nearly equally prominent (DIN = 93.92 and 91.13, respectively). They are also words that could refer to individuals and actions from various regions and historical periods. Collocates from both SPUCz and SYN2015 are informative in understanding the discourse-semantic spin of these lemmas (Table 10.10).

Table 10.10 Collocates (case-insensitive) for *separatista* in SPUCz and SYN2015

separatista Collocates (SPU Cz)	logDice (≥5)	Freq (≥3)	separatista Collocates (SYN2015)	logDice (≥5)	Freq
stydět (all as nestydím '[I] am not ashamed of')	11.752	4	**proruský 'pro-Russian'**	11.719	47
terorista 'terrorist'	11.069	4	**doněcký 'of Donetsk'**	9.156	7
označit 'label'	9.461	4	**luhanský 'of Luhansk'**	8.943	5
za 'as'	7.179	7	donbas 'Donbas'	8.715	5
"	5.416	5	doněck 'Donetsk'	8.559	7
na 'to'	5.224	8	**slavjanský 'of Slaviansk'**	8.342	3
být 'to be'	5.205	13	slavjansk 'Slaviansk'	8.272	3
a 'and'	5.164	10	**kurdský 'Kurdish'**	8.151	4
který 'rel pron'	5.056	3	**čečenský 'of Chechnya'**	7.891	3
Rusko 'Russia'	5.028	3	**vlámský 'Flemish'**	7.681	3
			podporovaný 'supported'	7.475	7
			ukrajinský 'Ukrainian'	7.453	11
			odtržení 'separation'	7.438	3
			kyjev 'Kiev'	7.232	5
			ozbrojenec 'an armed man'	7.171	3
			ukrajina 'Ukraine'	7.117	15
			ovládaný 'controled'	7.008	5
			příměří 'truce'	6.708	3
			ozbrojený 'armed'	6.678	7
			skotský 'Scottish'	6.66	5
			vůdce 'leader'	6.247	10
			východ 'Eastern'	5.783	13
			pozorovatel 'observer'	5.533	3
			rusko	5.344	11
			armáda	5.143	11

The range for collocates is set at (−3, +3), the minimum collocate frequency in the corpus at 5, and the minimum collocate frequency in the span at 3.

The collocates for 'separatist' in SYN2015 suggest discussions about territorial issues (regional names within a larger territory in different parts of the world), ethnic-national loyalty and affiliations (e.g., 'pro-Russian', 'of Donetsk', 'Luhansk', 'Kurdish', 'of Slaviansko', 'of Chechnya', 'Flemish'), and armaments (in bold style). In contrast, such collocates are fewer in SPUCz and are primarily part of expressions reporting false and unfair negative labeling ('terrorist', 'to be ashamed of', 'as', 'to label', 'to be') (indicated by gray shading):

6. Podle slov zástupců veřejnosti Donbasu, všichni, kdo se odvažují mít vlastní názor, se hned prohlašují **za separatisty** a napomahače [sic] teroristů. (https://cz.sputniknews.com/svet/20150417274162/)
   'According to the words of the representatives of the Donbas public, everybody who dares to have an opinion of their own is immediately proclaimed **as separatists** and accomplices to terrorists.'
7. Mimochodem, v Česku se **za** označení separatista **nestydím**. Vášnivými separatisty **byli** zakladatelé českého státu Tomáš Garrigue Masaryk a Karel Kramář. (Jiří Just, https://cz.sputniknews.com/politika/201503211137897/)
   'By the way, **I am not ashamed of being labeled as** a separatist. The founders of the Czech state Tomáš Garrigue Masaryk and Karel Kramář were passionate separatists.'

KL-links in SPUCz further point to the type of discourse in which *separatista* is embedded. Table 10.11 suggests that *separatista* belongs to a discourse not only about armed conflict ('conflict', 'of military') but also about economic hardships, anti-Russian actions, presence of accomplice(s), and propaganda, as illustrated by KL-links such as 'sanctions', 'to impose [sanctions]', 'medium' (normally *media* in the plural), and 'anti-Russian' (bold style). The KL is represented as part of Western discourse, which unfairly denigrates the fighters defending their home.

Table 10.11 KL-links for *separatista* 'separatist'

Separatista KL-links	Count
Ukrajina 'Ukraine'	6
ukrajinský 'of Ukraine'	5
Rusko 'Russia'	4
Donbas 'Donbas'	3
ruský 'of Russia'	3
východ 'east'	3
kontrolovaný 'controlled'	2
Rusín 'Rusyn'	2
představitel 'representative'	2
domobrana 'home-defense'	2
konflikt 'conflict'	2
vojenský 'of military'	2
pomahač 'accomplice'	2
oznamovat 'to announce'	2
vyzývat 'to call, challenge'	2
kyjevský 'of Kiev'	2
sankce 'sanction'	2
uvalit 'to impose [sanctions]'	2
protiruský 'anti-Russian'	2
médium (used in pl) 'media'	1

8. V zemi se zakládají iniciativní skupiny a internetové zdroje se seznamy „zrádců vlasti, **separatistů** a pomahačů ruských okupantů," dodal senátor. (https://cz.sputniknews.com/svet/201504102364 07/)
   'In the country active groups and internet sources are being established with the lists "of traitors of the motherland, of **separatists**, and accomplices of Russian occupiers," the senator said.'

The context for 'separatists' in SPUCz shows a shift from what is largely observed in the general representative corpus of Czech. Its discourse-semantic function is altered by the syntactic constructions in which the lemma occurs and by the prominent links to other prominent KLs. *Separatista* in SPUCz suggests that it is an unfair label used against people who disagree with the official Ukrainian view.

Genocida 'genocide' is another illustrative example of discourse-semantic spin. Table 10.12 shows collocates of this lemma in both SPUCz and SYN2015.

The collocates for this KL in SYN2015 suggest mass killings ('murdering', 'massacre'), the locations of their occurrence ('Rwanda', 'Armenia', 'Cambodia'), their victims and culprits ('Armenian', 'of Rwanda', 'Nazi'), and denial of such actions ('denying') (bold style). The collocates in SPU, in contrast, show that the reference to genocide is likely to be embedded in a sentence related to *Donbas* (in gray shading).

The top four KL links for *genocida* from SPUCz show that the KL is linked to both the Armenian genocide ('Armenian') (bold style), and the conflict in Donbas in Ukraine (gray shading) (Table 10.13).

Table 10.12 Collocates for *genocida* 'genocide' in SPUCz and SYN2015

Collocates (SPUCz)	logDice	Freq	**Collocates genocida (SYN2015)**	**logDice**	**Freq**
armén 'Armenian'	12.559	7	**rwanda 'Rwanda'**	10.102	17
přiznat 'to acknowledge'	10.771	4	**popírání 'denying'**	9.142	8
obyvatel 'resident'	9.148	4	**rwandský 'of Rwanda'**	8.871	5
donbas 'Donbas'	8.724	6	**armén 'Armenian'**	8.794	6
za 'as'	5.966	3	**genocida 'genocide'**	8.781	8
.	4.136	10	**arménský 'of Armenia'**	8.602	6
a 'and'	3.842	4	**kambodža 'Cambodia'**	8.336	5
v 'in'	3.686	4	**nacistický 'Nazi'**	7.785	14
,	1.934	3	**vraždění 'murdering'**	7.323	3
			masakr 'massacre'	7.093	5
			lidskost 'humaneness'	6.952	3
			schvalování 'approval'	6.893	3

Table 10.13 KL-links for *genocida* 'genocide'

KWLink	**Count**
Armén 'Armenian'	13
Donbas	8
ukrajinský 'of Ukraine'	4
Ukrajina 'Ukraine'	3

9. Jeden z novinářů položil ukrajinskému politikovi následující otázku: „Kdy zastavíte **genocidu** na Donbasu?" (https://cz.sputniknews.com/svet/201505154 11642/)
   'One of the journalists asked the Ukrainian politician the following question: 'When will you stop the **genocide** in Donbas?"'

10. Za hlavní úkol dneška označil Janukovyč nastolení míru a zdůraznil přitom, že to, co se děje na jihovýchodě Ukrajiny, není nic jiného než **genocida** obyvatel Donbasu. (https://cz.sputniknews.com/svet/20150623590005/)
    'Yanukovych declared establishment of peace as today's most important task, and emphasized on this occasion that what is happening in the South-Eastern Ukraine is nothing other than **genocide** of the Donbas residents.'

The semantic scope of this KL is thus expanded to apply to Donbas.

The previous subsections ("KWs (Key Inflected Word Forms)," "Key Lemmas (KLs)," and "Collocates and Key Lemmas Links (KL links): Contextual Reading of Words") have explored discourse contents in SPUCz. KWs, KLs, collocations, and KL-links exemplify the predominant themes and images of Russia and Ukraine. The following sections will explore the morphosyntactic features of selected KLs to demonstrate that morphemes help identify an internally consistent rhetoric in SPUCz: the discourse position or implicit ideology of the target corpus.

Keymorph Analysis: A Glimpse into Discourse Position

This section first explores predicates and their grammatical subjects, then the grammatical case marking of selected KLs. These morphosyntatic features serve as keys to unpack what constitutes alternativeness in SPUCz discourse.

Opinion Predicates and Their Grammatical Subjects: Alternative Sources

SPUCz yields a number of keyed verbs expressing opinions and speech (*verba dicendi*) (DIN $\geq$ 75.5). We looked at the verbs that yielded three or more occurrences of subject nouns (Table 10.14).

Table 10.14 Grammatical subjects of keyed *verba dicendi* and opinion verbs (with FQ ≥ 3)

poznamenávat 'remark'		**podotýkat 'note (imperf.)'**		**podotknout 'note (perf.)'**		**zdůrazňovat 'emphasize (imperf.)'**		**ironizovat 'ironize'**		**zdůraznit 'emphasize (perf.)'**		**vyslovit 'express'**	
Subject	**FQ**	**Subject**	**FQ**	**Subject**	**FQ**	**Subject**	**FQ**	**Subject**	**FQ**	**Subject**	**FQ**	**Subject**	**FQ**
list 'newspaper'	4	časopis 'magazine'	6	ministr 'minister'	5	list 'newspaper'	9	list 'newspaper'	2	prezident	20	**Putin**	3
expert	4	politolog 'political scientist'	4	**Putin**	3	expert	4			premiér 'prime minister'	10	většina 'majority'	3
novinář 'journalist'	3	autor 'author'	4	expert	3	analytic 'analyst'	4			ministr 'minister'	10		
autor 'author'	3	novinář 'journalist'	3	senátor	3	agentura '[news] agency'	4			**Putin**	9		
						Lagowski[a]	3			**Lavrov**	8		
						novinář 'journaist'	3			šéf 'head, boss'	5		
										Ušakov	4		
										diplomat	3		
										Peskov	3		
										Kerry	3		
										Hollande	3		

The most frequent subject nouns split into two major categories: external sources (media, journalists, experts, and analysts) (gray shading) and the major representatives of the Russian government (Putin, Lavrov, and Ušakov) (bold style).

Grammatical subjects confirm the formal aspects of *Sputnik*'s self-representation: an "alternative news portal," not an explicitly pro-Kremlin press agency. The subjects are Russian officials as well as media-expert sources; grammatical subjects representing the political leaders of the EU and the USA are relatively scarce. The results do not inform of the content of what is stated. The partiality of reported content in SPUCz is explored in the following section.

Predicates Reporting Victimization

The grammatical subjects of keyed verbs reporting unfavorable actions (below) can inform who in particular is viewed as taking negative actions and who is affected by those actions in texts. By verbs of unfavorable actions (VUs), we mean those verbs that report events in which a culprit and victim can potentially exist.[25]

Table 10.15 shows that VUs gravitate towards the passive voice in SPUCz more than in SYN2015. The chi-square statistic of distribution passive voice among corpora is 59.794 ($p < 0.0001$).

[25] Subjects were manually checked and categorized.

Table 10.15 Passive and active voices for verbs of unfavorable action (VUs)

	SPU				SYN2015		
Predicates	**DIN**	Passive voice total	Active voice total	Total passive and active	Passive voice total	Active voice total	Total passive and active
torpédovat 'to torpedo'	96.9214	0	5	5	3	28	31
démonizovat 'to demonize'	95.0535	1	6	7	9	30	39
ostřelovat 'to shoot, to shell'	94.2045	6	15	21	23	140	163
obstavit 'to freeze [assets]'	93.663	5	0	5	10	27	37
uvalit 'to impose [sanctions]'	91.7726	9	11	20	92	208	300
znepokojit 'alarm, pf'	91.4103	26	1	27	140	230	370
sestřelit 'to shoot down'	90.8411	12	7	19	57	225	282
destabilizovat 'to destabilize'	90.4447	0	5	5	6	48	54
podkopat 'to undermine pf'	88.9727	0	5	5	12	61	73
porušovat 'to violate, impf'	88.2318	4	37	41	53	739	792
podkopávat 'to undermine impf'	88.1279	0	7	7	5	110	115
zmařit 'to thwart'	86.0015	8	5	13	65	208	273
vyprovokovat 'to provoke'	84.921	4	14	18	34	338	372
pobouřit 'to outrage'	84.3693	4	5	9	66	209	275
postrkovat 'to push'	83.7646	0	9	9	8	199	207
bombardovat 'to bombard'	81.4461	0	11	11	62	222	284
zkreslovat 'to distort'	80.3308	0	6	6	7	155	162
znepokojovat 'to alarm, impf')	79.6402	3	14	17	3	603	606
Total FQ		82	163	245	655	3780	4435
%		33.5%	66.5%	100%	14.8%	85.2%	100%

As to the subjects of passive and active voice forms, Russia appears more often in the passive voice than the active voice of VUs (Table 10.16)[26]:

[26] The subjects were manually identified and include instances where the subject is implicit and/or is mentioned in the surrounding discourse.

Table 10.16 Subjects of passive and active voices for VUs

Passive voice	Russia	USA, Europe, NATO	others	total
Passive voice FQ	29 (35.4%)	15 (18.3%)	38 (46.3%)	82
Active voice FQ	8 (4.9%)	72 (44.2%)	83 (50.9%)	163

The results are significant (the chi-square statistic of Russia appearing in context of passive versus active voice is 37.133, $p < 0.0001$). The numbers are consistent with the image of Russia as a victim discussed below in 8.3.2. SPUCz clearly presents itself as a portal that draws information not only from Russian government officials, but also from experts. The portal, however, shows a consistent pattern to impress upon the reader that Russia is the victim of troubles, rather than the instigator. Such use of passive voice is known to represent event participants as "affected by the actions of others" (Fairclough, 1995, p. 112).

Grammatical Case: Implicit Rhetoric

Grammatical case in discourse is not extensively explored in English-based quantitative discourse analysis. However, when a specific grammatical case is used with unusually high frequency relative to the other cases, it contributes to the image of the referent. Furthermore, case marking KMA of several lemmas reveals a pattern of relationship among discourse participants.

This section will contrast the prominence of grammatical cases[27] for two sets of KLs: two presidents (Putin and Poroshenko) and their states (*Rusko* 'Russia' and *Ukrajina* 'Ukraine'). It is an expansion of KMA presented in Fidler and Cvrček (2017) and Cvrček and Fidler (forthcoming).

Putin vs. Poroshenko

The notion of grammatical case interactions with semantics has been discussed in Jakobson on Russian case (1936/1984). The more recent study by Janda and Clancy provides a comprehensive description of the semantics of Czech grammatical case in the cognitive linguistics framework (2006). The nominative case is most likely of all the cases to signal agency. The dative case in Czech is most likely to signal that the referent, although an important participant in discourse ("potential competitor" in Janda & Clancy, 2006, pp. 96–107), is represented as the experiencer or even a victim of actions (pp. 60–95). The instrumental case reports means

[27] DIN here (marked with the asterisk) is calculated differently than for KLs. The prominence of each case is calculated relative to all occurrences of a given lemma in SPUCz and SYN2015, respectively (i.e., not relative to the number of tokens in the corpus) as in Table 10.17.

by which actions are carried out (pp. 180–198); while the preposition *s* 'with' suggests that the referent is portrayed as a companion (pp. 204–207).

The DIN values in Table 10.17 clearly show that Putin is represented as an active participant: most prominently as an agent and secondarily as a partner in joint actions.[28] The relative grammatical case prominence for Putin gives rise to an image of a strong leader who also works collaboratively with others.

11. Peskov: **Putin**^{nom} vysvětlil Obamovi, že prohlášení o vojsku RF na Ukrajině jsou mylná (https://cz.sputniknews.com/svet/201506266037731/).
    'Peskov: **Putin**^{nom} explained to Obama that the statements about the troops of the Russian Federation were erroneous.'
12. Kerry označil jednání s **Putinem**^{instr} a Lavrovem za upřímná (https://cz.sputniknews.com/svet/201505123930451/)
    'Kerry described the negotiations with **Putin**^{instr} and Lavrov as honest.'

Poroshenko in Table 10.17 projects the opposite image. The dative case is more keyed than the other cases. When contrasted with Putin, the Ukrainian president is portrayed as a recipient and experiencer of actions possibly carried out by someone else.

13. Jak se informuje na webu organizace, hlavní výtky adresované **Porošenkovi**^{dat} se týkají vyšetřování masových vražd během euromajdanu v Kyjevě (https://cz.sputniknews.com/svet/201506085233191/)
    'As the organization describes on the web, the main criticisms addressed to **Porošenko**^{dat} concerns the investigation of mass murders during the Euromaidan in Kiev'
14. Nedá se s naprostou jistotou říct, že **Porošenkovi**^{dat} hrozí fašistický převrat, ale situace s radikály […], musí vyvolávat ostražitost nejen u ukrajinské moci, ale i v USA a Evropské unii, zdůrazňuje Stephen Cohen. (https://cz.sputniknews.com/politika/20150304345441/)

Table 10.17 Prominence of grammatical cases: Putin and Porošenko

Case[a]	Putin (DIN)	Porošenko (DIN)
Nominative	12.24	1.81
Genitive	−30.91	0.18
Dative	−49.78	29.41
Accusative	−26.37	−10.70
Instrumental	6.10	−25.60

[a]The raw frequencies of the locative case are not shown here since their numbers are miniscule.

[28] The instrumental case is highly collocated with the preposition *s* 'with' in Czech.

'It's not possible to state with absolute certainty that a fascist revolution threatens **Porošenko**^{dat}, but the situation with the radicals [...] must generate wariness not only in the Ukrainian authorities, but also in the USA and EU, Stephen Cohen emphasizes.'

A pattern of rhetoric emerges when we compare the results from Table 10.17 and the case marking for Russia (*Rusko*) and Ukraine (*Ukrajina*) in the following section.

Russia vs. Ukraine

The case endings for Russia and Ukraine present the mirror image of the prominence of grammatical cases for Putin and Poroshenko (Table 10.18).

The dative case and the instrumental case are the most prominent for *Rusko*. Russia tends to be represented as an experiencer (even a victim) and a potential competitor (dative case) and a companion (instrumental case).

15. Kanadská vláda rozšířila seznam sankcí proti **Rusku**^{dat}, [...] (https://cz.sputniknews.com/byznys/201506306200971/).
    'The Canadian government expanded the list of sanctions against **Russia**^{dat} [...]'
16. A musím znovu opakovat, že si přejeme dobré vztahy s **Ruskem**^{instr}, [...], řekla Merkelová. (https://cz.sputniknews.com/politika/20150612544229/)
    'And I must repeat once more that we wish for good relationships with **Russia**^{instr}, [...], said Merkel.'

In (15), Russia is the victim of sanctions. (16) represents Russia as a partner in international relations.

In contrast, the highly keyed cases for *Ukrajina* are the nominative and the genitive. The nominative is likely to represent the explicit agent of actions. The genitive

Table 10.18 Prominence of grammatical cases: *Rusko* 'Russia' and *Ukrajina* 'Ukraine'

Rusko			Ukrajina		
Case	Word form	DIN	Case	Word form	DIN
Nominative	Rusko	11.02	Nominative	Ukrajina	9.70
Genitive	Ruska	1.05	Genitive	Ukrajiny	9.81
Dative	Rusku	35.79	Dative	Ukrajině	2.10
Accusative	Rusko	15.53	Accusative	Ukrajinu	−15.34
Locative	Rusku	−61.49	Locative	Ukrajině	−3.30
Instrumental	Ruskem	31.09	Instrumental	Ukrajinou	−33.79

case is used to represent source (movement away from the entity) and goal (movement into the entity) (Janda & Clancy, 2006, pp. 23–42), or a part of the whole (pp. 42–53). The genitive case can also report the participants (subject and object) of nominalized events. The meanings associated with the genitive suggest unusually frequent references to parts *of Ukraine*, and Ukraine as an entity which forces move into and out of. Ukraine is also likely to be a participant of nominalized actions: expressions where it is uncertain who is responsible for the action and who is affected by the action, when the action takes place, and to what degree the action is likely. Ukraine is presented as a place where forces come and go, a place likely to occur in texts contrasting different parts of the country, and a place associated with actions whose details are unclear.

17. **Ukrajina**^{nom} zaslala MZV RF protest proti údajné účasti ruských vojenských příslušníků v bojových akcích na Donbasu, […] (https://cz.sputniknews.com/svet/20150519428192/).
    '**Ukraine**^{nom} sent to the FMRF [Foreign Ministry of the Russian Federation] a protest against the alleged participation of Russian army members in the combat actions in Donbas, […]'
18. Projekt „finlandizace" **Ukrajiny**^{gen} navržený Zbigniewem Brzezinským, poradcem prezidenta USA Jimmyho Cartera pro národní bezpečnost, předpokládá změnu **Ukrajiny**^{gen} v trh otevřený jak pro Rusko, Tak i pro Západ bez její integrace do jakéhokoliv vojenského svazku. (https://cz.sputniknews.com/politika/2015030430480/)
    'Project 'Finlandization' **of Ukraine**^{gen} proposed by Zbigniew Brzeziński, US President Jimmy Carter's National Security Advisor, presumes transformation **of Ukraine**^{gen} into an open market for Russia as well as the west without its integration into any type of military alliance.'
19. Závěrečný dokument summitu zdůrazňuje podporu územní celistvosti **Ukrajiny**^{gen} a obsahuje výzvu k naprostému splnění minských dohod o Donbasu. (https://cz.sputniknews.com/politika/20150523446675/)
    'The final document of the summit emphasizes support for the territorial integrity of **Ukraine**^{gen} and contains an appeal for total fulfillment of the Minsk Protocol.'

In (17), Ukraine is the agent of an action. Ukraine in (18), read in context, is likely to be the direct object of two nominalized actions ("Finlandization" and "transformation"). The nominal phrase evokes uncertainty about the responsible agent for these actions, the time, the manner, and the likelihood of these actions. The genitive in (19) is used in a context that concerns the wholeness vs. potential division of Ukraine.

Implicit Rhetoric on Kremlin Leadership

Prominent case-making morphemes for the four lemmas—*Rusko*, *Ukrajina*, *Porošenko*, and *Putin*—result in an implicit rhetoric that involves the Russian and Ukrainian leaderships. Ukraine is a state that takes actions, as it were, on its own.

The country is a locus for moving forces and is associated with division and actions with unclear details. These properties point to an image of Ukraine as an unstable and divided state; the observation is consistent with the results from the previous sections: "KWs (Key Inflected Word Forms)," "Key Lemmas (KLs)," "Collocates and Key Lemmas Links (KL Links): Contextual Reading of Words." President Poroshenko is portrayed as non-agentive, i.e., an insufficiently decisive and passive leader of such a country. This relationship between the morphemes gives rise to questions about the adequacy of Poroshenko's leadership in Ukraine.

On the contrary, case marking for Russia represents the state as a receiver, experiencer, a victim (although a potential competitor), and a companion, according to SPUCz. Such a view of Russia corresponds to the image of a mistreated state that actually wants to cooperate with others; this can be also gleaned from KL-links and the subject of passive voice forms of VUs. In relation to this image of Russia, the strong agency attributed to Putin can then be viewed positively: Russia, which is subject to international mistreatment, needs a strong leader who is also a negotiator. The portrayal of Russia and Putin that emerges from relative prominence in grammatical case marking thus justifies Putin's presidency. Furthermore, the contrast between the Russian and Ukrainian leaderships implicitly endorses the legitimacy of actions by Russia towards Ukraine.

This section first examined *verba dicendi*. The subjects of verbs of reporting suggest that the information presented includes apparently diverse views and statements by experts, journalists, and Russian political representatives. A deeper exploration of SPUCz using KMA, however, captures the implicit pro-Kremlin rhetoric built into SPUCz. The results obtained from KMA can explicitly pin down what constitutes this "alternative" news. KMA provides a more dynamic analysis than KWA: while KWA reports on the prominence of "groups" of ideas, KMA reports on how keyed lemmas consistently and implicitly relate to one another throughout the corpus and contribute to the resulting message. The following section further corroborates this observation.

Density of Prominent KLs in Sentences

A sentence with multiple KLs, i.e., with a high density of KLs, is expected to draw more of the reader's attention as more striking lemmas co-occur. A set of such sentences can be considered as a "distilled extract" of the entire corpus.

Table 10.19 below categorizes the top 107 sentences with high KL density.[29] Among the sentence categories, the most frequent are those that convey a positive

[29] The sentences were examined by each co-author independently first. The co-authors then discussed their differences and reached a mutually acceptable categorization.

Table 10.19 Sentence categories with high KL density (top 107)

Category	Number of sentences	%
Positive evaluation of Russia	34	34.8
Negative evaluation of Ukraine	28	26.2
Situations that might threaten Russia	21	19.6
Negative evaluation of Russia	7	6.5
Positive evaluation of Ukraine	3	2.8
Others	14	13.1
Total[a]	107	100

[a]The numbers are slightly larger than 100, as some of the sentences were used more than once and/or altered only slightly and placed in different contexts. These sentences, however, were not considered true duplicates as their functions are expected to differ in different contexts

evaluation of Russia. They may show Russia's military power, its determination, or its cooperation with superpowers (e.g., China), for example:

20. Irácký voják také hovořil o značné převaze ruských zbraní nad zbraněmi americkými. (https://cz.sputniknews.com/politika/20150525452335/)
    'The Iraqi soldier also talked about the significant superiority of Russian weapons over American weapons.'

The next most frequent sentence types are those that provide a negative evaluation of Ukraine: Ukraine's violation of the Minsk agreements, its weakening economic power, and Ukrainian extremism (example 21):

21. „Tři tanky ukrajinských ozbrojených sil vjely z ukrajinského týlu na území Kondrašovky, což je porušením minských dohod." (https://cz.sputniknews.com/svet/20150326166660/)
    '"Three tanks of the Ukrainian armed forces drove out of the Ukrainian rear onto the territory of Kondrašovka in a violation of the Minsk agreements."'

There were also a fair number of sentences describing situations that might threaten Russia. They report NATO expansion towards the east, anti-Russian propaganda in the western media, and the possible arms supply to Ukraine:

22. Lavrov: USA porušují Smlouvu o nešíření jaderných zbraní, když rozmísťují taktické jaderné zbraně na území pěti států. (https://cz.sputniknews.com/politika/20150422294771/)
    'Lavrov: The USA is violating the treaty on the non-proliferation of nuclear weapons while it is deploying tactical nuclear weapons on the territory of five states.'

The other types of sentences include negative evaluations of Russia, for example:

23. Moldavští politici mnohokrát vyzývali ke stažení ruských vojsk z regionu, protože jejich přítomnost tam pokládají za okupaci. (https://cz.sputniknews.com/politika/20150318120831/)

'The Moldavian politicians repeatedly called for the withdrawal of Russian forces from the region because they consider their [the Russian forces'] presence there as an occupation.'

There were only a few sentences presenting a positive evaluation of Ukraine:

24. Podle slov Harfové vyslovují experti ministerstva zahraničí mínění, že domobranci porušují příměří častěji, než ukrajinští vojáci. (https://cz.sputniknews.com/svet/201506045064581/)
'According to Harf's words the experts at the ministry pronounce the international opinion that the home-defenders are violating the truce more often than Ukrainian soldiers.'

Table 10.19 indicates that SPUCz gravitates towards presenting a positive image of Russia and situations that threaten Russia. The corpus also describes Ukraine negatively much more often than it does Russia. The sentences with the largest density of KLs impress on the reader that Russia is strong, determined, and an internationally cooperative partner; at the same time, it is notable that there is serious concern over threats to Russia. These results are consistent with the results of the KMA that shows Putin's strong leadership as well as the image of Russia under threat.

Conclusions

Multi-level Discourse Prominence Analysis (MLDPA) reveals language patterns that are prominent against the background of general language usage. Departure from more general patterns is presumably impactful to the reader. Although this paper presents samplings of prominent components of discourse, they help us understand the "alternativeness" in *Sputnik* and the extent to which similar properties are consistently observed on different levels of the language.

Examination of verba dicendi shows that *Sputnik* builds its image of a news-opinion portal that draws on diverse sources and views (experts, journalists, analysts, and political scientists). The results are consistent with the preliminary observation that the preposition *podle* 'according to' is unusually frequent in *Sputnik*. Although quantitative analysis does not allow for evaluation of the *type* of experts cited, MLDPA provides other ways to show the pervasiveness of pro-Kremlin ideology.

KWs and KLs—as isolated words—suggest that SPUCz expresses empathy towards Ukrainian separatists, and concern about anti-Russian actions and Russophobia. These prominent lexical units serve as a starting point for researchers to focus on aspects of Russia and Ukraine. KL context provides further details on the image of Russia and Ukraine. The adjective 'Russian' suggests economic concerns, while 'Ukrainian' occurs in the context of conflict and instability. Differences between Russia and Ukraine can also be observed in the contextual information for amplifiers and stance adverbs in SPUCz. Stance adverbs occur more often with Ukraine's actions, while amplifiers occur more often with Russia's actions. A sampling of the KLs 'separatist' and 'genocide' is symptomatic of the contrast between Russia and Ukraine. By placing the words where they are not entirely anticipated (i.e., by shifting the context), SPUCz creates a different image of each of these KLs. *Separatista* in SPUCz, in contrast with general corpus SYN2015, is used as a label that is unfairly used against the people who disagree with the Ukrainian government. *Genocida*, a word that accompanies empathy towards victims, is used for description of the situation in Donbas. Sentences with higher density of KLs present a positive image of Russia, while simultaneously suggesting that Russia is under threat.

KWs, KLs and KL-collocates, KL-links, and KL-density all show a consistent contrast between Ukraine and Russia. Ukraine is described as unstable and conflict-ridden, while Russia speaks with conviction and determination but is under threat. Comparison of selected KLs between SPUCz and SYN2015 suggests discourse-semantic spin directing empathy towards the Ukrainian separatists. These probes are based largely on lexical information at different levels.

The morphosyntactic portion of MLDPA (keymorph analysis) found a large distribution of passive voice for keyed VUs. It identified Russia as their predominant grammatical subject and confirmed the consistent representation of Russia as a victim in SPUCz discourse. More importantly, this part of MLDPA indicates the implicit predominant rhetoric within SPUCz. The results were drawn from morphosyntactic features of lemmas with little lexical information about specific events: *Putin*, *Porošenko*, *Rusko*, and *Ukrajina*—four of the seed words (also KLs). The relative prominence of case endings of these lemmas suggests an implicit *relationship* between each state and its leadership. The case endings for *Ukrajina* and *Porošenko* point to the inadequate presidency in Ukraine. In contrast, the case endings for *Rusko* and *Putin* point to the representation of a victimized state and a need for a strong presidency in Russia. Case thereby suggests a consistent pattern of (de) legitimization of state leadership in Russia and Ukraine and possibly legitimization of Russian actions.

MLDPA is a method that consists of three parts. KWs and KLs serve as the starting point, which directed us to zoom in on the representations of Russia and Ukraine. The contextual information for KLs and the density of KLs facilitate our understanding of consistent topics and the image of Russia as a state under threat. Keymorph analysis further corroborates this image of Russia. Furthermore, KMA was shown to be a powerful tool to probe an overarching rhetorical structure and ideology—the legitimization and delegitimization of states and presidencies.

MLDPA is grounded in the corpus linguistic notion of keyness applied not only to the lexicon but also to the cognitive linguistic notion of morphemes as meaning-bearing units. This approach provides quantitative data to study the discourse position of a text, which is central to discourse analysis. Using the data from *Sputnik*, the present study demonstrates the applicability of MLDPA to probe implicit rhetoric and ideology in many types of discourse.

Acknowledgments This paper was supported in part by program Progres Q08 *Czech National Corpus* implemented at the Faculty of Arts, Charles University and the Brown University Humanities Research Funds. The authors would also like to thank Katie Krafft for data collection.

References

Altshuler, D. (2010). Aspect in English and Russian flashback discourses. *Oslo Studies in Language, 2*, 75–107.

Baker, P., & McEnery, T. (2005). A corpus-based approach to discourse of refugees and asylum seekers in UN and newspaper texts. *Journal of Language and Politics, 4*(2), 197–226.

Baker, P. (2005). *The public discourse of gay men*. London: Routledge.

Baker, P. (2009). The question is, how cruel is it? Keywords in debates on fox hunting in the British House of Commons. In D. Archer (Ed.), *What's in a word-list?* (pp. 125–136). London: Ashgate.

Bertels, A., & Speelman, D. (2013). 'Keywords method' versus 'Calcul des Spécificités'. *International Journal of Corpus Lingustics, 18*(4), 536–560.

Biber, D. (1993). Using register-diversified corpora for general language studies. *Computational Linguistics, 19*(2), 219–241.

Biber, D. (2006). *University language: A corpus-based study of spoken and written registers*. Amsterdam: John Benjamins.

Biber, D., Johansson, S., Leech, G., Conrad, S., & Finegan, E. (1999). *Longman grammar of spoken and written English*. Harlow, UK: Longman.

Caldas-Coulthard, C. (1994). "On reporting reporting: The representation of speech in factual and factional narratives", ed. In *Malcolm Coulthard, advances in written texts analysis, 295–308*. London: Routledge.

Chvany, C. (1990). Verbal aspect, discourse saliency, and the so-called perfect of result in Modern Russian. In N. B. Thelin (Ed.), *Verbal aspect in discourse* (pp. 213–236). Amsterdam: John Benjamins.

Culpeper, J. (2002). Computers, language and characterisation. An analysis of six characters in *Romeo and Juliet*. In U. Melander-Marttala, C. Ostman, & M. Kyto (Eds.), *Conversation in life and in literature: Papers from the ASLA symposium* (Vol. 15, pp. 11–30). Uppsala, Sweden: Association Suedoise de Linguistique Appliquee.

Culpeper, J. (2009). Keyness: Words, parts-of-speech and semantic categories in the character-talk of Shakespeare's Romeo and Juliet. *International Journal of Corpus Linguistics, 14*(1), 29–59.

Culpeper, J., & Demmen, J. (2015). Keywords. In D. Biber & R. Reppen (Eds.), *The Cambridge handbook of English corpus linguistics* (pp. 90–105). Cambridge, UK: Cambridge University Press.

Cvrček, V., & Fidler, M. (forthcoming). More than keywords: Discourse prominence analysis of the Russian web portal *Sputnik Czech Republic*. In A. Salamurovič & M. Berrocal (Eds.), *Language in politics in Slavic-speaking countries*.

Desclés, J.-P., & Guentschéva, Z. (1990). Discourse analysis of aorist and imperfect in Bulgarian and French. In N. B. Thelin (Ed.), *Verbal aspect in discourse* (pp. 237–261). Amsterdam: John Benjamins.

Fidler, M., & Cvrček, V. (2015). A data-driven analysis of reader viewpoints: Reconstructing the historical reader using keyword analysis. *Journal of Slavic Linguistics, 23*(2), 197–239.

Fairclough, N. (1995). *Media discourse*. London: Hodder Education.

Fidler, M., & Cvrček, V. (2017). Keymorph analysis, or how morphosyntax informs discourse. *Corpus Linguistics and Linguistic Theory*. https://doi.org/10.1515/cllt-2016-0073. Accessed 29 Sept 2018.

Fielder, G. (1990). Narrative context and Russian aspect. In N. B. Thelin (Ed.), *Verbal aspect in discourse* (pp. 263–284). Amsterdam: John Benjamins.

Fisher-Starcke, B. (2009). Keywords and frequent phrases of Jane Austin's *Pride and Prejudice*. A corpus-stylistic analysis. *International Journal of Corpus Linguistics, 14*(4), 492–523.

Groll, E. Elias. (2014). Kremlin's 'Sputnik' newswire is the buzzfeed of propaganda. *Foreign Policy*. https://foreignpolicy.com/2014/11/10/kremlins-sputnik-newswire-is-the-buzzfeed-of-propaganda/. Accessed 3 July 2017.

Heritage, Timothy. (2013, December 9). Putin dissolves state news agency, tightens grip on Russia media. *Reuters World News*. http://www.reuters.com/article/us-russia-media-idUS-BRE9B80I120131209. Accessed 17 July 2017.

Hopper, P., & Thompson, S. (1980). Transitivity. *Language, 56*(2), 251–299.

Jäger, S., & Maier, F. (2016). Analysing discourses and dispositives: A foucauldian approach to theory and methodology. In R. Wodak & M. Meyer (Eds.), *Methods of critical discourse studies* (3rd ed., pp. 109–136). London: Sage.

Jakobson, R. (1984). Contribution to the general theory of case: General meanings of the Russian cases. In L. R. Waugh & M. Halle (Eds.), *Roman Jakobson. Russian and Slavic grammar. Studies 1931–1981* (pp. 59–103). Berlin: Mouton.

Janda, L. A. (1993). The shape of the indirect object in Central and Eastern Europe. *The Slavic and East European Journal, 37*(4), 533–563.

Janda, L. A., & Clancy, S. (2006). *The case book for Czech*. Bloomington, IN: Slavica.

Kresin, S. (1998). Deixis and thematic hierarchies in Russian narrative discourse. *Journal of Pragmatics, 30*(4), 421–435.

Křen, M., Cvrček, V., Čapka, T., Čermáková, A., Hnátková, M., Chlumská, L., et al. (2016). SYN2015: Representative Corpus of contemporary written Czech. In N. Calzolari, K. Choukri, T. Declerck, S. Goggi, M. Grobelnik, B. Maegaard, et al. (Eds.), *Proceedings of the tenth international conference on language resources and evaluation (LREC'16)* (pp. 2522–2528). Portorož, Slovenia: ELRA http://www.lrec-conf.org/proceedings/lrec2016/index.html. Accessed 29 Sept 2018.

MacFarquhar, Neil. (2016, August 28). A powerful Russian weapon: The spread of false stories. *The New York Times*. https://www.nytimes.com/2016/08/29/world/europe/russia-sweden-disinformation.html. Accessed 17 July 2017.

Machin, D., & Mayer, A. (2012). *How to do critical discourse analysis: A multimodal introduction*. Los Angeles: Sage.

Mahlberg, M. (2007). Clusters, key clusters and local textual functions in Dickens. *Corpora, 2*(1), 1–31.

Scott, M. (2010). Problems in investigating keyness, or cleansing the undergrowth and marking out tails…. In M. Bondi & M. Scott (Eds.), *Keyness in texts* (pp. 43–57). Amsterdam: John Benjamins.

Scott, M. (2013). *WordSmith tools manual. Version 7.0*. Liverpool, UK: Lexical Analysis Software http://www.lexically.net/downloads. Accessed 29 Sept 2018.

Scott, M., & Tribble, C. (2006). *Textual patterns: Keyword and corpus analysis in language education*. Amsterdam: John Benjamins.

Smoleňová, Ivana. (2015, June). The pro-Russian disinformation campaign in the Czech Republic and Slovakia. Types of media spreading pro-Russian propaganda, their characteristics and frequently used narratives. *Prague Security Studies Institute (PSSI)*. http://www.pssi.cz/download/docs/253_is-pro-russian-campaign.pdf. Accessed 17 July 2017.

Sonnenhauser, B. (2008). Aspect interpretation in Russian—A pragmatic account. *Journal of Pragmatics, 40*(12), 2077–2099.

Stewart, D. (2010). *Semantic prosody. A critical evaluation*. New York: Routledge.

Straková, J., Straka, M., & Hajič, J. (2014). Open-source tools for morphology, lemmatization, pos tagging and named entity recognition. In *Proceedings of 52nd annual meeting of the Association for Computational Linguistics: System demonstrations, Baltimore, Maryland, June 2014* (pp. 13–18). Stroudsburg, PA: Association for Computational Linguistics.

Stubbs, M. (2005). Conrad in the computer: Examples of quantitative stylistic methods. *Language and Literature, 14*(1), 5–24.

Tabbert, U. (2015). *Crime and corpus. The linguistic representation of crime in the press.* John Benjamins: Philadephia.

Ueda, M. (1992). *The interaction between clause-level parameters and context in Russian morpho-syntax: Genitive of negation and predicate adjectives.* Munich, Germany: Otto Sagner.

Walker, B. (2010). Wmatrix, key concepts and the narrator in Julian Barnes's *Talking It Over*. In D. McIntyre & B. Busse (Eds.), *Language and style* (pp. 364–387). Basingstoke, UK: Palgrave Education.

Williams, R. (1976). *Keywords: A vocabulary of culture and society*. New York: Oxford University Press.

Wilson, A. (2013). Embracing Bayes factors for key item analysis in corpus linguistics. In M. Bieswanger & A. Koll-Stobbe (Eds.), *New approaches to the study of linguistic variability. Language competence and language awareness in Europe* (pp. 3–11). Frankfurt, Germany: Peter Lang.

MIX
Papier aus verantwortungsvollen Quellen
Paper from responsible sources
FSC® C105338

If you have any concerns about our products,
you can contact us on
ProductSafety@springernature.com

In case Publisher is established outside the EU,
the EU authorized representative is:
Springer Nature Customer Service Center GmbH
Europaplatz 3, 69115 Heidelberg, Germany

Printed by Libri Plureos GmbH
in Hamburg, Germany